CLIENTS AND LAWYERS

Contributions in Legal Studies
Series Editor: *Paul L. Murphy*

Crime and Punishment in Revolutionary Paris
Antoinette Wills

American Legal Culture, 1908-1940
John W. Johnson

Governmental Secrecy and the Founding Fathers: A Study in Constitutional Controls
Daniel N. Hoffman

Torture and English Law: An Administrative and Legal History from the Plantagenets to the Stuarts
James Heath

Essays on New York Colonial Legal History
Herbert S. Johnson

The Origins of the American Business Corporation, 1784-1855: Broadening the Concept of Public Service During Industrialization
Ronald E. Seavoy

Prologue to Nuremberg: The Politics and Diplomacy of Punishing War Criminals of the First World War
James F. Willis

The Network of Control: State Supreme Courts and State Security Statutes, 1920-1970
Carol E. Jenson

Drugs and Information Control: The Role of Men and Manipulation in the Control of Drug Trafficking
Jerald W. Cloyd

State Supreme Courts: Policymakers in the Federal System
Mary Cornelia Porter and G. Alan Tarr, editors

The Future of Our Liberties: Perspectives on the Bill of Rights
Stephen C. Halpern, editor

Tightening the Reins of Justice in America: A Comparative Analysis of the Criminal Jury Trial in England and the United States
Michael H. Graham

The Development of Law on the Rocky Mountain Frontier
Gordon M. Bakken

CLIENTS AND LAWYERS

Securing the Rights of Disabled Persons

SUSAN M. OLSON

Contributions in Legal Studies, Number 28

GREENWOOD PRESS
Westport, Connecticut • London, England

Library of Congress Cataloging in Publication Data

Olson, Susan M. (Susan Marie), 1949-
Clients and lawyers.

Contributions in legal studies, ISSN 0147-1074 ;
no. 28)
Bibliography: p.
Includes index.
1. Physically handicapped—Transportation—Law and legislation—United States. 2. Physically handicapped—Legal status, laws, etc.—United States. 3. Attorney and client—United States. 4. Actions and defenses—United States. I. Title. II. Series.
KF480.O44 1984 346.7301'3 83-11724
ISBN 0-313-24015-8 (lib. bdg.) 347.30613

Library of Congress Catalog Card Number: 83-11724
ISBN: 0-313-24015-8
ISSN: 0147-1074

First published in 1984

Greenwood Press
A division of Congressional Information Service, Inc.
88 Post Road West
Westport, Connecticut 06881

Printed in the United States of America

10 9 8 7 6 5 4 3 2 1

To Kris, Pat, Kathryn
and all the others

Contents

Acknowledgments

Thanks are due to many people for their contributions to this book. Michael Barkun, Marie Provine, Richard Schwartz, Douglas Biklen, and Michael Sawyer of Syracuse University were important in shaping its first incarnation. My colleagues at Minnesota, Frank Sorauf, Sam Krislov, Paul Murphy, and the late Harold Chase read the manuscript and made helpful and encouraging comments. Research support from the National Science Foundation (Grant No. SOC78-16211) and from Syracuse University made possible the trips to interview the disabled plaintiffs and their lawyers. I owe thanks to Sharon McCrea, who transcribed the taped interviews and offered an interested ear for my progress reports when I was far from my academic colleagues; to Jacalyn Plagge, who typed the final draft; and to Anne Wall. My greatest appreciation, however, must go to the many persons who so graciously gave me their time for interviews and who generally seemed pleased to tell me about their lawsuits. Having a chance to talk with people who have overcome so many handicaps and achieved so much made the research a personally as well as intellectually rewarding experience.

Introduction

In 1977 a journalist declared in *Newsweek* magazine that the United States is in the midst of "one of the great unnoticed revolutions in U.S. history: the ever-increasing willingness, even eagerness, on the part of elected officials and private citizens to let the courts settle matters that once were settled by legislatures, executives, parents, teachers—or chance."[1] The article in which this comment occurred represents one of a small swell of complaints heard in the middle and late Seventies about a perceived increase in the "lawyerization" or "judicialization" of American life.

These popular complaints have two different emphases. Some focus on the role of lawyers and courts in facets of private life, such as divorce, personal injury, real estate transactions, and probate.[2] Complaints in this sphere tend to be that lawyers are greedy, high-handed, uncaring, or simply too expensive. Other popular excoriations focus on courts' actions in the public sphere on issues such as desegregation, abortion, and prison conditions.[3] In this, the popular press has a close counterpart in scholarly social science and legal literature.[4] Criticism of "judicial activism" has been heard for years from some scholars on the grounds that this takes away control over social policy from the majority and its duly elected representatives.

A possible common thread in the criticisms of lawyers and courts on the personal and policy levels is a sense of loss of control over important decisions in one's life. On the policy level court policy making is problematic because courts are not accountable to majority opinion as much as the other policy-making branches of government are. Indeed, they are not supposed to be, but we do expect courts not to be too far ahead of or behind majority views on most subjects.

On the personal level individuals feel considerable ambivalence about their relationships with private lawyers. While we want our lawyer to prevent, cure, or at least shield us from our legal difficulties, we are often dissatisfied with the results. Twenty-eight percent of women responding to a survey about divorce lawyers reported that they were dissatisfied with their lawyers.[5] Complaints to lawyer-discipline agencies and malpractice suits "soared" in the late Seventies.[6] At the base of some of the unhappiness is uncertainty about the extent to which a lawyer is, in Hobbes' terms, an actor or an agent, that is, one who acts independently and takes initiative or one who acts only on the instructions of another.[7]

Confusion about the degree of autonomy of lawyers becomes politically significant when courts make policy at the behest of lawyers representing groups of people who are not formally part of the suit or who at least do not personally speak on their own behalf. The problem of knowing whom exactly the lawyers represent is greatest in public interest litigation, as evidenced by the endless debates over who determines the public interest.[8] The problem is almost as great in relation to populations who are presumed to need the protection of courts precisely because they are not certain to know their own interests, such as mentally disabled people and children.

With other types of clients, presumably, the lawyer's role is reduced from identifying the interests that need defending to merely applying his or her more sophisticated understanding of the legal and judicial system to obtain the interests identified by the client, but the line between these tasks is not clear. The survey on divorce lawyers found misunderstandings about whether the lawyer is expected only to respond to questions directly asked or is also expected to anticipate potential questions the client *should* ask.[9] That this problem exists even in personal litigation suggests the need to look closely at lawyer–client relations in social policy litigation. The extent to which lawyers or clients are directing the litigation may influence the substantive policy sought, the participants' attitudes toward the process, which may in turn influence their subsequent involvement with the judicial or political system, and the broader public's perception of the litigation.

This book describes the development of a style of social policy litigation which features greater participation by clients and goals and strategies different from the classic model of social reform litigation, as practiced by the NAACP. This new style is more integrated conceptually and practically with nonjudicial political strategies for achieving social change. Treating litigation more like other politics, it reduces the emphasis on the lawyer as expert. This new style arguably has the potential for achieving some kinds of results better than the NAACP model—fewer problems with a formal court victory going unimplemented, less client ignorance of and alienation from the judicial system, and more lasting involvement of people in political action.

To make this argument, this book brings together the concerns of two different sets of literature—that on interest group litigation, which tends to concern choices of strategy and conditions of success or failure with an emphasis on the lawyer's role, and that on mass political behavior in the form of political participation, community organization, and voluntary association and interest group membership. These two sets are used to inform and expand what little literature there is which expressly addresses questions of the client role in litigation.

The book does not claim that the new style of group litigation is a salvation for all the problems of all groups trying to use the courts for political relief or even that it is necessarily the "wave of the future" in group litigation. There is still a place for the familiar NAACP-style litigation; the new style requires certain conditions which may not always be present. Nevertheless, social reform litigation which involves the client more and achieves some success in obtaining the group's goals can happen and has happened.

The example presented is litigation occurring in the mid-Seventies over the provision of public transportation accessible to persons with physical disabilities. The disability rights movement produced groups which were able to initiate and pursue litigation at the grassroots level without its being taken over by lawyer-dominated national interest groups. Their use of the courts was highly politicized, in the sense of approaching litigation with many of the same assumptions with which they simultaneously pursued their goals in other political channels, and they achieved at least a moderate success. It is important that scholars of interest group litigation recognize this new style, exemplified by the accessible transit litigation, as a significant political use of the courts and a form of grassroots political participation.

The organizational plan of the book combines analytical issues concerning social reform litigation raised in other studies with evidence from the accessible transit cases and the disability rights movement. Chapter 1 presents the development of conditions in the larger political environment that have made possible the new style of litigation and introduces the characteristics of that style. Chapter 2 presents the argument that the extent of client participation is significant for the achievement of long-term success of litigation goals. Chapter 3 examines the political context of the accessible transit cases with a review of the development of the disability rights movement and accessibility laws. Chapter 4 introduces the five cases of accessible transit litigation studied in depth and the clients and lawyers bringing them. Chapter 5 uses these cases to illustrate the characteristics of the new style of litigation. Chapter 6 specifically looks at how this new style helped to protect disabled litigants from some of the risks of litigation encountered by client groups in the past. Chapter 7 discusses the various determinants of client participation that can be gleaned from these case studies in combination with the literature on involvement in other political or quasi-political activities. Chapter 8 looks at factors other than client participation which influenced the success or failure of the transit access cases. Finally, chapter 9 draws some conclusions about the applicability of findings based on these lawsuits for social reform litigation generally, and for the women's movement in particular.

Notes

1. Jerrold K. Footlick, "Too Much Law?" *Newsweek*, January 10, 1977, p. 44.
2. E.g., Vivian Cadden, "The Case Against Divorce Lawyers," *McCall's*, November 1976, pp. 169+; Margaret Daly, "What Are Your Rights with a Lawyer?" *Better Homes and Gardens*, November 1975, pp. 40+; "Those #*%&!!! Lawyers," *Time*, April 10, 1978, pp. 56–59+; "Lawyers Giving Public a Raw Deal?" *U.S. News and World Report*, December 1, 1980, pp. 45–46; C. Salzberg, "Should You Trust Your Lawyer?" *Working Woman*, September 1980, pp. 30–31; Ted Gest, "Why Lawyers Are in the Doghouse," *U.S. News and World Report*, May 11, 1981, pp. 38–41.
3. E.g., William F. Buckley, "Curb the Courts?" *National Review*, May 26, 1972, pp. 606–7; Jerrold K. Footlick, "We've Got Too Much Law!" *Reader's Digest*, May 1977, pp. 96–100; F. Hunt, "Lawyers' War Against Democracy," *Commentary*, October 1979, pp. 45–51; John M. Ashbrook, "Are Judges Abusing Our Rights?" *Reader's Digest*, August 1981, pp. 77–80. See also, Jerold S. Auerbach, "A Plague of Lawyers," *Harper's*, October 1976, pp. 37–44.
4. To mention only a few examples from this vast literature, representing various points of view on judicial review: Charles L. Black, Jr., *The People and the Court: Judicial Review in a Democracy* (New York: The Macmillan Co., 1960); Alexander Bickel, *The Least Dangerous Branch* (Indianapolis: The Bobbs-Merrill Co., 1962) and *The Supreme Court and the Idea of Progress* (New York: Harper and Row, 1970); Herbert Wechsler, *Principles, Politics and Fundamental Law* (Cambridge: Harvard University Press, 1961); Charles Hyneman, *The Supreme Court on Trial* (New York: Atherton Press, 1963); Howard E. Dean, *Judicial Review and Democracy* (New York: Random House, 1966); Louis Lusky, *By What Right? A Commentary on the Supreme Court's Power to Revise the Constitution* (Charlottesville, Va.: The Michie Co., 1975); and Raoul Berger, *Government by Judiciary: The Transformation of the Fourteenth Amendment* (Cambridge: Harvard University Press, 1977).
5. Cadden, "The Case Against Divorce Lawyers," p. 169.
6. Gest, "Why Lawyers Are in the Doghouse," p. 38.
7. Thomas Hobbes, *Leviathan*, ed. Michael Oakeshott (New York: Collier Books, 1962), chap. 16, pp. 125–26.
8. E.g., Frank J. Sorauf, "The Public Interest Reconsidered," *Journal of Politics*

19 (1957): 616–39; Glendon Schubert, *The Public Interest* (Glencoe, Ill.: The Free Press, 1960); Virginia Held, *The Public Interest and Individual Interests* (New York: Basic Books, 1970); Clarke E. Cochran, "Political Science and the 'Public Interest,' " *Journal of Politics* 36 (1974): 327–55; Barry M. Mitnick, "A Typology of Conceptions of the Public Interest," *Administration & Society* 8 (1976): 5–28.

9. Cadden, "The Case Against Divorce Lawyers," p. 169.

CLIENTS AND LAWYERS

Chapter 1

The Changing Environment of Social Reform Litigation

Pluralist theory emphasizes the importance of interest groups in the functioning of all institutions of the American political system, and courts are no exception.[1] Indeed, because the court's role has traditionally included the protection of minority rights, Clement Vose points out, "there is a special appropriateness for small, organized interests to work through litigation."[2] Other factors, such as the geographical decentralization of the federal courts, have made litigation a practical as well as appropriate means of influencing federal decision making.

As Vose has documented, minority interest groups have been using the courts at least since the turn of the century, but the strategy has become particularly widespread in the latter half of the century. The greater availability of low-cost legal assistance to more groups through federally-funded legal services and the public interest law movement as well as court decisions in the 1960s liberalizing doctrines about standing and attorney's fees contributed to the march to the courts.[3] Perhaps the greatest stimulus to the use of litigation as a political strategy, however, was the success of the National Association for the Advancement of Colored People (NAACP). By the time of *Brown v. Board of Education*[4] in 1954, the NAACP and its affiliated Legal Defense Fund (LDF) had won 34 of 38 cases before the Supreme Court.[5]

The desegregation litigation of the NAACP and the LDF was the first planned campaign of affirmative use of the courts for social change, and it has been the model for many other groups. The NAACP's approach is still the prototype of social reform litigation in the political science literature. American government textbooks and books on interest groups tend to use the NAACP as their example of group litigation. Social reform litigation is much more varied than this one model, however. Litigation strategy reflects particular issues and historical circumstances.

The NAACP developed its strategy precisely because blacks were excluded from other channels of policy making. Facing statutes that were blatantly discriminatory, but duly enacted, the NAACP lawyers had to rely on constitutional arguments to challenge the unfavorable laws. The elements of the NAACP strategy, such as encouraging the publication of law review articles to provide scholarly support for their legal arguments, soliciting *amicus curiae* briefs, coordinating test cases in several geographic locations, and developing full trial records to facilitate appeal, were all aimed toward the establishment of constitutional precedent.

Such careful litigation planning was possible because the NAACP was the preeminent national organization working through the courts for black civil rights at the time. Through its volunteer National Legal Committee, the NAACP staff not only enjoyed the advice of prominent lawyers around the country interested in civil rights, but also enlisted their cooperation in pursuing the goals and methods of the national organization when they took charge of cases at the trial court level.[6] Furthermore, the other organizations for black advancement existing at the time were not using litigation as a strategy. The Urban League, for instance, concentrated more on economic issues, such as persuading employers to hire blacks.[7]

The NAACP clients did not challenge the lawyers for control of the litigation planning any more than did other organizations. Local groups and individuals were not eager to go into court at all, because at the time the litigation campaign began, blacks risked immediate reprisals for any attempt to challenge the status quo. The NAACP membership scattered around the country in local branches helped to identify willing plaintiffs and raise money, but had little autonomy.[8] In short, the NAACP lawyers were able to supervise and control desegregation litigation to an extent unmatched since by any other group litigating on any other issue.

A great deal has happened in the history of social reform movements in America since *Brown v. Board of Education*.[9] While the use of litigation is still popular, litigation style and strategy have changed, reflecting changes in the environment and the participants. Three developments in particular have influenced social reform group litigation. The first two are broad sociopolitical changes, while the third is a more narrow legal change.

(1) The growth of collective "rights consciousness" has produced more numerous, more assertive litigating groups. Furthermore, within those groups, challenges to professional expertise in the name of "citizen participation,"

"community control," or "consumer representation" have resulted in the lawyers having less complete control over the direction of litigation.

(2) The increase in statutory and regulatory responses to social problems has created multiple pressure points within government for achieving policy goals. Changes requiring less than a new constitutional interpretation can be sought through nonjudicial channels.

(3) Access to the judiciary has expanded through the use of legal mechanisms for articulating collective problems, especially organizational standing to litigate on behalf of group members. While this entry to the courts has already closed a little from its widest opening in the early Seventies, it has not returned to its original narrow confines.

The consequence of this multiplication of participants and opportunities to effect change is that social reform group litigation has become more decentralized with less agreement on or coordination of goals and strategies. The greater participation of nonlawyers in decision making and the greater realization by lawyers of the limitations of judicial pronouncements alone to induce change have resulted in a melding of political and legal strategies. Some litigation has become so integrated with political activity outside the courts that its goal is as much to increase bargaining leverage externally as to secure victory in court, as an examination of the interrelatedness of the three environmental changes and their ramifications for social reform litigation reveals.

Collective Rights Consciousness

The first of the three changes in the political environment of social reform litigation in the past thirty years is the growth of collective rights consciousness—the recognition that problems previously thought to be personal are instead collective and the rising sense of entitlement to relief from those problems. Although sometimes there is a strong self-help element as well, rights consciousness often results in a demand that the society or government take responsibility for and do something about the problems.

Group rights consciousness did not, of course, emerge suddenly in the mid-twentieth century. Its roots lie in the social dislocation created by industrialization and urbanization in the nineteenth century. Both social and economic relationships underwent what Mauro Cappelletti calls "massification."

> Because of the "massification" phenomena, human actions and relationships assume a collective, rather than a merely individual, character: they refer to groups, categories, and classes of people, rather than to one or a few individuals alone. Even basic rights and duties are no longer exclusively the individual rights and duties of the eighteenth or nineteenth century declarations of human rights

inspired by natural law concepts, but rather meta-individual, collective, "social" rights and duties of associations, communities, and classes.[10]

Rights consciousness seems to exist in ambiguous interrelationship with the government's assumption of responsibility for social problems. In some situations government action is a response to the demands of rights-conscious citizens, while in other situations it may be the conferral of rights by an authoritative source which stimulates the rights consciousness of the group. For example, political mobilization of people with disabilities really began only after several pieces of beneficial legislation were passed but then went largely unenforced.

Generally, there is a dialectical relationship of sorts between rights-conscious groups and government actions. Some commentators credit the NAACP litigation campaign, particularly its victory in *Brown v. Board of Education*[11] with stimulating the mass movement phase of the civil rights movement, usually dated from the Montgomery, Alabama, bus boycott which began less than six months after the Supreme Court's implementation decree in *Brown II*.[12] In the words of Richard Kluger: "It [*Brown*] meant that black rights had suddenly been redefined; black bodies had suddenly been reborn under a new law. Blacks' value as human beings had been changed overnight by the declaration of the nation's highest court."[13]

Participation in mass action tactics, such as boycotts, marches, and sit-ins, further heightened group rights consciousness and increased self-esteem.[14] This in turn led to greater demands for the recognition of rights such as an end to housing and employment discrimination.

This process was not confined to blacks. The rhetoric of President Kennedy's "New Frontier" and President Johnson's "Great Society" raised expectations that government could and would tackle all social problems. The blurring of expectations and rights led Daniel Bell to label the trend disparagingly, "the revolution of rising entitlements."[15] The Sixties saw the "rights revolution" spread to even more groups—senior citizens, environmentalists, native Americans, and consumers, to name only a few.

The federal government's largest effort, the War on Poverty, launched in 1964, drew its inspiration from what Samuel Krislov calls the "twin strands of the civil rights movement: the moral-ethical emphasis on analysis of problem areas and the quasi-existentialist emphasis on action and personality transformation through effective individual action."[16] Strategically, it combined the litigation approach of the NAACP and the emphasis on community organizations and indigenous leadership of Saul Alinsky, who had long before recognized the connection between direct participation and political consciousness.[17]

The activism of the Warren Court in addressing the problems of racial discrimination led many of the new groups to seek redress through the courts. The Supreme Court encouraged further use of the Equal Protection Clause on behalf of other minority groups by decisions favoring the interests of indigent criminal defendants,[18] welfare recipients,[19] and illegitimates.[20] The executive director of the ACLU describes the tendency to organize and litigate:

> Each legal success encouraged other groups to emulate blacks and organize to demand their rights. By the late 60s most of the "disenfranchised"—the groups in American society which traditionally had been denied their rights by reasons of race, sex, or institutional status—had created some organized efforts to win their rights.[21]

Direct popular participation and a corresponding challenge to traditional sources of authority and expertise continued to be major themes. The War on Poverty endorsed a right to participate when "maximum feasible participation" was mandated in the Economic Opportunity Act of 1964.[22] In some instances the rhetoric escalated, and "community control" became the watchword. University governance, stockholders' meetings, and the administrative bodies of social services of all sorts became targets for claims of citizen/consumer/client participation. A main theme of the public interest law movement in the late Sixties was the lack of accountability of government agencies and "big business" to the people they purportedly served.

Groups also began to question the necessity of involving lawyers in issues which traditionally attorneys had monopolized. Controversies over "community control" engulfed some neighborhood legal centers.[23] A movement began to remove lawyers from small claims and conciliation courts. Even the appearance of "divorce yourself" kits and advice on "how to avoid probate" represented a challenge to the idea of the passive client who puts his or her fate totally in a lawyer's hands.

Social reform litigation could not help being touched by this trend. Groups that were already organized and mobilized had no need for the consciousness-raising function of litigation envisioned by antipoverty lawyers.[24] Local organizations did not always call in lawyers affiliated with a national organization to take over a lawsuit, as had been the typical pattern in earlier NAACP and church-state litigation.[25] A few people expressly advocated the sharing of litigation decisions by lawyers and clients.[26] The growth of rights consciousness created more numerous and more aggressive groups interested in litigating and expecting to play a bigger role in their lawsuits. No longer could a small group of lawyers control the litigation strategy in any of the major issues of the day.

The Proliferation of Rights and Sources of Redress

Paralleling the growth of collective rights consciousness was the tremendous growth of statutory and regulatory concern for social problems. The same conditions which gave rise to rights consciousness also produced large-scale government intervention into social ills. The battle over the government's role in addressing these problems was finally won in the Depression, when the Supreme Court at last capitulated to the pressures for expanded federal and state efforts to regulate the economy and related social problems.

World War II, Korea, and eight years of the Eisenhower administration slowed new initiatives on domestic problems, but President Kennedy's "New Frontier" followed by President Johnson's "Great Society" and "War on Poverty" resumed large-scale federal intervention into social ills. The return of eight more years of Republican administrations in 1968 did not diminish the pace. The Occupational Safety and Health Act, the Consumer Product Safety Act and the Equal Employment Opportunity Act—to name just a few from the Seventies—created new regulatory agencies to make and enforce rules concerning aspects of daily life.[27]

In the Eighties, new opposition to federal regulatory programs is apparent. While it is dubious that the government will ever return to so limited a role as it played before the 1930s, if it should, the change would undoubtedly affect social reform litigation strategies.

The significance of the long-term development for social reform groups which use litigation as a strategy for obtaining their policy goals is that new statutes and regulations create new legal grounds on which to sue. It is not necessary to argue that a grievance is a violation of constitutional rights if there are already statutes and regulations which, if enforced, would provide the desired protection. The statutes may indeed be highly general and thus shift controversy to the regulation making and enforcement stages, but litigants may be better off if they can show that the government at least intended to do something about their problem.

A second consequence of regulatory proliferation is that groups may be able to utilize many tactics simultaneously because more than one channel exists through which the goals can be obtained. Claims based on statutory rather than constitutional rights are as much within the purview of the legislature as of the courts. The relevant administrative agency can sometimes be "reached" through the legislature or through a bureaucratically higher level.

Contrast this with the situation of the NAACP at the time it began its desegregation campaign. In the first place, widespread voter disenfranchisement kept blacks from exercising any political influence in the states maintaining segregation by statute. Representatives of the same states were sufficiently influential in Congress to keep the issue from arising there, even if other members of Congress had seen it as a national responsibility. The NAACP had to go to the courts and establish that racial segregation violated constitutional rights before it could obtain redress. By comparison, a black person experiencing racial discrimination today has many more channels to try. State or local human rights commissions, the U.S. Department of Education, the Equal Employment Opportunity Commission, the Office of Federal Contract Compliance, and the Justice Department now handle discrimination in various contexts.

The availability of multiple pressure points was first realized and exploited fully by the public interest law movement in the late Sixties. Although a number of groups which could appropriately be called public interest organizations, such as Consumers Union and the National Wildlife Federation, are much older, the beginning of the public interest law movement could probably be dated from the publication of Ralph Nader's *Unsafe at Any Speed* in 1965, which prompted the passage of legislation regulating a powerful manufacturing industry in the interest of general consumers. Notably, Nader did not first gain attention by litigating. The Nader Study Group Reports on a multitude of consumer-related issues became well known long before he organized the Public Citizen Litigating Group.

The public interest law movement is a multi-strategy, multi-forum movement. Law is only one of four major strategies of influence used by public interest groups which Jeffrey Berry identifies in his study of eighty-three public interest groups in Washington, D.C.[28] The other three are embarrassment and confrontation, information, and constituency influence and pressure. These broad strategies encompass a variety of different tactics for specific situations.

Even though litigation is only one of many strategies used by the public interest groups to achieve their goals, lawyers have played a major and perhaps dominant role in the public interest movement. Ralph Nader is a lawyer and in the late Sixties young lawyers flocked to work with him. These lawyers and those working for other public interest causes developed a notion of "flexible lawyering" to encompass the variety of activities in which they engaged.[29] Litigation itself had new goals in addition to winning the case: educating the public about the issues in contention, encouraging supporters inside the bureaucracy, and increasing one's future negotiating power.[30]

Hand in hand with other political tactics, plaintiffs could use litigation to pressure their adversary to the negotiating table when he or she was not willing to negotiate without such pressure. If litigation and out-of-court pressures and negotiating occurred simultaneously, it was even possible for the plaintiffs to win a satisfactory settlement and still actually lose the lawsuit. The extreme form of this approach is to use litigation as a form of harassment to cost the defendant so much time and money that he or she is willing to concede.[31] It would be grossly unfair to classify most social reform litigation as harassment, but litigating to cause delay has been a popular and successful strategy in some areas, such as environmental protection.[32]

Negotiated settlements are possible, of course, only if the parties' positions have some room for compromise, and certain types of issues are more negotiable than others. Some researchers have suggested that disputes over tangible, divisible remedies are more likely subjects for compromise than intangible, largely symbolic principles.[33] Some injuries which become the subjects of litigation are almost entirely matters of principle. For example, violations of church-state separation are injuries only because the First Amendment to the U.S. Constitution says that there shall be no laws respecting the establishment of religion. Litigation on such issues is much more likely to remain focused on seeking constitutional precedents from appellate courts.

Nevertheless, the history of Establishment Clause litigation shows how the litigators of even wrongs against principle may seek a variety of goals. Frank Sorauf's study of church–state litigation from 1951 to 1971 identifies three general categories of goals among separationist groups: 1) remedy, a solution for their immediate grievance; 2) constitutional principle, the separation of church and state for its own sake; or 3) organizational or ideological goals, attention for their ongoing separationist movement.[34]

What is unique about constitutional litigation is that a necessary condition for its success is a definitive declaration by the U.S. Supreme Court. Either of the other two types of goals—remedy or organizational or ideological advancement—can often be obtained by means other than appellate litigation or even without any litigation at all. Remedy-oriented litigation can be decentralized with no need to coordinate suits in different localities, unlike constitutional litigation, which may require coordination to avoid bad precedent. Remedy in the sense of an end to the immediate grievances can be obtained any time the defendant decides to yield. There might also be a policy maker at a higher level than the defendant with the power to award the desired outcome. Finally, the publicity sought for organizational ends can also be obtained from many activities other than lawsuits.

Where the meaning of a statutory or constitutional provision is in question, how a decision is reached is important, beause the precedent will be interpreted in order to resolve similar situations in the future. In contrast, reasoning is relatively unimportant when the focus is an immediate problem at hand rather than potential future situations. A decision by the defendant to yield, for whatever reason, is as good as or better than getting a court to order the defendant to yield. Courts recognize this when they encourage litigants to reach a settlement before proceeding to full trial.

When the plaintiff's goal is remedy or organizational or ideological gains, statutes or regulations may provide the basis for a satisfactory resolution without the need for ultimate legal vindication. When the plaintiffs' goal is establishing constitutional precedent, however, there is no alternative to an appellate court decision. Short of amending the Constitution, there is no constitutional counterpart to an out-of-court settlement.

Judicial Vehicles for Group Litigation

The third change affecting interest group litigation since *Brown* is closely related to the first two. To accommodate the demands of organized interests, court rules determining the parties permitted to participate in the judicial process had to change. This is the issue of standing. Occasionally, the new statutes and regulations explicitly established causes of action for individual suits or recognized categories of persons eligible to sue under the new law.[35] More often, however, legislation did not specify whether it created a private cause of action so that courts were left to decide.[36]

Even if a statute is recognized as creating a private cause of action, the question remains of who is qualified to bring such a suit. Traditionally, the right to sue was limited to individuals who could establish that they had been personally injured in some legally protected right—most commonly a property right. As Samuel Krislov puts it (with a nod to Jerome Frank): "The theory of trial by duel precludes a generous view of the right to intervene."[37] Some mechanisms for group participation in litigation have existed for a long time, however, such as the *amicus curiae* or "friend of the court" brief. Class actions, which join as direct parties in a suit all persons "similarly situated," were not new when the NAACP used them in challenging segregation, but their popularity grew along with the increase in group litigation.

The Development of Organizational Standing

An important development in the representation of collective interests in court was the liberalization of standing for associational or organizational plaintiffs to litigate on behalf of their members.[38] Although trade associations began to bring affirmative suits to advance their members' claims early in this century, the Supreme Court first clearly sanctioned an organizational representation theory in 1963 in *National Motor Freight Traffic Association, Inc. v. United States.*[39] This occurred at the same time that the Court was also upholding an organization's right to sponsor political litigation in *NAACP v. Button*.[40]

Up to this time the NAACP had sued in its own name only in those suits arising from attacks on the organization itself, as in *Button*, or on its members for belonging to the organization, as in *NAACP v. Alabama*.[41] At the time of *Button*, however, two law review commentators predicted the future trend of organizations suing on behalf of their members when those members could have sued in their own right without suffering any harm greater than inconvenience:

> The candid recognition by all the Justices in the *Button* case of the judiciary's responsibility to determine public policy in interest group struggles might lead the Court to conclude that a group can have standing to assert positively (as well as to defend as in *NAACP v. Alabama*) in its own name the rights of its members without having to produce formal complaints signed by individuals. Such a ruling would constitute a dramatic change in judicial doctrine, though probably less of one in practice. The history of use of the judicial process by interest groups indicates that they have looked on the necessity of an individual plaintiff as no more than a burdensome formality and that courts have rarely been willing to look behind the complaint form.[42]

The successes of the NAACP inspired other groups to go to the courts and many litigated in their own names. Only a minority were denied standing, as courts had a growing "disposition to allow associations to appear as representatives of their members and to grant them standing to seek to vindicate the interests of those members."[43] Some public interest groups began to press for the right to litigate the interest of the general public rather than just their specific members in areas like environmental quality. The majority of the Supreme Court rejected so broad an aegis in *Sierra Club v. Morton*, but for the first time unqualifiedly stated: "It is clear that an organization whose members are injured may represent those members in a proceeding for judicial review."[44]

The zenith of organizational standing was reached in 1973 in *United States v. Students Challenging Regulatory Agency Procedures* (SCRAP).[45] In subsequent terms, however, the Court began to scrutinize standing more closely again. In *Warth v. Seldin*[46] and *Simon v. Eastern Kentucky Welfare Rights Organization*,[47] organizations were denied standing to bring actions on their members' behalf, but the denials were due more to the nature of the claimed injury and lack of particularity of the injury to the members rather than from rejection of organizational representation per se. The Supreme Court's most recent summary of the requirements for organizational standing appeared in *Hunt v. Washington Apple Advertising Commission*:

Thus we have recognized that an association has standing to bring suit on behalf of its members when: (a) its members would otherwise have standing to sue in their own right; (b) the interests it seeks to protect are germane to the organization's purpose; and (c) neither the claim asserted, nor the relief requested, require the participation of individual members in the lawsuit.[48]

The Elusive Goal of Representativeness in Judicial Proceedings

Collective participation in litigation—whether through *amicus* briefs, class actions, or organizational standing—raises questions of representativeness, though this may mean something different to the court than it does to the parties. From the court's viewpoint, any time a few persons present issues on behalf of a larger group, the question arises whether the active parties are adequate representatives of the class or whether passive members of the group have divergent interests. This problem of representativeness is inherent in any pluralistic process, where interests are aggregated into groups rather than each individual's speaking for him- or herself.

In a class action suit the judge must make such a determination in certifying the class for purposes of the suit. Because members may be legally bound by the outcome, notice of the suit is required so that passive members of the class may make themselves active participants or withdraw if they have conflicting views. This could also be an issue with organizational plaintiffs suing on behalf of their members, since members obviously do not always agree with the policies of the organization. This issue, which courts have hardly touched, potentially leads to scrutiny of the degree of democracy of a group's internal procedures.

Organizations with members are generally assumed to represent their true interests, but it is sometimes necessary to define what constitutes membership. The Supreme Court in *Hunt v. Washington*[49] developed the criteria quoted earlier for the functional equivalent of membership in terms of control to determine whether a state agency could have standing to represent Washington apple growers. Since then, at least one federal district court has denied standing to a public interest organization because its contributors and supporters were not the equivalent of members in the degree of control they exercised over the organization.[50]

The litigants' conception of representativeness, in contrast to the courts', is more politicized in the sense of adopting assumptions drawn from pluralist politics in other arenas and acting on those assumptions in a process I call "stacking the plaintiffs." One assumption fundamental to any decision-making process is the significance accorded the identity and number of the participants. Formally, the law creates rights and duties which adhere to persons because of their legal relationships, regardless of who they are or how many they are. The influence of differences in power is more readily acknowledged in legislative politics than in the courtroom. Ideally, the legal system is a process of applying "preexisting norms impartially (that is, unaffected by the identity of the parties.)"[51] Wechsler's concept of "neutral principles" also captures this quality of adjudication.[52]

In reality, deviation from this ideal occurs both in the norms and their application. The differential success of different plaintiffs has now been widely documented: "haves" win more than "have nots,"[53] and blacks and other racial minorities are treated differently from members of the racial majority.[54] Although the power imbalances that exist in society may be lessened in litigation, the judicial process retains some of them.

Recognizing this, litigating groups strategically select plaintiffs who best represent the total aggrieved population. Their criteria for "best" representative, however, are likely to include many other considerations in addition to which person's situation is most similar to the situations typical for the group—the sole concern of the court. This degree of stacking the plaintiffs is not particularly new. For example, in the Establishment Clause lawsuits studied by Sorauf in which the interest group lawyers were involved early enough to help in selecting the named plaintiffs, the lawyers sought individuals with the "right public image" (nonatheists and respected members of the community) and those whose position made them relatively less vulnerable to reprisals in the event of hostility to the litigation.[55]

Another plaintiff response to questions of representativeness is to have more people become actively or visibly involved in the litigation so that their support or agreement is manifest. This is particularly useful if the participants represent variations on the common interest in the problem being litigated, so that a kind of "ticket balancing" of plaintiffs occurs. Class actions are frequently used as much to emphasize the breadth and variety of the problem as to include formally in the outcome of the suit all those who are "similarly situated."[56]

Working with multiple named plaintiffs may be administratively awkward, however, and they may fight among themselves about issues that arise during the litigation. Class actions have the disadvantage of notice requirements and other technical hurdles, such as the $10,000 minimum for diversity jurisdiction.[57] For these reasons, an organization suing on behalf of its members may be an attractive plaintiff. From a practical point of view an organization may have more money and/or expertise to contribute to a lawsuit than individuals would. An organization is also evidence that an established group exists if one is seeking certification for a class action suit.

On an overtly political level, organizers of a suit may believe that an organizational plaintiff simply would have more credibility with the court because of its reputation for professionalism or its experience in previous litigation. Lawyers readily acknowledge that such considerations influence the use of *amicus* briefs. A public interest lawyer in the mental health field said: "[W]e want to have all of the major professional organizations that have an interest represented in that brief because the more heavyweight the organizations the more weight that brief will be given by the court. Or so we assume."[58]

Bringing in a class of plaintiffs or an organizational plaintiff may have another purpose as well, one which replaces a second traditional assumption of the legal system with a more political one. A construct of absolute rights and duties would hold that not only is one person's right as important as any other person's right, but also that at least sometimes one person's right is as important as the rights of many persons put together.[59] "The isolates, the loners, the nonconformists, the dedicated, the fearful, the moralizers, and the independent spirits may invoke the judicial power on much the same terms as majorities might invoke the power of the legislatures."[60] Nevertheless, in adjudication as well as legislation it is psychologically difficult to avoid the conclusion that if one person's grievance should be redressed, then the cause of many persons suffering the same grievance is even more compelling.

This last point is at the very heart of interest groups' entry into the judicial process. Groups often assume that the number of aggrieved parties—the size of one's constituency—ought to affect the outcome of the judicial process just as it rightfully does in a democratic legislative process. Lawyers as well as laypersons may hold this assumption.[61] The result is an effort to enlist a number of individuals or, better yet, organizations with large memberships in support of a suit as parties: plaintiffs or *amici*.[62]

All of these strategic considerations may culminate in multiple organizational plaintiffs for a lawsuit, which can marshall huge numbers of presumed supporters of the suit. Including groups which fall along different points on an ideological spectrum shows the court that the suit has broad political support. The assumption of the litigation organizers is that not only the number of people or organizations one can line up on one's side is counted, but also who the people or groups are—with the implication that some groups carry more prestige or "clout" than others. This clearly violates the legal presumption that only certain characteristics of a party are relevant to the weight of a claim.

More than thirty years ago the courts became aware of and criticized a similar tendency for multiple *amicus* briefs to be filed in suits in order to add the strength of numbers and influence to one side rather than to contribute to the intellectual and legal debate on the issue. The emphasis on the size and power of the member newspapers in the American Newspaper Publishers brief in a 1946 case, *Craig v. Harney*, led Mr. Justice Jackson to charge the brief writers with attempted intimidation.[63]

Amicus briefs are at least expected to contribute to the substantive argument of a case. Multiple organizational plaintiffs are likely to be even more overtly political. Including many people among the potential beneficiaries of the suit could be accomplished by a class action. Class action members are largely anonymous, however. Multiple organizational plaintiffs, which add little more than their names, their numbers, and their diversity, are understandable only as an effort to lobby the court.

This is not to say that the availability of organizational standing—any more than the presence of group rights consciousness or statutes and regulations—requires that the game of litigation be played by the same rules, assumptions, and strategies as the game of politics. Nevertheless, the developments in these areas do make it possible. Case-specific factors, such as the number and identity of the parties involved (both lawyers and clients) and the strength of the case on purely legal grounds, also influence whether the lawyers simply go into court with one or more representative plaintiffs, make their legal argument, and wait for the judge to interpret the law in their favor or whether the lawyers and clients recruit as many supporters in the form of plaintiffs or *amici* as they can and simultaneously pressure the defendants both in court and out to give them the remedy they seek.

One example of social reform litigation influenced by these developments in the political environment is the litigation over accessible public transit. Between 1972 and 1978 a total of twenty-four lawsuits was filed by disabled individuals or organizations of disabled people against local, state, and federal transit agencies in an effort to obtain public transportation accessible to persons with disabilities.[64] A detailed look at the origins, participants, goals, strategies, and successes or failures of six of the twenty-four suits reveals a style of social reform litigation very different from the NAACP prototype.

The new style of litigation includes the following characteristics: (1) The lawsuits tend to be decentralized with little or no coordination among similar suits, in contrast to the centrally controlled approach of the NAACP. (2) The assumption drawn from legislative politics that the size and political clout of a constituency influences decision makers seems to affect the recruitment of plaintiffs. (3) The suits tend to be oriented more toward obtaining a remedy for the immediate grievance than toward establishing constitutional precedents. (4) At the same time as they litigate, the plaintiffs pursue the same issue in nonjudicial political arenas.

The common thread in these four characteristics is greater client involvement than is typical in social reform litigation. The political assumptions result in the recruitment of multiple plaintiffs rather than an individual plaintiff. The remedy orientation is due to clients having more influence in shaping the litigation goals. The remedy orientation of the goals and the manpower available from many active plaintiffs make the use of multiple strategies both possible and desirable. Multiple strategies both create opportunities for many people to get involved and require such participation if they are to succeed. Finally, the decentralized pattern is a reflection of these suits being grassroots, client-controlled efforts rather than lawyer-controlled national campaigns. The important questions, then, are the significance of greater client involvement, the causes of it in the accessible transit litigation, and the likelihood that greater client participation is not just a fluke of this particular issue but a possibility in other social reform litigation.

Notes

1. The mainstay of the literature of interest group pluralism is David B. Truman, *The Governmental Process: Political Interests and Public Opinion*, 2d ed. (New York: Knopf, 1971).
2. Clement E. Vose, *Constitutional Change: Amendment Politics and Supreme Court Litigation Since 1900* (Lexington, Mass.: Lexington Books, 1972), p. 330.
3. In recent years the Supreme Court has again restricted the possibility of attorneys' fees and has slowed the broadening of the standing rules. See text p. 12.
4. 347 U.S. 483 (1954).
5. Joel F. Handler, *Social Movements and the Legal System: A Theory of Law Reform and Social Change* (New York: Academic Press, 1978), p. 26.
6. Vose, *Caucasians Only: The Supreme Court, the NAACP, and the Restrictive Covenant Cases* (Berkeley: University of California Press, 1959), p. 158ff., notes that NAACP supervision "did not produce perfect coordination in brief writing and oral argument by the attorneys" in the four consolidated restrictive covenant cases. Control by NAACP staff attorneys was somewhat more complete in the school desegregation cases. See Richard Kluger, *Simple Justice: The History of Brown v. Board of Education and Black America's Struggle for Equality* (New York: Vintage, 1977).
7. *Report of the National Advisory Commission on Civil Disorders*, by Otto Kerner, Chairman (New York: Bantam, 1968) (hereinafter cited as *Civil Disorders*), pp. 220–21.
8. Even today, policies of the organization are set at the top, and local branches can be disciplined for deviating from them, according to Frank G. Bowe, Jan E. Jacobi, and Laurence D. Wiseman, *Coalition Building: A Report on a Feasibility Study to Develop a National Model for Cross-Disability Communication and Cooperation* (Washington, D.C.: American Coalition of Citizens with Disabilities, 1978), p. 15.
9. 347 U.S. 483 (1954).
10. Mauro Cappelletti, "Vindicating the Public Interest Through the Courts: A Comparativist's Contribution," *Buffalo Law Review* 25 (1976): 646.

11. 347 U.S. 483 (1954).
12. *Brown v. Board of Education II*, 349 U.S. 294 (1955).
13. Kluger, *Simple Justice*, p. 749.
14. *Civil Disorders*, pp. 225–30.
15. Daniel Bell, "The Revolution of Rising Entitlements," *Fortune*, April 1975, p. 98.
16. Samuel Krislov, "The OEO Lawyers Fail to Constitutionalize a Right to Welfare: A Study in the Uses and Limits of the Judicial Process," *Minnesota Law Review* 58 (1973):213.
17. Saul Alinsky, *Reveille for Radicals* (New York: Vintage, 1969), chap. 10.
18. *Griffin v. Illinois*, 351 U.S. 12 (1956); *Douglas v. California*, 372 U.S. 535 (1963).
19. *Shapiro v. Thompson*, 394 U.S. 618 (1969).
20. *Levy v. Louisiana*, 391 U.S. 68 (1968).
21. Aryeh Neier, "Protest Movements among the Disenfranchised," *Civil Liberties Review* 1 (1973): 50.
22. Section 202 (a)(3) of Title II of the Economic Opportunity Act (1964).
23. Robert Borosage et al., "The New Public Interest Lawyers," *Yale Law Journal* 79 (1970):1124–27.
24. Ibid., p. 1079, e.g., advances litigation as a device for consciousness raising, as do writers John Denvir, "Towards a Political Theory of Public Interest Litigation," *North Carolina Law Review* 54 (1976):1144-47 and Stuart A. Scheingold, *The Politics of Rights: Lawyers, Public Policy, and Political Change* (New Haven: Yale University Press, 1974), pp. 134–35.
25. On the earlier pattern, see Vose, *Caucasians Only;* Kluger, *Simple Justice;* and Frank Sorauf, *The Wall of Separation: The Constitutional Politics of Church and State* (Princeton: Princeton University Press, 1976), p. 150.
26. Thomas K. Gilhool, "The Uses of Courts and of Lawyers," in R. Kugel and A. Shearer, eds., *Changing Patterns in Residential Services for the Mentally Retarded* (Washington, D.C.: President's Committee on Mental Retardation, 1976); in the context of personal injury litigation rather than social reform litigation, see Douglas E. Rosenthal, *Lawyer and Client: Who's in Charge?* (New Brunswick: Transaction Books, 1977).
27. This trend is discussed at length in Theodore J. Lowi, *The End of Liberalism: The Second Republic of the United States,* 2d ed. (New York: Norton, 1979), especially chap. 5.
28. Jeffrey M. Berry, *Lobbying for the People: The Political Behavior of Public Interest Groups* (Princeton: Princeton University Press, 1977), p. 263.
29. Philip Selznick, "Social Advocacy in the Legal Profession in the United States," *Juridical Review* (1974): 124, and Gilhool, "Uses of Courts," p. 174.
30. Charles R. Halpern and John M. Cunningham, "Reflections on the New Public Interest Law: Theory and Practice at the Center for Law and Social Policy," *Georgetown Law Journal* 59 (1971): 1095.
31. Litigation for harassment purposes has been conducted by, for example, the Church of Scientology. See Ron Shaffer, "Church of Scientology Attacks Investigators and Critics," *Washington Post*, 16 August 1978, p. A4. Church founder L. Ron Hubbard is quoted as saying, "The purpose of a suit is to harass and discourage rather than to win. The law can be used very easily to harass, and enough harassment on somebody who is simply on the thin edge anyway . . . will

generally be sufficient to cause his professional decease. If possible, of course, ruin him utterly."

32. See chap. 2 in Handler, *Social Movements and the Legal System.*

33. Joseph R. Gusfield, *Symbolic Crusade: Status Politics and the American Temperance Movement* (Urbana: University of Illinois Press, 1963).

34. Sorauf, *Wall of Separation,* p. 92.

35. E.g., the Water Pollution Prevention and Control Act, *U.S. Code,* vol. 33, sec. 1365.

36. This issue has been particularly important in some disability rights litigation. See, for example, *Lloyd v. Regional Transportation Authority,* 548 F.2d 1277 (7th Cir. 1977) and *Trageser v. Libbie Rehabilitation Center,* 590 F.2d 87 (4th Cir. 1978), cert. denied 442 U.S. 947 (1979).

37. Krislov, "The Amicus Curiae Brief: From Friendship to Advocacy," *Yale Law Journal* 72 (1963): 696.

38. A full discussion of the liberalization of standing appears in Karen Orren, "Standing to Sue: Interest Group Conflict in the Federal Courts," *American Political Science Review* 70 (1976):723–41.

39. 372 U.S. 246 (1963).

40. 371 U.S. 415 (1963).

41. 357 U.S. 449 (1958).

42. Robert H. Birkby and Walter F. Murphy, "Interest Group Conflict in the Judicial Arena: The First Amendment and Group Access to the Court," *Texas Law Review* 42 (1964): 1037–38.

43. Dale Gronemeier, "From Net to Sword: Organizational Representatives Litigating Their Members' Claims," *University of Illinois Law Forum* (1974): 667, citing *National Automatic Laundry and Cleaning Council v. Shultz,* 443 F.2d 689, 693 (D.C. Cir. 1971).

44. 405 U.S. 727, 739 (1972).

45. 412 U.S. 669 (1973).

46. 422 U.S. 490 (1975).

47. 426 U.S. 26 (1976).

48. 432 U.S. 333, 343 (1977).

49. Ibid. at 344–45.

50. *Health Research Group and Public Citizen, Inc. v. Kennedy,* 82 F.R.D. 21 (1979).

51. Marc Galanter, "Why the 'Haves' Come Out Ahead: Speculations on the Limits of Legal Change," *Law and Society Review* 9 (1974): 96.

52. Herbert Wechsler, "Toward Neutral Principles of Constitutional Law," in Wechsler, *Principles, Politics, and Fundamental Law* (Cambridge: Harvard University Press, 1959).

53. Galanter, "Why the 'Haves' Come Out Ahead."

54. E.g., Fred Kort, "Content Analysis of Judicial Opinions and Rules of Law," in Glendon Schubert, ed., *Judicial Decision-Making* (New York: Free Press, 1963); Stuart S. Nagel, "Using Simple Calculations to Predict Judicial Decisions," *American Behavioral Scientist* 4 (1960): 24–28; Roger Benjamin and Choong Nam Kim, *American Indians and the Criminal Justice System in Minnesota* (Minneapolis: Center for Urban and Regional Affairs, 1979).

55. Sorauf, *Wall of Separation,* pp. 107, 147.

56. Debby Kaplan, Director of the Disability Rights Center in Washington, D.C.,

interviewed in Washington, January 5, 1979, noted: 'I would favor a class action whenever there's a class involved if a particular case is only illustrative of a broader problem. Otherwise the court is not going to understand the broader implications of the case." Of course, a class action also protects a suit from becoming moot if the named plaintiff or plaintiffs die, lose interest, or change their relevant status during the litigation.

57. The United States Supreme Court required the notice to class action members in *Eisen v. Carlisle & Jacquelin*, 417 U.S. 156 (1974), and the jurisdictional minimum in *Zahn v. International Paper Company*, 414 U.S. 291 (1973).

58. This quotation and subsequent quotations without specific references come from persons interviewed by the author between 1978 and 1981. These persons are listed in the bibliography, but are not identified in the text.

59. Ronald Dworkin, *Taking Rights Seriously* (Cambridge: Harvard University Press, 1977), chap. 7.

60. Sorauf, *Wall of Separation*, p. 156.

61. E.g., Gordon Harrison and Sanford M. Jaffe, "Public Interest Law Firms: New Voices for New Constituencies," *American Bar Association Journal* 58 (1972): 476.

62. On occasion, the reverse strategy of minimizing one's numbers may be preferred. Some disabled activists allege that organizations representing blind persons have chosen this strategy, refusing to join disability coalitions. See chapter 3, especially pp. 43, 48-49.

63. 331 U.S. 367, 397 (1946).

64. During the course of this study, I learned of three more such lawsuits filed—two in 1979 in New York and Nevada and one in 1980 also in New York.

Chapter 2

Lawyer Domination and the Risks of Litigating

As Richard Kluger notes in his study of the NAACP's desegregation campaign: "It is one of the idiosyncrasies of American constitutional law that cases of profound consequence are often named for plaintiffs whose involvement in the original suit is either remote or merely fortuitous. So it was with the Brown of *Brown v. Board of Education.*"[1] Indeed, social reform litigation in many areas has often seen the lawyers playing a more prominent role than the clients.

In the NAACP test cases, even when the clients took some initiative in generating the lawsuits, they generally receded to a passive role once the NAACP lawyers took over.[2] Frank Sorauf reports a similar pattern in First Amendment litigation sponsored by national organizations.[3] Joel Handler not only cites numerous examples of this in public interest litigation, but also suggests reasons why it occurs, such as the free rider problem among clients in group litigation, the lack of organizational ties between lawyer and client, and the need of the lawyers for the litigation limelight to keep their financial support coming in.[4]

Other reasons for lawyer domination are particularly associated with litigation with the goal of obtaining a constitutional precedent from the Supreme Court, in contrast to remedy-oriented litigation. Because of the danger of setting bad precedents, constitutional litigators must be very cautious and pick only cases that are sure winners (as closely as that can be predicted). This means cases with uncluttered issues and full trial court records, which are best achieved with the kind of central supervision exercised by the national office of the NAACP in its cases. With control over strategy, the NAACP could coordinate sequential cases from various geographical areas and retain the initiative over the decision to appeal cases lost in the lower courts, contributing to its success rate at the Supreme Court.

Success defined in terms of the number of cases won before the Court, however, masks the biggest problem of litigating with the goal of setting constitutional precedent: once it is achieved, the decision may not necessarily be enforced. Constitutional litigation campaigns, like those of the NAACP, are based on a belief in the efficacy of legal rule change—what Stuart Scheingold calls the "myth of rights."

> The assumption is that litigation can evoke a declaration of rights from courts; that it can, further, be used to assure the realization of these rights; and, finally, that realization is tantamount to meaningful change. The myth of rights is, in other words, premised on a direct linking of litigation, rights, and remedies with social change.[5]

This myth of rights deeply penetrates American political culture. The formal constitutional basis of our government puts politics within a framework of rules about who has which capacities and rights and how the rules can be changed. The process of appellate court decision making further suggests that social change can be accommodated and encouraged by judges' applying and interpreting the rules of the past to new situations with an eye to their precedential value in the future.

Beyond the wisdom or error of the rule announced in any given judicial decision, however, lies the problem of translating that decision, that determination of rights and obligations, into behavioral changes that really make up social change. Courts are notably lacking in direct enforcement powers. They rely primarily on recognition of their legitimacy to win compliance with their decisions. The weight of that legitimacy in American society should not be underestimated—it gives court victories considerable symbolic value. But research of the past fifteen years has documented the numerous occasions when court decisions do not bring about immediate, universal changes in past behavior.[6] Rules are not self-executing; they require an enforcement mechanism. No better evidence for that exists than the slow and painful process of school desegregation.

Even litigation which recognizes the importance of field-level implementation for true success often does not involve any greater client participation than constitutional litigation has. A recent study by Joel F. Handler of the determinants of successful social reform litigation acknowledges that the achievement of tangible, as opposed to symbolic, outcomes requires two steps: "First, new norms must be established or existing ones revalidated; second, the norms must somehow be implemented in the field."[7] Furthermore, in contrast to the precedent-oriented interest groups traditionally studied in political science, Handler, a law professor, examines what he calls "law reform" efforts, which are characterized by a focus on "enforcing laws already on the books" and by advocacy which takes place not just in the courtroom but "wherever important decisions are made."[8] Certainly, the accessible transit litigation would fall into this category.

Nevertheless, Handler does not find clients to be an important factor in the success or failure of such law reform. In fact, he finds both the lawyers and the client groups to be unable to provide long-term monitoring of a court decision to ensure its implementation. As a result, the variable which Handler finds to be the most important in determining success is what he calls the bureaucratic contingency.[9] By this he means whether the benefit sought can be provided with a one-time decision made at the top, requiring minimal administrative discretion at the field level and minimal time to implement. Decisions which must be implemented by many scattered decision makers are much more difficult to monitor. Thus, the best solution to the problem of doing follow-up is to avoid the need for it altogether.

The lawyers' and clients' inabilities to stay involved for the long term are due to different factors. The public interest lawyers he studied tended to pursue their own priorities and interests independent of the clients unless they happened to be organizationally linked to the client group. Frequent new litigation was both the source of the lawyers' intrinsic rewards from using their legal skills and the main vehicle of publicity which kept their funds coming in from foundations and contributors. They also lacked the technical and political resources for long commitments to behind-the-scenes negotiations or routine monitoring of compliance with a court decision.[10]

The client groups Handler studied, on the other hand, tended to be large groups seeking collective goods, which made them susceptible to the free rider problem: that rational persons will not contribute to the group because they can get the advantage of the collective benefits without helping to attain them, unless selective incentives are available to induce them to cooperate. Among Handler's groups only the organizational staff or leaders had the material selective incentives of salary and prestige for working for the collective good. They spent most of their time cultivating a group of mass contributors, who had only purposive incentives for contributing to the organization, that is, the good feelings one gets from helping to accomplish a goal. Handler argues that such an incentive is rarely strong enough to survive for a long time or to resist rival appeals for the contributions.[11] Keeping the contributions coming in took so much of the time of the paid staff that they were unable to undertake the long-term follow-up to ensure the implementation of a legal victory.[12]

Handler's theory would not predict the active client involvement in the litigation and its aftermath which occurred in the transit access cases. His theory does accord with the typical pattern in social reform litigation, however. To account for the transit litigation, one needs to turn to another model of social reform.

It is the tradition of community organizing, rather than social reform litigation, that has long asserted the possibility of grassroots people pursuing their own interests and goals. Organizing a community to pursue its own political interests has been an alternative political strategy, independent of litigation, at least since Saul Alinsky's activities in the Forties, with roots in the labor movement and earlier protest groups.[13] If social reform litigation clients could be similarly mobilized to take the responsibility for following up litigation to ensure its fulfillment, then presumably having a favorable bureaucratic contingency, in Handler's terms, would be less critical and more social reform lawsuits would achieve ultimate long-term success.

If client groups are to be able to do this, however, they must emerge from the litigation process as healthy and strong organizations. The question, then, becomes the compatibility of litigation and community organizing as political strategies—whether the two can work hand in hand or whether there is something about litigation that inevitably subordinates the client to the lawyer and ultimately emasculates the client.

Litigation and Community Organization: Possibilities and Problems

The Possibilities: Creating or Strengthening Organizations

Although the NAACP had sometimes left a new or revitalized local chapter in the wake of a lawsuit, creating such groups was never a primary purpose of the Legal Defense Fund lawyers.[14] The combination of litigation and community organizing was first widely articulated as a political strategy in the War on Poverty during the Sixties, when antipoverty lawyers found their clients often feeling hopeless and defeated by life.

People must believe that they can do something about their problems before they will organize to act upon them, so in the antipoverty movement, consciousness raising became an explicit goal of litigation. Activist lawyers and legal scholars asserted the ability of litigation to change complainants' perception of a problem from a personal discontent to a political demand, turning despair into indignation.[15] Litigation legitimates a complaint by asserting the violation of some rightful claim. It legitimates the feeling of being wronged and reinforces the inclination to fight back. Scheingold writes of "altering self-conceptions by imparting. . . a sense of 'legal competence'."[16] For Edgar and Jean Cahn, legal advocacy is "emancipating" and it "enhances the capacity of individuals to cope on their own, to secure justice, and to avoid injury."[17]

The vehicle usually envisioned for this emancipation was the class action test case. A class action test case would reveal the universality of many people's grievances and encourage them to band together to solve their problems. The change of perception might also affect the general public and the courts themselves. Formulating a cause in legal terms might attract moderate allies who would not be sympathetic to a direct action strategy.[18] Gary Bellow makes the direct connection between litigation and political organizing:

> If litigation is directed toward the different goal of organizing, the potentials and methods in pursuing a law suit significantly change. In such a context, law suits can consciously be brought for the public discussion they generate, and for the express purpose of influencing middle class and lower class perspectives on the problems they illuminate. They can be vehicles for setting in motion other political processes and for building coalitions and alliances. . . . It is on this base that the coalitions and publicity can be built and the groups can be organized to limit previously invisible authority.[19]

The culmination of this vision is what Scheingold calls the "politics of rights." Legal rights won through litigation become resources for organizing politically the disadvantaged group and those potential allies responsive to legal norms. In this way legal victories could be monitored by the intended beneficiaries to see that they are enforced. Political demands would become political issues when "pressed by effective political organizations."[20]

While Scheingold sees lawyers and litigation as useful primarily in this consciousness-raising and initial organizing stage, the arguments of others stress the contributions of litigation to an ongoing organization. Litigation can produce new information through processes such as discovery, create new forums for additional debate, and cause delay—all of which can be used by organizers.[21] Community organizations can reciprocate by providing ideas and leads for future lawsuits, recruiting individual clients and assuring their availability, collecting data for the suits, and legitimating them within the community by their participation.[22]

Astute organizational leaders should be able to take advantage of a lawsuit to generate publicity and legitimacy for their groups. Litigation is often newsworthy, and a press conference held to announce a development in a lawsuit may bring the organization and its goals to the attention of potential new supporters. These are the types of activities that Sorauf identified with his third category of litigation goals, organizational or ideological gain.[23] In the context of largely precedent-oriented First Amendment litigation, such a goal may appear dangerous and selfish. In the context of remedy-oriented litigation, it is an appropriate part of the "politics of rights"—educating the potential beneficiaries of the litigation and the wider public about the issues in hopes of mobilizing their support.

Emerging occasionally in the beneficent visions of litigation, however, is an underlying worry about the possible incompatibility of litigation and community organizations. For example, Handler outlines a number of risks to a social reform group of choosing litigation as a political strategy, in addition to the danger that the lawyers may try to shape the litigation to meet their own goals:

> Using the legal system itself may exact a high price. The lawyers, with the leaders, often assume a dominant position with regard to tactics and strategy once the group goes the legal route. The membership is confronted with a mysterious procedure and trade language; the specialists take over. There is a danger that the nonlegal activity of the group will languish pending the outcome of the litigation. There will be the inevitable delays that can sap the enthusiasm of the membership. Using the courts might mean framing the issues that, while legally sound, lose political and purposive appeal. [sic][24]

We will look in more detail at four of these potential dangers for reform groups in litigation: the costs in money and human energy, deception by symbolic victories, the slow pace of litigation, and subservience to lawyers.

The Problems: Undermining Organizations

The most obvious danger is for a group to make financial commitments it cannot sustain. Litigation is expensive, especially if complex fact situations are being disputed and it is necessary to gather extensive evidence or to assemble witnesses. The cost is a major reason why groups often sponsor test case litigation; individuals alone could not carry the financial burden.[25]

Of course, the clients in social reform litigation often do not pay all or even any of the costs of the litigation.[26] A group such as the NAACP relied on contributions from its nationwide membership or grants from foundations to support its litigation because its clients were usually poor. Government-funded legal sevices for the poor and foundation-funded public interest law centers emerged in the Sixties to provide low- or no-cost legal assistance for particular causes. Frequently, however, while the lawyers' salaries are paid by these sources, clients may have to contribute to any cash outlays the litigation requires.

Any contribution the client group makes to the suit in time as well as money is likely to require a trade-off with some other priority of the organization. Especially if group members do play the active role in litigation and its subsequent activities envisioned by the "politics of rights" view, it will be time- and energy-consuming. Other activities of the group could suffer, or discord might occur among members with different opinions about the group's priorities.

A second danger is that groups may fail to understand that a court victory is only the beginning of the battle and that continued efforts may be necessary to ensure that the court's decision is enforced. This concern is basic to the idea of combining litigation and community organization. Drawing on Murray Edelman's sense of the manipulative power of political symbols, Scheingold warns litigants against succumbing to the "myth of rights" common in American culture—the belief that a legal declaration of a right translates automatically into the realization of that right.[27] Winning a lawsuit can create a false sense of success and reduce the impetus for long-term organizing.

The slow pace of litigation, the third danger, may occasionally be a benefit, but it also brings great risks. Delays can be used to gather information, raise money, or recruit supporters, but this is more likely to be needed by the defendants than by the plaintiffs, who had the initiative in deciding when to bring the suit in the first place. When a group has initiated a lawsuit, long delays can sap a group's enthusiasm. It is hard to keep up the momentum for fund-raising or to milk a suit for publicity when little or nothing seems to be happening. Furthermore, a lawsuit often involves a series of interim decisions—motions and counter-motions and possibly appeals of these—before a decision on the merits is reached. Losing at one of these preliminary stages could be so discouraging that a group might decide not to go on.[28]

The damage caused by even small defeats has long been recognized by community organizers. A staff member of the National Welfare Rights Organization has stated: "Of course it is harmful for poor people to do battle and lose. Losing only confirms their worst expectations and makes future battles less likely. For this reason, professional organizers never acknowledge a defeat: every action results in a 'victory.' "[29] This view contrasts sharply with Sorauf's observation about constitutional litigation: "It is often easier to reach the highest appellate court—the goal of constitutional litigation—if one loses his case. In a manner of speaking, one 'loses' one's way to the Supreme Court."[30]

An additional risk of the slow pace of litigation is that the faster pace of developments outside of the courtroom may resolve the issue *de facto* before the court declares who wins the legal battle.[31] Donald Horowitz notes a striking example of this in the efforts of the Philadelphia Area-Wide Council to litigate its right to participate in the city's Model Cities program. When the group lost its funding, it went to court to regain it and ultimately won the suit. But in the intervening period of almost three years, the Area-Wide Council had completely disintegrated as a functioning organization, and another rival group had become well established in the neighborhood.[32]

The fourth and most fundamental danger to groups from litigation, the one most commonly noted in the literature, is that a lawsuit may become dominated by the lawyer and that the organizational members will lose control over "their" issue.[33] It is little wonder that such a concern exists, for lawyer domination has been common in the history of social reform litigation, as noted at the beginning of this chapter. Lawyer domination of a lawsuit is, of course, consistent with the traditional model of lawyer-client interaction, as described by Douglas Rosenthal. The traditional model calls for the client to rely completely on the lawyer to solve his or her problem. Such passivity is justified on the grounds that legal problems have technical solutions beyond the comprehension of most clients and that professionals can be trusted to give competent, disinterested service on the client's behalf.[34]

Lawyer Domination: The Short- And Long-Range Dangers

In social reform litigation lawyer domination can have two different aspects: (1) controlling the content and management of the lawsuit and (2) creating dependence on the lawyer, impairing the organization's ability to function in the long run. Rosenthal is primarily concerned about the short-run effects because the litigation he studied is individual and apolitical—personal injury litigation. Dependence of an individual on a lawyer to solve personal problems can develop, of course, but a personal injury suit itself does not typically involve a lawyer-client relationship continuing much beyond the resolution of the suit. An award of money damages is likely to be a single transaction or, if not, is at least relatively simple to monitor.[35] In contrast, monitoring the outcome of a social reform lawsuit may involve the lawyer and clients in a long-term relationship.

Who Controls the Substance of the Litigation?

Rosenthal proposes a participatory model of lawyer-client interaction as an alternative to the traditional model. He believes that many of the decisions in a lawsuit which the traditional model presumes are routine, technical, and inaccessible to most nonlawyers are, indeed, "open choices" which are individualized in each case and understandable to the layperson.[36] The decisions in a personal injury suit that Rosenthal argues are open and should be discussed by a lawyer with the client include whether to sue at all, the ground rules of the lawyer's and client's mutual contact, the lawyer's fee, the preparation of the case, the best time to sue, whether to seek a jury trial or special trial preference, various issues of settlement strategy, and the preparation for examination before trial.

Most of these decisions are also important in a social reform lawsuit and appropriate for joint lawyer-client consideration. There are two additional issues frequently "open" in a social reform suit, which are almost always taken for granted in a personal injury case: whom to sue and what type of remedy to request. The question of whom to sue is likely to be only partially open. If the suit challenges the practices of a public institution or agency, for example, one must name as defendants the officials with the legal capacity to provide the relief sought. That much is a technical legal requirement, which only the lawyer might know. Naming other defendants, however, is optional and may be influenced by political considerations concerning past or potential allies outside of the courtroom. The client may have definite opinions about this point and could make such decisions once informed by the lawyer of any legal risk in naming or failing to name certain officials.

Client involvement in the choice of relief to be sought is even more important because the lawyer may not be aware of the differential impact of different remedies on the client. Mental health litigation provides a good example. A "right to treatment" suit seeks better conditions for residents of an institution, whereas a "least restrictive alternative" suit usually seeks to release a person from an institution and provide him or her with community-based services. Clearly, the ramifications for the client of the two remedies would be very different, and it is not necessarily the place of the lawyer to say what is in the best interest of the client. Another example is the debate over full-size buses on regularly scheduled routes versus door-to-door, demand-responsive mini-buses as the preferable mode of accessible transportation. The importance of client participation in this decision was noted by one accessible transit litigant:

> Lawyers don't always understand the need or what the eventual remedy should or could be. It's not like a malpractice suit where the only remedy is damages, money damages. . . . Here we're after accessibility; we're not after money; we're not after a slap on the other side's hand; we're not trying to prove a point. We're just trying to get access and use of a facility that, number one, we helped pay for and, number two, that legally we're entitled to use. And so it's important that lawyers in that sense understand their clients' needs and desires and work closely with them so that if you are winning a remedy, it has to be one that would be an effective remedy.

The choice of a remedy may have significant ideological overtones, as in the dislike of demand-responsive bus service because of its separate-but-equal connotations. One remedy may be a more long-range, ideal solution to a problem, while another may provide a more immediate solution. Social reform lawyers who work full-time in a particular area are likely to have ideological commitments to broad principles beyond a single lawsuit. This may bring them into conflict with their clients over remedies unless the lawyers also suffer from the immediate, day-to-day problem as much as the clients do or unless the clients have particular fortitude and similarly long-range goals.

In the area of school desegregation, for example, Derrick Bell has expressed concern about the gap between the belief of civil rights lawyers in school integration as an ideal and the desire of clients—parents and children—for educational improvement, whether in a segregated or integrated environment.[37] In the mental health litigation described above, a "least restrictive alternative" suit is preferred to a "right to treatment" suit by those persons committed to the belief that institutional life per se is bad for a person and that deinstitutionalization with community services is preferable. The lawyers of the Mental Health Law Project, for instance, are committed to the goal of deinstitutionalization and will no longer provide their services for persons wishing to bring a "right to treatment" suit.[38]

Even if they have no preference for any particular tangible remedy, lawyers may have their own goal of establishing an important legal precedent. The emphasis of their education on legal doctrine as a product of sequential appellate court decisions may create a bias toward seeking a definitive court decision rather than settling for a consent agreement.[39] For example, Sorauf found among First Amendment litigators that the local individuals or groups bringing the suits were likely to be more interested in a remedy to the problem at hand and less interested in constitutional precedent than were the national organizations providing the legal assistance, such as the American Civil Liberties Union (ACLU) or the American Jewish Congress (AJC).[40]

The tension is not limited to constitutional issues. The clients may be primarily interested in obtaining some service as soon as possible, which may most quickly be achieved through a compromise settlement with the defendant agency. The lawyer, on the other hand, may prefer to go to trial and, if necessary, appeal to get a court ruling that the agency has a statutory duty to provide the service.[41]

The possibility of lawyer-client conflict is increased when the lawyer is responsive to a constituency, different from the clients, from which the lawyer receives moral and financial support. This is a common circumstance in social reform litigation because its costs are so often paid by sources other than the client. The constituents may be of a social class different from the client's, as is often true in civil rights and civil liberties litigation,[42] or be of the same social class, as with community control of a poverty law center.[43]

Potential lawyer-client conflicts become manifest only if the client asserts a point of view different from the lawyer's, of course. There will be no overt conflict if the client is passive, as in Rosenthal's traditional model, or completely agrees with the lawyer. If prospective clients are inclined to assert opposing opinions, lawyers can often avoid conflicts by providing their services only to amenable clients who agree with them and/or are passive.

Because social reform clients often do not pay for the legal costs and lawyers' fees, the lawyers can (and must) be very selective about which clients they take.[44] The Mental Health Law Project cited above is an example. Other times clients are recruited after the decision to bring suit has been made.[45] In the case of ideologically motivated public interest clients, a mutually acceptable approach to the lawsuit may be carefully negotiated before the suit begins, so that the clients can be confident that their views are being represented without needing to be very actively involved.[46]

The upshot of this is that through negotiation, selectivity, or client passivity, lawyers with broad ideological commitments tend to dominate social reform litigation. The problem, however, is that such litigation often requires long-term supervision to ensure implementation of the remedy, which lawyers may not be willing to do. For this reason, the second aspect of lawyer domination of litigation, the creation or reinforcement of dependence in the clients, is particularly dangerous in social reform litigation. If the lawyers do not follow up the litigation and the clients are unable to do so without the lawyers' help, a legal victory could be stillborn for lack of continuing attention.

Do Lawyers Increase the Independence or the Dependence of Clients?

Even the proponents of litigation as a strategy for consciousness raising and organizing admit that it can backfire and create a dependence in the clients on the lawyer that reinforces feelings of helplessness. Especially when "tainted by racism," the Cahns warn that legal advocacy "can readily be converted into a form of imperialism by expertise which increases dependence and manipulates clients under the guise of providing assistance."[47] In the words of John Denvir:

> When litigation has undermined organization, the proper message has become distorted. Instead of showing the organized that the establishment can be defeated, thereby inciting other community efforts at organization and pressure, the litigation has taught only the lesson that the establishment can be defeated by lawyers. This proposition is not only false, it also reinforces the basic apathy that organization attempts to overcome.[48]

Supporters of litigation as a strategy acknowledge that the problem lies with the role that the lawyer plays, but they are vague about solutions or even about when consciousness raising and organizing through litigation will "work" and when it will not. Denvir continues: "This [undermining organization], however, is not a weakness of litigation itself, but a misconception of certain attorneys of exactly what their proper role should be in organizational attempts and a misconception by the organized of the abilities of attorneys that encourages deference to them."[49]

Out-and-out critics of the test case approach have discussed the problem in more detail, emphasizing class differences between lawyers and clients and the tendency of lawyers to protect their professional interests. Harry Brill found the lawyers of the San Francisco Neighborhood Legal Assistance Foundation to be more eager to maintain their reputations among the local influentials as neutral mediators than they were to advocate vigorously the positions of their clients. But class actions were a strategy that appeared to be as direct an assault on the problems as the clients' own: "Class action provided the lawyers with a politically militant language that justified their bypassing other legal alternatives, yet could still persuade the organizers that they were serious about their anti-Establishment convictions."[50]

Stephen Wexler, former house counsel for the National Welfare Rights Organization, is another critic of litigation because of its tendency to be dominated by the lawyer. He rejects most litigation as a phony "lawyer's game" and recommends avoiding it altogether, unlike Brill, who recommends individual legal aid rather than test cases as the best way to help poor people. Wexler favors lawyers' doing other work in support of community organizations, such as writing training materials and rights manuals, training lay advocates, and preparing people for confrontation situations.[51]

The whole debate over the compatibility of litigation and organizing is part of the larger issue of the relationship between action and consciousness. The importance of personal participation is a fundamental tenet of organizing because of the belief that self-esteem is increased by doing something for one's self instead of having it done by others. Saul Alinsky staked his whole strategy on this psychological premise.

> It is impossible to overemphasize the enormous importance of people's doing things themselves. It is the most common human reaction that successful attainment of objectives is much more meaningful to people who have achieved the objectives through their own efforts. The objective is never an end itself. The efforts that are exerted in the actual earning of the objective are part and parcel of the achievement itself. . . . It is part of what great religious schools of thought call the dignity of man. It is living in dignity to achieve things through your own intelligence and efforts.[52]

The black civil rights movement, for example, falls into strategic and rhetorical stages which reflect changes in consciousness and participation. During the early years participation was confined to a relatively small number of persons and organizations. Indeed, as the only major litigator in the field, the NAACP was able to coordinate and control the desegregation litigation.

Following the impact of *Brown v. Board of Education*[53] on the rights consciousness of black Americans, noted in chapter 1, the mid-Fifties saw mass action strategies beginning, such as marches, boycotts, and work stoppages, which involved large numbers of persons in directly protesting their situation. As tactics escalated to sit-ins and other obstructive demonstrations, people found that "putting one's body on the line" brings about a change in consciousness.[54] The result was increased self-esteem, epitomized by the Sixties' rallying cry, "Black is beautiful!"

This link between participation and consciousness may be particularly important for oppressed or devalued social groups, but intense involvement can create increased commitment to any cause. Michael Barkun and James Levine's study of a suburban Chicago open housing project in the summer of 1965 describes this link between direct personal involvement and consciousness among a group of middle-class whites.

> The meetings were longer than was necessary simply to conduct business because they functioned not only to transact business but also to mold and strengthen individual attitudes. The tactics (ranging from attitude surveys to petitions to vigils) did constitute a grab-bag, but their latent function was not to change the environment but to provide an arena in which attitudes could be tested through action. . . . The slow ascent from interviewing and fact-gathering to vigils in front of real estate offices did not represent the stages in a calculated campaign of social change, but rather the stages in innumerable personal journeys of commitment.[55]

This example suggests that political strategies fall into a tacit hierarchy according to the participants' level of consciousness. More abstract or intellectual activities seem to correspond to lower levels of consciousness and commitment, and more physical activities, especially if obstructive or destructive, seem to correspond to higher levels. How then does litigation fit into such a hierarchy of strategies? Obviously, it is relative to the times and to the group. What would be considered a moderate strategy among blacks in the Sixties would be considered radical among parents of disabled children in the Sixties or even in the Seventies.

Litigation is unique in being the only political strategy which requires a citizen or citizen group to obtain the assistance of an expert—a lawyer. There are professional organizers, lobbyists, and public relations experts, of course, but amateurs undertake such activities constantly, unlike the relatively rare and controversial *pro se* litigant. As a result, litigation may be rejected by groups that are aware of the psychological dimensions of strategy choice and for whom consciousness raising is a goal.

This was the case with the open housing project studied by Barkun and Levine. The latent function of building commitment lying behind the tactical choices resulted in a strong rejection of litigation as an approach to combatting housing discrimination, even though several legal grounds for such a challenge existed and the project had several lawyers who had volunteered to undertake a suit. In the first place, the slow pace of litigation would likely have made a suit last beyond the scheduled duration of the project, but litigation was rejected for two other reasons as well. It would involve only a few people with specific skills and thus go against the norm of mass participation. Secondly, because the project leaders knew little about the legal issues, they would have had almost no control over the lawyers. The role they preferred for the lawyers was providing information when requested and making sure the project did nothing illegal.[56]

The two aspects of lawer domination—control of the content of the lawsuit and creation of dependence on the lawyer—are surely related. As the open housing leaders sensed, dependence develops when the clients are ignorant of the contents of "their" suit, when the lawyer has made the major and minor decisions about its formulation. This is why Rosenthal's idea of "open choices" is so important. If clients can share in the concrete, day-to-day decisions arising from the lawsuit itself, their chances of becoming dependent on the lawyer in the long run are much smaller.

The Impact of Litigation on the Accessible Transit Clients

The impact that litigating had on the disability groups in the transit access lawsuits fell somewhere between the very positive and very negative pictures that occur in the literature. While no group achieved great attention, acclaim, increased financial support, and new members flocking in with raised consciousness, neither did any group suffer the disastrous extreme of losing all control over the suit to the lawyer, losing interest in the issue, losing members, and collapsing.

The transit access cases generally escaped domination by their lawyers because in each of the six suits studied in detail at least one client was actively involved in all phases of the litigation. In some of the cases an organized group of clients both played a major role in formulating the lawsuit itself and did considerable follow-up to ensure that their gains were realized. In general, the clients' efforts were relatively successful, although their success came less from outright victories in court than from negotiation, political pressure, and advocacy "wherever important decisions are made," in the style of Handler's law reform model.

The accessible transit litigation was much closer to Handler's law reform model than to the NAACP constitutional model. In terms of Sorauf's categories of goals, the accessible transportation litigation was primarily oriented to remedy and secondarily to organizational and ideological gains, with scarcely any concern for constitutional precedents. The lawsuits were, in a sense, two steps removed from the main type of goal of the NAACP, the ACLU, and the AJC. In the first place, the transit suits were argued primarily on statutory rather than constitutional grounds. Although equal protection of the laws and the right to travel were sometimes included among the legal bases for a complaint, laws passed by Congress that endorse the principle that public transportation should be accessible to persons with disabilities were the major bases for relief claimed.

Litigation seeking the interpretation of an existing legal rule may be no more efficacious than litigation seeking to change a legal rule, of course. The problem of translating the rule into policy—implementing the rule—still remains. In this regard, the transit access suits deviated yet a second step away from the interest group litigation for constitutional development. Though the transit suits formally requested judicial interpretation of statutory law, in reality they emphasized getting immediate relief more than getting a binding interpretation of a statutory right.

With the elevation of remedy over principle, the court's authority is no longer unique; the plaintiffs may be able to get what they want through a negotiated settlement with the relevant government agency as well as through a court order. Thus, the litigation becomes as important for the pressure it can put on nonjudicial policy makers as it is for the actual decision of the court.

It is here that Sorauf's third type of goal—organizational, ideological, or publicity gains—comes into play. Strengthening the organization and increasing public awareness of the issues are particularly important when nonjudicial policy makers are approached. In some of the transit access lawsuits, the plaintiffs simultaneously conducted the lawsuit and carried out many other tactics to achieve the same goal, such as legislative lobbying, public relations campaigning, and demonstrating. In the process, assumptions about decision making in one institution get applied to others. Although the courts are specifically constituted as nondemocratic or antimajoritarian institutions, litigants try to influence the judges by the weight of numbers as well as the weight of argument.

This kind of strategy is similar to Scheingold's concept of the "politics of rights," his recommended antidote to the "myth of rights." Rather than assuming that court declarations of rights will be translated into remedies which themselves will constitute the change desired by the litigants, rights should be treated as resources for mobilizing the intended beneficiaries of those rights. Scheingold suggests that real changes will occur only when and if the beneficiaries organize and follow up the court decisions through other political channels. The disabled litigants in the accessible transportation litigation played the politics of rights much more than they succumbed to the myth of rights.

Although these cases are closer to Handler's model than to the NAACP model, they tend to be more successful than his theory would predict. Both the plaintiff groups and the lawyers in the disability rights litigation had characteristics different from the expectations of Handler's theory, which enabled them to pursue their issue over a longer time period. Accessible transportation is certainly a collective good, and the number of potential beneficiaries is large even if only those persons who cannot now ride public transportation are counted. This should make the plaintiff groups susceptible to the free rider problem and in need of some type of selective incentive to overcome it. While a few of the active participants in these suits had salaried positions which paid them for their advocacy of disabled persons' needs, most did not. Purposive incentives were certainly there, but Handler may be right that they alone are inadequate to motivate group action for an extended conflict.

The biggest shortcoming of Handler's theory as applied to disability rights litigation is that he discounts the importance of solidary (i.e., social or fraternal) incentives as a strengthening factor among social reform groups. The groups he studied tended to be either dispersed and anonymous or made up of persons, such as very low-income people, who he believes respond primarily to material incentives. In the disability rights movement, however, solidary incentives have played a major role and helped give the groups in this study more endurance for long-term struggles than Handler would expect.

Handler's analysis of the lawyers concludes that they are no more likely to do extensive follow-up to ensure implementation than the groups themselves, though for different reasons. In the transit access cases, however, the lawyers did not act as independently of the clients as Handler predicts even though not one of them was organizationally linked to the client groups. Although there was a little bias toward litigation over other strategies among some of the lawyers, this did not prevent the use of simultaneous activities in other arenas to reach the desired goal.

The whole lawyer-client relationship evident in the transit access cases differed from Handler's expectations and from the pattern in NAACP or church–state litigation. National organizations like the NAACP or the AJC that have conducted planned litigation campaigns typically have their own legal staff or are primarily composed of lawyers. As a result, the lawyers rather than the clients tend to dominate the lawsuits, determining the legal strategy and recruiting clients who are willing to cooperate with the chosen strategy.

In the transit access litigation the interest groups involved either had close ties with the clients or were the clients themselves. The lawyers were not permanently associated with the groups, and the clients were more likely to have decided to litigate and then sought out a lawyer to represent them than the reverse. As a result, the clients played a greater role in shaping the litigation than in the typical suit sponsored by a national organization. The clients also then remained active in monitoring the court decisions or negotiated agreements they had won. The reasons for the difference of this pattern from Handler's expectations lie in the development of the disability rights movement as a whole.

Notes

1. Kluger, *Simple Justice*, p. 407.
2. Kluger, *Simple Justice*.
3. Sorauf, *Wall of Separation*, pp. 150 and 154.
4. Handler, *Social Movements and the Legal System*, pp. 5–14 and 25–33.
5. Scheingold, *The Politics of Rights*, p. 5. For a pessimistic view of the prospects of using law and courts to protect persons with disabilities, see Wolf Wolfensberger, *A Balanced Multi-Component Advocacy/Protection Scheme*, Law and Mental Retardation: A Monograph Series (Toronto: Canadian Association for the Mentally Retarded, 1977), pp. 41–42.
6. This research is often referred to as the "impact studies." Two collections of these studies are Stephen Wasby, *The Impact of the United States Supreme Court: Some Perspectives* (Homewood, Ill.: Dorsey Press, 1970) and Theodore Becker and Malcolm M. Feeley, eds., *The Impact of Supreme Court Decisions*, 2d. ed. (New York: Oxford University Press, 1973).
7. Handler, *Social Movements and the Legal System*, p. 36.
8. *Ibid.*, p. 3.
9. *Ibid.*, pp. 18–22.
10. *Ibid.*, pp. 25–33.
11. Handler does note that organizations such as Common Cause occasionally manage to survive with primarily purposive incentives for members. *Social Movements and the Legal System*, p. 9.
12. *Ibid.*, pp. 5–14.
13. Alinsky, *Reveille for Radicals*, and William A. Gamson, *The Strategy of Social Protest* (Homewood, Ill.: Dorsey Press, 1975).
14. Kluger, *Simple Justice*, p. 17, describes the birth of one such local branch in conjunction with a lawsuit.
15. Denvir, "Political Theory of Public Interest Litigation," pp. 1143–46; Borosage et al., "New Public Interest Lawyers," p. 1079; Arthur R. Matthews, Jr., and Jonathan A. Weiss, "What Can Be Done: A Neighborhood Lawyer's Credo," in Elihu Katz and Brenda Danet, eds., *Bureaucracy and the Public: A Reader in Official-Client Relations* (New York: Basic Books, 1973), p. 444.

16. Scheingold, *Politics of Rights,* p. 135.

17. Edgar S. Cahn and Jean Camper Cahn, "Power to the People or the Profession?—The Public Interest in Public Interest Law," *Yale Law Journal* 79 (1970): 1041.

18. Borosage et al., "New Public Interest Lawyers," p. 1079.

19. Quoted in Borosage et al, p. 1087.

20. Scheingold, *Politics of Rights,* p. 139.

21. Denvir, "Political Theory of Public Interest Litigation," pp. 1137–43.

22. Harry Brill, "The Uses and Abuses of Legal Assistance," *The Public Interest* 31 (1973): 47.

23. Sorauf, *Wall of Separation,* p. 92.

24. Handler, *Social Movements and the Legal System,* p. 33.

25. Krislov, *The Supreme Court in the Political Process* (New York: Macmillan, 1965), pp. 41–42; Herbert Jacob, *Justice in America: Courts, Lawyers, and the Judicial Process,* 2d ed. (Boston: Little, Brown and Co., 1972), pp. 133–34.

26. Sorauf, *Wall of Separation,* pp. 150–51.

27. Scheingold, *Politics of Rights,* p. 5; Murray Edelman, *Politics as Symbolic Action: Mass Arousal and Quiescence* (New York: Academic Press, 1971).

28. Henry di Suvero, "The Movement and the Legal System," in Jonathan Black, ed., *Radical Lawyers: Their Role in the Movement and in the Courts* (New York: Avon Books, 1971), pp. 67–68.

29. Stephen Wexler, "Practicing Law for Poor People," *Yale Law Journal* 79 (1970): 1058 n.9.

30. Sorauf, *Wall of Separation,* p. 122.

31. di Suvero, "The Movement and the Legal System," pp. 67–68.

32. Donald L. Horowitz, *The Courts and Social Policy* (Washington, D.C.: The Brookings Institution, 1977), chap. 3.

33. Cahn and Cahn, "Power to the People," pp. 1021–22 and 1040; Denvir, "Political Theory of Public Interest Litigation," p. 1144; Brill, "Uses and Abuses of Legal Assistance," p. 54; Wexler, "Practicing Law for Poor People," p. 1053.

34. Rosenthal, *Lawyer and Client,* p. 13.

35. Handler, *Social Movements and the Legal System,* p. 25.

36. Rosenthal, *Lawyer and Client,* p. 13.

37. Derrick A. Bell, Jr., "Serving Two Masters: Integration Ideals and Client Interests in School Desegregation Litigation," *Yale Law Journal* 85 (1976): 470.

38. According to Norman Rosenberg, attorney, Mental Health Law Project, interviewed in Washington, D.C., October 17, 1978.

39. Bell, "Integration Ideals and Client Interests"; Sorauf, *Wall of Separation,* pp. 86–88; Scheingold, *Politics of Rights,* especially chap. 10; Judith N. Shklar, *Legalism: An Essay on Law, Morals and Politics* (Cambridge: Harvard University Press, 1964); Brill, "Uses and Abuses of Legal Assistance."

40. Sorauf, *Wall of Separation,* pp. 86–88 and 92.

41. The decision when to settle rather than to press a case further is so fundamental, however, that it is one of only two issues which even most of the lawyers Rosenthal surveyed agreed should be discussed with the client. *Lawyer and Client,* p. 113. The degree of lawyer influence on the client's perception of an acceptable settlement can be considerable, of course. Ibid., p. 69.

42. Bell, "Integration Ideals and Client Interests."

43. Borosage, et. al. "New Public Interest Lawyers," pp. 1125–27.
44. Robert L. Rabin, "Lawyers for Social Change: Perspectives on Public Interest Law," *Stanford Law Review* 28 (1976): 234.
45. Ibid., p. 235; also Sorauf, *Wall of Separation*, p. 154.
46. Rabin, "Lawyers for Social Change," p. 234.
47. Cahn and Cahn, "Power to the People," p. 1040.
48. Denvir, "Theory of Public Interest Litigation," p. 1144; see also Borosage et al., "New Public Interest Lawyers," p. 1079.
49. Denvir, "Theory of Public Interest Litigation," p. 1144.
50. Brill, "Uses and Abuses of Legal Assistance," p. 51.
51. Wexler, "Practicing Law for Poor People," pp. 1056–58.
52. Alinsky, *Reveille for Radicals*, pp. 174–75.
53. 347 U.S. 483 (1954).
54. *Civil Disorders*, pp. 225–30.
55. Michael Barkun and James Levine, "Protest in Suburbia: Case Study of a Direct-Action Movement," *Syracuse Law Review* 20 (1968): 42.
56. Ibid., p. 36.

Chapter 3

The Political and Legal Context of the Accessible Transit Litigation

The particular configuration that the transit access litigation assumed is the result of the political and legal context in which it occurred. It was clearly a product of the "new environment" discussed in chapter 1. The clients were highly rights conscious; the lawsuits relied on statutory and regulatory law more than constitutional law; and organizational plaintiffs were frequently involved.

It is little wonder that the styles of the litigation brought by the NAACP and the disability rights movement differ. Despite some similarities in the treatment of racial minorities and disabled people, important differences in the nature of the discrimination they have faced as well as the timing of their efforts to combat the discrimination have led to differences in strategy.

The most benign interpretation of the situation of people with disabilities is that well-intentioned but misguided charity has been insufficient to compensate for the thoughtless construction of the physical environment in ways that inhibit their ability to function independently in society. A less benign interpretation is that able-bodied people are afraid of and repelled by disabled people because they are a reminder of everybody's vulnerability. By this account, society has chosen to keep them out of sight and out of mind, and present institutional arrangements are now reinforced by a group of experts on problems of disabled people who have a vested interest in keeping things the way they are.

Regardless of which interpretation one prefers, attitudes toward disabled persons, as publicly expressed, are usually couched in terms of sympathy or perhaps pity.[1] There is no question that residual sympathy for them has protected some disabled militants from the harshest response meted out to other demonstrating minorities. Furthermore, legislation seeming to benefit people with disabilities has often passed with little or no opposition.[2]

One consequence of this was to delay the development of rights consciousness among people with disabilities because many felt they were already being taken care of. Eventually, however, people began to realize that they had rights which were not being enforced and started to organize politically to pursue those rights. Nevertheless, a number of factors have made it difficult to organize people with disabilities into a unified political movement, and one result of this is the decentralization which characterized the transit access litigation.

Rights Consciousness: Disability Rights as a Political Movement

The disability rights movement is based on two premises—the importance for disabled people of (1) political activism by disabled people themselves and (2) cooperation across disability groups. Each of these has occurred in the past, but rarely at the same time or for any extended period until the 1970s. In its present form, the disability rights movement is a product of several historical roots as well as a few specific precipitating events. Persistent centrifugal forces within the disabled population, however, make it extremely difficult to organize. Understanding the accessible transit litigation is impossible without knowing the larger political context in which it took place.

One Movement from Four Roots

The disability rights movement as it exists today was clearly influenced by the civil rights and Vietnam War eras, but it also draws on three older strands: *provider groups*, early disabled *consumer groups*, and *parent groups*. These three types of organizations plus the new post-Sixties consumer groups will be briefly described in order of their historical appearance.[3]

Provider groups are organizations devoted to providing services to disabled persons or to performing research on the causes and cures of disabilities. If they are membership organizations at all, their members are primarily professionals in the fields of medicine, rehabilitation, or education, the majority of whom are likely to be able-bodied. Examples include the Council for Exceptional Children, National Rehabilitation Association, and Council of State Administrators of Vocational Rehabilitation. Some such groups have existed as long as there has been organized charity—perhaps from the early Christian era.[4] Groups that are research-oriented and some that are service-oriented tend to be disability-specific as a focus for their work. Some organizations, such as the National Spinal Cord Injury Foundation (formerly the National Paraplegia Foundation) are research-oriented at the national level, but the local chapters are much more concerned with the daily living problems of persons with spinal cord injuries.

Consumer groups is a term describing organizations of, by, and for disabled individuals themselves. The term is less than ideal because it emphasizes the members' status as recipients of services, but it does suggest the tensions that have surfaced repeatedly between service-providing professionals and persons with disabilities.

Deaf people and blind people were the first to organize themselves in this country. The National Association of the Deaf (NAD) was founded in 1880 and still exists today. The first national organization of blind people was the American Blind People's Higher Education and General Improvement Association, founded in 1895, which has been succeeded by a number of different organizations.[5] Both deaf and blind people have long been politically active. The NAD was fighting employment discrimination against deaf persons as early as the first decade of this century. State laws prohibiting deaf persons from obtaining drivers' licenses were frequent targets of NAD action until the 1940s. Representatives of the National Federation of the Blind frequently testified on legislation concerning blind persons in the 1940s and 1950s.

These two disability groups have rarely worked together politically, however. They have traditionally taken opposing stands on the appropriateness of public assistance for persons with their impairments, the National Association of the Deaf vigorously opposing any subsidies, such as tax exemptions, and organizations of the blind equally vigorously supporting assistance programs for visually impaired persons.[6] The blind and deaf communities have experienced major internal schisms as well. Deaf groups have particularly been divided over the preferability of manual or oral means of communication. Organizations of the blind have taken different positions on many government aid programs and on the advisability of alliances with other disability groups.[7]

Persons with hearing and visual impairments rarely joined the few early cross-disability consumer organizations, such as the Indoor Sports Club, founded in 1930, and the National Association of the Physically Handicapped (NAPH), founded in 1958. Still active today, both of these organizations include political activities in their formal statements of purpose, but they are very moderate by today's standards, emphasizing "public education" and projects in cooperation with civic, religious, and fraternal organizations.[8] Another major goal, which sometimes overshadows the more political ones, is to provide social and recreational activities for disabled persons excluded from other opportunities.

In 1958 a number of groups of physically disabled persons came together and founded the National Congress of Organizations of the Physically Handicapped. Its geographical scope has never been truly nationwide, however, and its focus is more on assistance to member groups with their programs and structure and on service as a clearinghouse of publications and literature than on national political action.[9]

Even these early organizations, however moderate by today's standards, emphasize disabled persons doing things for themselves rather than being dependent on professionals or other able-bodied people. Only persons with disabilities are accepted as full members of either the Indoor Sports Club or NAPH, with able-bodied persons welcome as auxiliary or associate members.

Latent tensions between consumers and providers have occasionally been more explicit. An organization called the American Federation of the Physically Handicapped was politically active in the 1940s and early 1950s but it disbanded in 1958. Its president, Paul A. Strachan, testified repeatedly at Congressional hearings on vocational rehabilitation legislation, often locking horns with representatives of the National Rehabilitation Association. In 1950 testimony, Mr. Strachan complained:

> We are very tired, Mr. Chairman, of the unfair present situation, which permits these opulent directors of states' rehabilitation services to come to Washington as frequently as they desire, and, without being registered as lobbyists, in fact, lobby all over the place. . . . Such lobbying never benefited the handicapped, and never will benefit the handicapped. These boys are concerned, solely, in benefiting themselves.[10]

Similar dissatisfactions with professionals led to the development of the third major strand of the disability rights movement—*parent groups*. In the late Forties and early Fifties, parents of disabled children began meeting together to share their problems and to work for better services for their children. For example, parents of children with mental retardation, cerebral palsy, and muscular dystrophy formed the National Association for Retarded Children (now the National Association for Retarded Citizens), the United Cerebral Palsy Associations, and the Muscular Dystrophy Association. These organizations tend to be single-disability groups, perhaps because of their emphasis on obtaining services for the children's specific needs. Because many of them, in the absence of available services, became involved in providing service themselves, the organizations are now often run by professional staffs with parental involvement limited to a greater or lesser advisory role.[11]

When parents organized thirty years ago, they undoubtedly did so because they believed their children were unable to speak for themselves. In the Seventies, however, persons with those disabilities, including mental retardation and severe cerebral palsy, began organizing and speaking out themselves. The fourth strand of the disability rights movement is a product of the social upheavals of the Sixties—specifically, the black civil rights movement, the citizen participation emphasis of the War on Poverty, and the consumer movement nurtured by Ralph Nader. All three of these movements challenged the previously accepted relationships between individuals and the government and other big institutions, and the post-Sixties consumer groups continue that spirit.[12]

Militant groups of disabled persons appeared first in places which were centers of other militant political movements, such as Berkeley, California, and New York City. The rhetoric, the tactics, and to some extent the participants of the new disability organizations emerged from these other movements.[13] Distrust of medical and rehabilitation professionals became a major theme of the new militance rather than a latent or sporadic tension. As Berkeley's Center for Independent Living relates its history:

> Political consciousness grew as they became aware of the degree to which control over their lives had been taken over by medical and rehabilitation professionals. They thus came to realize that the concerns about self-determination raised by the black and student movements had considerable relevance to their own lives as disabled people.[14]

Around the country other groups motivated by similar sentiments sprang up. A group calling itself Disabled in Action organized in New York City in 1971 and made news with a protest demonstration blocking Manhattan traffic with wheelchairs. Over the next three years local groups adopting the same name, Disabled in Action, began in New Jersey, Philadelphia, and Baltimore. In 1974 in Minneapolis/Saint Paul, Minnesota, the United Handicapped Federation was organized with the specific aim of following Saul Alinsky's philosophy of confrontational politics. By the same year other groups had sprung up around the country with such colorful names as SO FED UP (Students Organization for Every Disability United) at Brooklyn College, MIGHT (Mobility Impaired Grappling Hurdles Together) at the University of Texas, and WARPATH (World Association to Remove Prejudice Against the Handicapped) in Florida.[15]

The post-Sixties consumer groups are responsible for revitalizing a political approach to the problems of disability, but the disability rights movement as a whole is trying to draw on the resources of the older groups as well. A catalyst for the coming together of the four disparate and at times conflicting types of organizations was the struggle over the passage of the Rehabilitation Act of 1972, which was vetoed by President Nixon. Since the end of the American Federation of the Physically Handicapped's zealous activity described above, consumer groups had typically left lobbying on vocational rehabilitation legislation to the provider groups. This is partially because debate often focused on issues largely irrelevant to consumers, such as which federal agency should have responsibility for administering the programs.[16]

The 1972 legislation, however, promised significant changes in the philosophy and direction of vocational rehabilitation programs toward greater assistance for severely disabled persons. The bill was vetoed, reintroduced early in the next year, and vetoed again, taking disabled people by surprise. President Nixon criticized the bill for exceeding his budget by adding what he saw as new medical or welfare functions that "serve only to dilute the resources of the vocational rehabilitation program and impair its continued valuable achievements in restoring *deserving* American citizens to meaningful employment." (Emphasis added.)[17] Even though a reduced bill finally passed as the Rehabilitation Act of 1973, the struggle profoundly affected some disabled persons. In the words of Rita Varela:

> Both vetoes shocked disabled Americans and stirred them to action. Groups such as [the Massachusetts Council of Organizations of the Handicapped], Disabled in Action, and others staged protests. The defeats and the demonstrations pulled together groups from across the country and turned their energies to a national issue that affected all of them. The bill that was finally enacted, known as the Rehabilitation Act of 1973, changed the lives of disabled people, but so did the realization that their community could no longer afford to let professionals carry the sole burden for shaping national rehabilitation policies.[18]

One outcome of this realization was the founding of the American Coalition of Citizens with Disabilities (ACCD) in 1974. The members of its first board of directors campaigned vigorously among all elements of the disability community for the concept of cross-disability cooperation in order to increase their numbers and combined political clout. They were convinced that because disabled people had been organizationally fragmented, no one group had a large enough constituency to get beyond lower level staff people into higher policy-making circles.[19]

Although ACCD is now the closest equivalent for disabled people of the NAACP for blacks before 1955, its coalition structure and its emphasis on organizational members reflect the decentralization in the disability rights movement. Consumer groups predominate, but its seventy-five organizational members in 1979 also included provider and parent groups. After a year-long study of alternative organizational models in 1976–77, the board of directors chose an ongoing open coalition model as the structure best able to integrate the disparate elements of the disability rights movement. A permanent central staff would maintain services and promote cooperative activities without trying to replace existing groups or force a greater ideological unity than was possible.[20]

Cooperation among old and new consumer groups, parent and professional groups, has been made more possible by the growing responsiveness of the older groups to the outlook of the post-Sixties militants. Different organizations are in different degrees of ferment over the push for consumer power and the new activist change strategies. For some, participation in litigation is a radical step that must be extensively debated and cautiously entered. Others have no reservations about litigating or lobbying, but stop short of protest marches and, particularly, obstructive demonstrations. On the other hand, militant groups committed to full membership participation question tactics that involve only a few persons, such as litigation. Finally, there are still a few groups of both consumers and providers that seem scarcely touched by the raised consciousness of the Seventies.

Who Are "the Disabled"?

The prospects for a strong, unified disability rights movement are still uncertain. ACCD leaders admit that a truly nationwide grassroots movement has not yet fully blossomed. A further look at the tremendous centrifugal forces among disabled people themselves—much less the parents and professionals—will reveal the difficulties in forging a national organization strong enough to exercise central control over litigation or any other political activities.

One factor, implied already by the history of consumer organizations, is that there is a generation gap among persons with disabilities, although the movement attempts to speak for all of them. Services and opportunities for disabled persons have improved only slowly until the very recent past, so that older disabled individuals are likely to have fewer years of education and possibly also an inferior quality of education than younger disabled individuals. As recently as 1972, estimates were made that one million children, one sixth of all the disabled children of school age, were excluded from any form of education.[21]

Similarly, when most middle-aged or older disabled people were young, vocational rehabilitation services for nonveterans were available only to persons with mild or moderate disabilities who had a clear potential for employment. Greater emphasis on persons with severe disabilities began only in 1965, gaining real priority only in 1973. Vocational rehabilitation services are still available only to persons with employment potential, but agencies now are prepared to commit more resources over a longer time period to help someone reach that potential.[22]

The consequence of this lack of education and services is that many older disabled persons remain more dependent and less exposed to the ideas of the larger world. Others who, by their own efforts, managed to obtain education and employment believe that these can be achieved without the rhetoric of rights and political stridency.

A second fragmenting factor, related to the generation gap, is that disabled people range across the political spectrum from conservative to liberal to radical. In this they do not differ from other parts of the American public, but it makes them very difficult to organize into a united political front. Disagreements over tactics, referred to above, are indicative of this problem. The spectrum is particularly evident in California, even among the disability groups involved in the transit litigation of this study. The San Raphael Indoor Sports Club is a primarily social organization with many older members with the experiences and consequent limitations just described. The California Association of the Physically Handicapped is primarily a lobbying group with a paid lobbyist in Sacramento. It has been divided over the issue of involvement in protest demonstrations. On the other end of the spectrum, Berkeley's Center for Independent Living is one of the most militant groups in the country.

Although the more radical groups have received the media coverage with their high-visibility demonstrations in wheelchairs, those trying to bring all elements of the disability rights movement together are aware of the conservatism of many of their number so often appeal to conservative themes. The announcement of an alliance between ACCD and the National Council of Senior Citizens emphasized programs that have the potential of taking people off public benefit rolls rather than "pie-in-the-sky" spending.[23]

A third centrifugal force among persons with disabilities, which the organizational fragmentation reflects, is the real difference in the concrete problems and experiences of persons with different kinds of disabilities. As the coordinator of consumer activities for United Cerebral Palsy Associations put it: "Persons disabled in different ways have as hard a time understanding each other's needs and perspectives, as the able-bodied have in understanding us as a group."[24] Different disabilities translate into different political priorities. Architectural and transportation barriers are the greatest problem for people in wheelchairs. Captioned television and TTY's (telephone-typewriter combinations) are needs solely of hearing-impaired people. Forced sterilization and institutional conditions have been issues primarily among persons with mental disabilities.

Certain disabilities impose inherent communication difficulties, particularly for blind and deaf people together. Perhaps because of this and because they organized earliest and separately, deaf and blind persons have been among the slowest to acknowledge a need for cross-disability cooperation. The by-laws of the National Federation of the Blind actually proscribe coalitions with other disability groups, which some disabled leaders attribute to a rejection by the Federation of the strength-through-numbers philosophy. Instead, critics assert that Federation leaders believe that asking for less in total is the best way to obtain the most benefits for blind individuals. It should be noted, however, that neither the blind nor the deaf community is unified on this matter. The American Council of the Blind and the National Association of the Deaf are active members of ACCD, and both the director and president of ACCD in 1979 were deaf.

A further example of the way differences among disabled people keep them apart is the remaining reluctance of some physically handicapped persons to be associated with persons with mental disabilities. Their reluctance is not surprising since so many people with physical disabilities, especially those persons with speech impairments, have been wrongly assumed to be retarded. Nevertheless, most advocates of cross-disability cooperation today wish to encompass both physical and mental disabilities on the grounds that the philosophy of emphasizing what people *can* do rather than what they *cannot* do is equally applicable to both.

The life experiences of disabled persons also differ drastically because their disabilities are acquired in so many different ways at different times in their lives: congenital defects, injuries or illnesses at birth or in infancy, slowly disabling diseases, or traumatic accidents at any time in life. The unconsidered impression of the broader public is often that most disabilities are congenital. This may be due to the great visibility of disabled children on money-raising posters and telethons. Many disabled persons today criticize such appeals for creating an image of all disabled people as perpetual children.[25] In fact, only one disabled person out of every six was born with the impairment.[26]

The variety of causes of disability gives rise to differing perspectives on oneself and one's disability. Many people consider segregated or integrated schooling to be the most important experience shaping their attitudes and expectations. One woman, disabled since infancy, described the differences particularly well:

> I think someone who becomes disabled later on in life has, number one, the fact that they were taught that to be disabled wasn't good. So when they become disabled, it's very difficult to acclimate, because you have all this stuff that you have to unlearn. But the positive side is that if you can begin to believe in yourself, you know that you are the same person, and that you still have contributions that you can make, and you're valuable, that you have the benefit of a regular education, and the benefit of growing up nondisabled, the fact that when you were nondisabled you were valued. So I think you can get in touch with those things and bring them to the surface, as opposed to people who were born disabled or became disabled early on in life, who don't have those experiences to call on. And so they have to learn them.

While some participants in the movement believe that leadership roles are more commonly taken by persons disabled later in life, others see no such tendency. Certainly many examples exist of prominent leaders disabled from birth or infancy. One disabled activist noted a tendency toward adult-disabled leaders now, but predicted that the movement would become even more radical if and when congenitally disabled people assume leadership because they have been more oppressed and discriminated against longer than the others. A different attitude toward the same situation was taken by a more conservative disabled woman who felt that activists who are disabled from birth had been sheltered and "don't know how to go out and tackle the world" and as a consequence do it "with more of a destructive attitude than constructive."

All these differences among disabled people—generational, ideological, physiological, and experiential—add up to the absence of any shared culture beyond the common experience with prejudice, stereotyping and discrimination. As the persons trying to organize them are well aware, disabilities cut across all ages, races, classes, religions, and geographical boundaries. Most people spend their early years within their own families where they are likely to be the only one with a disability. Few disabilities are hereditary, so parents do not already know how to deal with special problems created by disabilities. Concomitantly, there is no intergenerational political socialization or wisdom. Each generation has to learn things anew. This makes the disability rights movement different from an ethnic, religious, or regional civil rights movement, where many ties other than specific political goals help to hold the movement together. Again, a disabled activist articulates the problem best:

> There is no disabled culture. Disabled people don't come from any one part of the world. Disabled people don't eat any one kind of food. . . . Disability is not a cultural-specific thing that happens to people. Disability happens in every culture, in every minority group. In fact, one of the major problems for families that have individuals with disabilities as opposed to families that belong to one particular culture or tradition is that the parents don't know how to deal with a disabled child either. . . . They may feel terribly guilty about having a disabled child because they think there's something very bad or negative about it.
>
> And it's very, very difficult for a disabled person to have any self-pride or any feelings of self-worth, because there is no self-preserving environment. There's no family unit. So, for instance, with a Polish family or an Italian family or an African family where there's a certain pride in one's own identity and certain traditions and cultures, that certainly doesn't exist with disabled people.

Compared to the other major civil rights movements of the Sixties and Seventies, the disability rights movement is virtually entirely assimilationist. Most of the other minority rights movements are also partially assimilationist, as they seek an equal opportunity to participate in the institutions of society on equal terms.[27] Frequently, however, there is also a subtle or not-so-subtle separatist strain that draws on the kinds of cultural ties lacking among disabled people. Certain values perceived as different from those of the larger "WASP-male-heterosexual-dominated" society are valued and deemed worthy of preservation. Such values help form the core of a group identity for the minority group members.

Disabled activists make no such claims. On the one hand, consciousness raising and identity reinforcement are important in the movement, conveying the message that it is all right to be disabled and there is no reason to feel ashamed or guilty. On the other hand, in the words of one activist: "Nobody is going to say, 'Crip is wonderful!' " The ultimate goal of the disability movement is to eliminate disability as a significant social category altogether. Indeed, because of the cross-cultural nature of disability, persons with disabilities really are just like everybody else.

Problems of Organizing

This tremendous diversity among disabled people creates great problems in trying to organize them politically. Moreover, in addition to the differences just described, the disability rights movement has faced a number of structural and organizational problems. The first and perhaps the greatest is the vested interests arising from the traditional division of people along disability lines into organizations accustomed to making decisions without consulting other groups. This is the reason ACCD selected a coalition for its structure that would both preserve the autonomy of existing groups and at the same time forge ongoing links between different disability interests.[28] Even so, the older National Congress of Organizations of the Physically Handicapped felt that ACCD was trying to usurp its role and declined to join.

The second problem is the opposite of the first. Despite the existence of so many organizations of and for disabled people, there are still many people with disabilities who are very isolated and have minimal social contacts with persons outside of their immediate family. Physically and psychologically dependent on others, they are unlikely to see their needs in terms of rights to be pursued politically. According to one frustrated organizer, there is still considerable reliance among some disabled people on the good will of experts or the public.

This inclination may be exacerbated by a situation faced by the disability rights movement, which seems advantageous compared to the struggle of the black civil rights movement, but which creates some difficulties for organizing. Rather than needing to fight against explicitly discriminatory laws, a grassroots movement among disabled people came into being only after a good deal of beneficial legislation had already been passed. The good will and foresight of a few members of Congress, paticularly Senator Harrison Williams (D-N.J.) and Representatives John Brademas (D-Ind.) and Mario Biaggi (D-N.Y.), resulted in the passage of education, rehabilitation, transportation, and architectural accessibility statutes in the 1960s and 1970s.

The political problem of the disability rights movement has not been to get legislation passed, but to get it enforced. The record of enforcement of the Architectural Barriers Act of 1968 and the 1970 Urban Mass Transportation Act amendments was abysmal until consumers began to organize and protest.[29] Nevertheless, the movement must still combat the assumption of some disabled people that they must be protected because there are laws on the books. This is the legislative version of Scheingold's myth of rights at work.[30]

The glaring frustration of rights promised but unfulfilled has resulted in disabled activists in many communities and at the national level concentrating their attention more on lobbying the government to implement existing laws than on mobilizing the still reclusive disabled population into a larger grassroots movement. Although ACCD recognizes the need for more grassroots organizing, it is a slow process that consumes a great deal of a new organization's resources.

There are practical reasons as well for the concentration on implementing services and enforcing rights. People struggling with major handicaps in daily life are not likely to become very politically active. In the words of the director of ACCD: "When the effort merely to get out of the house or to understand the words of another human being is so great that it commands every available ounce of energy, a man's spirit can rarely soar."[31] People wanting to protest inaccessible transportation cannot get to meetings or demonstrations. People without jobs due to employment discrimination do not have the money to pay dues or to travel to conferences.

For this reason some groups have combined the provision of direct services needed by disabled people with political mobilization. Through its transportation, attendant referral, legal advocacy, counseling, job placement, wheelchair repair and many other services, the Center for Independent Living in Berkeley is able to reach thousands of persons with disabilities, few of whom would likely come out for political meetings alone. Its combination of income from grants, contracts, and fees for services also gives it a greater stability than organizations relying on contributions and occasional short-term grants.

Definitional Problems

Another problem of organizing the disability rights movement is knowing how to define the relevant population. More than any other minority group, "the disabled" is a socially defined category with amorphous boundaries. Determining if a person is disabled depends on social expectations and demands.[32] If the conventional expectation were that people should be able to lift their own weight in barbells, then all but

Olympic weightlifters would be disabled. On the other hand, if standards of normal intelligence were measured by the capacity to care for one's personal grooming and diet and to learn some basic routines, then many people now classified as mentally disabled would fall among the so-called normal. "The fine line between 'handicapped' and 'normal' has been arbitrarily drawn by the 'normal' majority," charges one commentator.[33] A person truly qualifies as handicapped only when he or she is so labeled by others.[34]

The social relativism of the category is the basis for the distinction made by some people in the movement between the terms *disability* and *handicap*. Although some groups and individuals continue to use the word *handicapped* to describe themselves, others feel it important to distinguish between the physical condition and barriers created by the social environment. As one man explains it:

> Cerebral palsy is my disability. There are a number of brain cells which are not functioning, which do not send the required signals to my legs. Okay, that is my disability. It's a definable set of medical criteria which gives rise to my physical being and my condition. That is as it was yesterday and as it will be for the foreseeable future, barring a miracle.
>
> A handicap, on the other hand, is in my view a sociological term which basically describes what society's perception of my limitations is and how I interact with those barriers that are presented by the society. Okay, to cite an example, if John can't get into the courthouse, he is handicapped. If he can get into the courthouse as an attorney, he is still disabled but he is no longer handicapped. He can practice law.

Although it uses *handicapped* rather than *disabled* and fails to distinguish between physiological and environmental causes of activity restrictions, the definition in effect for recent federal legislation also recognizes the conventional or relational quality of the category. The regulations implementing Section 504 of the Rehabilitation Act of 1973 state: " 'Handicapped persons' means any person who (i) has a physical or mental impairment which substantially limits one or more major life activities, (ii) has a record of such an impairment, or (iii) is regarded as having such an impairment."[35]

The second of these categories would include persons recovered from mental illnesses for example, who might still face discrimination. The third category explicitly recognizes that a disability may be solely in the eyes of the beholder. Persons falling into this category would include those with a cosmetically disfiguring scar or growth that leads others to shun them. Such discrimination has been incorporated into law, as in the Chicago Municipal Code provision, which stated:

> No person who is diseased, maimed, mutilated or in any way deformed so as to be an unsightly or disgusting object or improper person to be allowed in or

on the public ways or other public places in this city, shall therein or thereon expose himself to public view, under a penalty of not less than one dollar nor more than fifty dollars for each offense.[36]

Although Chicago repealed this law in 1974, a police officer in Omaha, Nebraska, arrested a man under a similar ordinance in the same year.[37]

Because of the indeterminateness of the definition of "disabled," accurate figures on the total number of disabled persons in the United States are difficult to obtain. One witness at 1972 Senate hearings placed the total number of physically disabled at 11.7 million,[38] but an Architectural and Transportation Barriers Compliance Board study on "Transportation Needs of Handicapped Individuals" totaled 13, 370,000 persons with "transportation dysfunctions."[39] Yet another study counted people with "activity limitations" and found 23,630,000 in this category, with 17,747,000 of them experiencing "major activity limitations."[40] Combining separately gathered figures for persons among the working-aged population, school-aged children, institutionalized people, and elderly people, ACCD arrives at a total estimate of 36 million disabled Americans.[41]

Positive Consequences of Negative Attitudes

What most unites people with different disabilities is undoubtedly the attitudes toward them of able-bodied people. "Whatever characteristics such individuals may or may not have had in common prior to their classification, it is their involvement in the classification that has generated the characteristics they all share—their social fate as members of a status category."[42] This attitudinal problem is a powerful centripetal force counteracting a great many of the divisions among disabled people discussed here that would appear to make political organizing problems virtually insurmountable.

Persons with disabilities are nearly the perfect example of people suffering from what Erving Goffman calls "stigma." Goffman defines a stigma as "an attribute that makes him different from others in the category of persons available for him to be, and of a less desirable kind."[43] In primitive times people associated disabilities with supernatural forces.[44] And still people with disabilities are vaguely feared by people without them. Some research has found that a negative evaluation of the disabling condition spreads to affect the evaluation of other nonimpaired characteristics of the disabled person.[45] Disabled people are a visible reminder that we all are mortal and vulnerable to disease and injury. Throughout history public policy has often been to isolate and institutionalize people with disabilities to get them out of sight and mind.[46]

One consequence of segregated schools and social clubs, however, is the formation of social ties among disabled people that now provide the foundation for political coalescence. Peer groups were already formed, ready to be politicized by the currents of the Sixties. As a woman with cerebral palsy put it: "Years ago belonging to a handicapped group was a last resort if you couldn't make it in society with normal friends. Now it's a step up to political action."

Unlike some stigmatized groups, such as poor people, disabled people are not generally perceived as morally to blame for their condition.[47] Instead, they are perceived as in need of and deserving "help" of some sort. Thus, agencies, societies, associations, and programs have been established to habilitate or rehabilitate persons with disabilities. Although much of this help has been specialized according to the type of disability, government programs in particular have tended to put all disabilities under the same bureaucratic roof, as with the Social Security Administration, the federal-state Vocational Rehabilitation program, and recently the emphasis on "mainstreamed" education for children.[48] The President's Committee on Employment of the Handicapped, formed in 1947, was one of the earliest contexts bringing disabled people together for quasi-political purposes.

It is the desire to influence these programs that is the second major centripetal force unifying people across disability lines. The initial impetus of the American Coalition of Citizens with Disabilities (ACCD) was the belief that politicians and program administrators are not likely to be responsive to the needs of those they perceive as a very small minority.[49] While the number of people with any single disabling condition, such as deafness, impaired vision, paralysis or amputation, or cerebral palsy is not great in relation to the national population, a constituency created through cross-disability cooperation could have more influence in higher decision-making levels in Washington.

The struggle over the passage of the Rehabilitation Act of 1973 probably did more than anything else to give the fledgling disability rights movement a sense of rights consciousness and of the possibilities arising from cross-disability cooperation. The efforts to get the law passed have already been described as the stimulus for the organization of the ACCD. The efforts to obtain regulations implementing one of its provisions constituted the next landmark in the formation of disabled persons into a political movement.

Section 504 of this act has been called the civil rights act for disabled people. In language almost identical to the nondiscrimination provision of Title VI of the Civil Rights Act of 1964, it states simply that "no otherwise qualified handicapped individual . . . shall, solely by reason of this handicap, be excluded from the participation in, be denied the benefits of, or be subjected to discrimination under any program or activity receiving federal financial assistance."[50] This sweeping provision has profound implications for persons with all kinds of disabilties, yet for three years after its passage almost no action was taken by the Department of Health, Education and Welfare (HEW) to implement it.

In February of 1976 a disabled individual filed suit in federal court to force HEW to promulgate regulations for Section 504.[51] The following July a district court judge so ordered, and work finally began. When the Carter administration came into office in January 1977, ACCD was quick to inform new HEW Secretary Joseph Califano of the urgency of completing and signing the regulations. Instead, the secretary ordered a new review of the regulations.

When in March it appeared to disabled leaders that changes were planned which would weaken the law's protections, they presented President Carter with a statement protesting the delays and the proposed changes. They set a deadline of April 4, 1977, for the regulations to be signed; otherwise, disabled people "would be forced to undertake nationwide action."[52] When the deadline was not met, on April 5 disabled people staged protest demonstrations and held meetings with officials in the ten cities around the country with regional HEW offices. Most of the demonstrations ended that day, but protesters in San Francisco began a sit-in that lasted until Secretary Califano signed the regulations on April 28.

The organizers of the demonstration hailed the signing as "the greatest struggle and victory of disabled people in the United States."[53] According to the director of ACCD at the time, even some of the more conservative members of ACCD who had dissociated themselves from the demonstrations before the fact were elated by the victory and embraced it as "ours." The "504 struggle" became a landmark for the disability rights movement and a rallying point for the idea of cross-disability cooperation.

Nevertheless, strong tendencies toward decentralization remained within the movement. Less than a month after the signing of the 504 regulations, the White House Conference on Handicapped Individuals was held. The Alternative Conference report issued by dissatisfied participants is militant in rhetoric and proposals, but it also emphasizes "the separate needs and specialized character of each handicap"[54] and calls for "the issues and concerns at this Conference [to] be analyzed and grouped according to each specific handicap in order to more fully and properly meet the needs of each handicapped group."[55]

Decentralization of Litigation

These centrifugal and centripetal forces within the disability rights movement make it very unlikely that any one organization could achieve a dominance in litigating the rights of disabled people comparable to the NAACP's litigation preeminence. None of the national disability organizations has in-house counsel equivalent to the NAACP's. The Paralyzed Veterans of America and the American Coalition of Citizens with Disabilities have at least one lawyer on staff, but they both coordinate general advocacy programs and would not be able to concentrate their time on a lawsuit. Litigation on behalf of deaf persons is done by the National Association of the Deaf Legal Defense Fund, but it enjoys no monopoly on litigation even of problems unique to deaf people.

The public interest law movement introduced the model of litigation centers which are not dependent on membership support, as in the NAACP model, but rely on government or foundation funding.[56] A few such disability rights litigating groups have developed. Among disability-specific organizations, the National Center for Law and the Deaf was originally funded in 1975 by the Department of Health, Education and Welfare and is now supported by Gallaudet College. It is the main alternative to the NAD Legal Defense Fund in this area. In the area of mental disabilities, the Mental Health Law Project and the Public Interest Law Center of Philadelphia (PILCOP) have brought a number of important lawsuits.

At least three cross-disability legal centers were operating in 1979: the Disability Rights Center in Washington, D.C., a Ralph Nader affiliate; the National Center for Law and the Handicapped in South Bend, Indiana;[57] and the Western Law Center for the Handicapped in Los Angeles. None of these organizations has had sufficient resources to undertake significant litigation efforts on its own. Their activities include providing research support to litigating attorneys around the country, disseminating public information on the rights of disabled people, participating in administrative procedures, filing *amicus curiae* briefs in appellate courts, and other general advocacy activities.

Even if one of these existing centers received a massive infusion of funds to increase its litigating capacity, it is unlikely that it could assume the role of coordinator of all disability litigation. The decentralization of past litigation has created a number of lawyers around the country who have acquired some expertise in disability issues. They would probably not be willing to submit to the decisions of any central litigation strategists.[58] Moreover, the diversified tenor of the whole disability rights movement and especially the emphasis on personal independence and self-help militate against a lawyer-run, nonmembership group dominating an important political tactic of the movement.

The development of rights consciousness among disabled people has brought forth a political movement that is beginning to overcome the fragmentation and is increasingly capable of fighting for the interests of persons with disabilities both in court and in other political arenas. The disability rights movement is an excellent example of the ability to take advantage of the growth of statutory and regulatory law to pursue one's ends. The peculiarity of the situation of disabled people, of course, is that in many cases the laws protecting their interests were on the books before there was a political movement to push for them. How this happened to occur and the ramifications it had for the enforcement of the laws are the subjects of the next section.

The Legal Basis of Accessible Transit Litigation

The lawsuits claiming a right to accessible public transportation were mostly brought on the basis of several federal statutes which were passed without much consideration or specificity. Some clarification of the contours of such a right has come about through pressure by disabled persons in the courts and in the federal rule-making process, yet the state of the law remains unsettled.

Passing the Legislation

Awareness of the problem of environmental barriers to the mobility of disabled people has been attributed to the results of the polio epidemic in the United States in the 1940s and 1950s. Polio struck people of all classes, so that people with middle- and upper-class expectations found themselves or their children paralyzed and cut off from schooling and jobs.[59]

In the late Fifties the federal government and voluntary associations concerned with disabled people, particularly the National Easter Seal Society, began to study the problem. The Easter Seal Society, together with the President's Committee on the Employment of the Handicapped, sponsored a committee of the American Standards Association (now the American National Standards Institute [ANSI]) to hold a national conference to discuss the technical specifications of access. In 1961 the committee issued a precise book of "Specifications for Making Buildings Accessible to and Usable by the Physically Handicapped," and the use of these standards was endorsed by many organizations.[60]

During the mid-Sixties there was a flurry of interest in the subject. Forty-four states, ninety-five cities, and forty-two metropolitan counties passed laws or ordinances endorsing accessibility for handicapped persons. A number of federal agencies voluntarily adopted the ANSI standards for their buildings. The 1965 Vocational Rehabilitation Act established the National Commission on Architectural Barriers to Rehabilitation of the Handicapped. The report produced by the commission three years later concluded that very little progress had been made in eliminating environmental barriers. It called for federal legislation mandating accessibility, and on August 12, 1968, the first Architectural Barriers Act was signed into law.[61]

Although this law covered only buildings, the attention to architectural barriers awakened interest in transportation barriers as well. The Department of Transportation contracted with Abt Associates to study the transportation needs of the handicapped in 1969.[62] In September of 1970, President Nixon expressed his support for the right of equal access to public transportation in his proclamation for National Employ the Physically Handicapped Week.[63]

The first statutory recognition of this right came without any committee hearings or discussion. During the floor debate of the 1970 amendments to the Urban Mass Transportation Act, Representative Mario Biaggi (D-N.Y.) introduced an amendment declaring as national policy that "elderly and handicapped persons have the same right as other persons to utilize mass transportation facilities and services." Section 16(a) goes on to provide that

> special efforts shall be made in the planning and design of mass transportation facilities and services so that the availability to elderly and handicapped persons of mass transportation which they can effectively utilize will be assured; and that all federal programs offering assistance in the field of mass transportation (including the programs under this chapter) should contain provisions implementing this policy.[64]

The amendment was adopted without opposition, and the record of the debate states that the amendment had been "well distributed and understood by the minority as well as the majority."[65]

During the following five years similar provisions were included in several other pieces of legislation. For instance, the Amtrak Improvement Act of 1974 authorizes the National Railroad Passenger Corporation to take "all steps necessary" to ensure that no elderly or handicapped passenger goes unserved, including the provision of special assistance or equipment.[66] The Federal-Aid Highway Act of 1973 states in a section entitled "Bus and Other Project Standards" that

> The Secretary of Transportation shall assure that projects receiving Federal financial assistance under [the Federal-Aid Highway Act of 1973] shall be planned and designed so that mass transportation facilities and services can effectively be utilized by elderly and handicapped persons who, by reason of illness, injury, age, congenital malfunction, or other permanent or temporary incapacity or disability are unable without special facilities or special planning or design to utilize such facilities and services as effectively as persons not so affected.[67]

The 1974 amendments of that act contain wording almost identical to that of the 1970 amendments to the Urban Mass Transportation Act, with some strengthening. "Construction and operation" are added to "planning and design" as aspects of mass transit services that must be available to the elderly and handicapped, and the more affirmative "effectively implement" replaces "should contain provisions implementing."[68] Finally, the Department of Transportation and Related Agencies Appropriations Act of 1975 directs that

None of the funds provided under this Act shall be available for the purchase of passenger rail or subway cars, for the purchase of motor buses or for the construction of related facilities unless such cars, buses and facilities are designed to meet the mass transportation needs of the elderly and the handicapped.[69]

The Struggle for Enforcement: Administrative Regulations and Judicial Remedies

That Congress intended some public transportation to be accessible to disabled persons seems indisputable. Nevertheless, little was done to translate the general policy statements of the legislation into enforceable duties on the part of transit operators. Exactly why nothing happened is difficult to determine. A 1977 report by the comptroller general on the Urban Mass Transportation Administration's (UMTA) actions to further mass transit for elderly and handicapped persons states simply that "UMTA did not believe it was required to issue regulations to implement the laws."[70]

Instead, it issued the following guidelines to grantees under its capital grant program shortly after the 1970 amendments passed: "In the planning and design of mass transportation facilities and equipment, reasonable efforts should be made to ensure that elderly and handicapped will be able to effectively use the facilities. A description of these efforts must be in the final application."[71] Any studies or plans that examined the transportation needs of elderly and handicapped persons, facts about their percentage of the population, programs and institutions devoted to their needs, and costs of special equipment and facilities were to be described. These guidelines notwithstanding, "grantees did not always have a clear understanding of what was required of them in addressing the transportation needs of elderly and handicapped persons," in the words of the comptroller general's report.[72]

Only when the disabled beneficiaries of these laws began to organize politically and push for the laws' enforcement were they taken seriously. The mobilization which occurred in the process of the passage of the Rehabilitation Act of 1973 and the boost to rights consciousness given by Section 504 of that act led many disabled people to feel that they had rights which were going unenforced. Since the executive branch had failed to bring to fruition the promise of the legislation, groups of disabled people around the country turned to the courts.

In general, the disabled litigants claimed in their suits that all transit equipment and facilities should be accessible to all persons, including those confined to wheelchairs. Transit operators, on the other hand, interpreted the law to mean that inaccessible equipment could be purchased if other specialized service was made available to disabled persons. Frequently named as co-defendants, UMTA officials supported the latter interpretation.

One of the earliest cases, *Disabled in Action of Baltimore v. Hughes,* was dismissed after the parties reached an out-of-court settlement in October 1974.[73] One of the agreements was that UMTA, which was named as a defendant along with Maryland and Baltimore transportation agencies, would within one year develop regulations to supplement the existing vague guidelines for Section 16 of the Urban Mass Transportation Act containing the "special efforts" requirement. Proposed regulations appeared on Feburary 26, 1975, but the final regulations were not published until April 30, 1976.[74]

Even when the regulations were finally signed, they still did not fully clarify the transit companies' obligations. They did not specify a mandatory program, but offered illustrations of different approaches that could constitute "special efforts," such as 1) a program for handicapped persons involving an expenditure of five percent of the funds a local area receives under the principal UMTA funding formula; 2) purchase of only wheelchair-accessible buses until one half of the fleet is accessible or, alternatively, provision of a substitute service that would provide comparable service; and 3) some other type of accessible system which would assure wheelchair users and semi-ambulatory persons ten roundtrips per week at fares comparable to mainline services.[75] The regulations were consistent with UMTA's general belief that localities should have flexibility in determining what services were best for their areas.

The regulations did not stem the flow of new lawsuits, which continued throughout this period, usually seeking to enjoin the purchase of new inaccessible buses. The lawsuits were not going well for the disabled plaintiffs, however. The comptroller general's review of UMTA activities reports that as of December 1976, UMTA had been involved in fifteen lawsuits concerning accessible transportation for elderly and handicapped persons. Court decisions had supported UMTA's position in ten of the suits, though the decisions were final in only two. Of the five remaining, three were pending in the courts, one had won a temporary injunction against the purchase of buses until the court decided on UMTA's motion for summary judgment, and the Baltimore case had been settled before the court ruled.[76]

Shortly thereafter, in January 1977 a breakthrough for the disabled litigants came when the Seventh Circuit Court of Appeals vacated a lower court decision that the Urban Mass Transportation Act, the Rehabilitation Act of 1973, and the Architectural Barriers Act of 1968 did not confer a private cause of action for disabled plaintiffs to sue the Chicago Transit Authority and the Regional Transportation Authority.[77]

The Court of Appeals judges went further and ruled that Section 504 of the Rehabilitation Act of 1973 establishes affirmative rights and that the plaintiffs could proceed directly in court because of the absence of an administrative remedy open to them.

Moreover, the judges noted that after the district court's opinion was issued, both the UMTA final regulations interpreting Section 16 of the Urban Mass Transportation Act and HEW's proposed regulations for Section 504 had appeared. They thus remanded the case for consideration on the merits consistent with the new regulations. Five months later the Eighth Circuit followed suit and remanded a case from Minneapolis-St. Paul that had been dismissed on the same grounds.[78] By the end of the year the Second Circuit had done the same.[79] On the other hand, the Fifth Circuit had affirmed a lower court ruling that granted the defendant's motion for summary judgment, finding that disabled persons have no constitutional right to public transportation and that minimal statutory requirements were being met.[80]

The court actions supporting the disabled plaintiffs are consistent with the observation made by Eric Peterson and others that courts are most likely to intervene in substantive issues if the statutory requirements are sufficiently specific and the defendants' deviation from the standards is sufficiently great.[81] Although no judgment is made here about the adequacy of the transit agencies' activities, it was clearly not until the vague statutory language had been clarified by regulations that the courts were willing to recognize any rights on the part of disabled plaintiffs. As the Seventh Circuit opinion notes, "we cannot fault the district court for its dismissal order. Without the benefit of any regulations, it is difficult to perceive what relief could have been afforded at that stage."[82]

Courts which looked to administrative regulations for guidance in interpreting the transportation rights of disabled people were not greatly helped because the regulatory picture became increasingly complex. The Section 16 regulations in 1976 were followed by the Transbus mandate of Secretary of Transportation Brock Adams in 1977, the HEW guidelines for implementing Section 504 in 1978, and the Department of Transportation's own Section 504 regulations in 1979.[83] Each appeared to affect the rights disabled riders could claim under the related statutes.

Consequently, the legal battles generally focused on precisely what the law required rather than whether local transit authorities were complying with it. None of the nineteen federal suits filed by the end of 1978 went to trial. Typically, the plaintiffs sought injunctions against the purchase of inaccessible vehicles and declaratory and/or injunctive relief stipulating their right to accessible service. The defendants typically moved for dismissal or summary judgment.

As additional regulations appeared, the pattern of court decisions became even more unpredictable than it was in 1976, but the disabled plaintiffs still did not do notably well in winning cases. While by mid-1979 there were still only two definitive losses in federal court where the judgments were final,[84] in only two other federal cases had the plaintiffs intially defeated the defendants' motions to dismiss or for summary judgment.[85] Five other cases, including the three discussed above, which initially lost in district court fared better on appeal in the Second, Fifth, Seventh, and Eight Circuits, at least on crucial procedural questions.[86] Appeals of two more lower court losses were pending in the Ninth and Tenth Circuits.[87]

Two of the cases which won on appeal lost again on remand, but at least one of them, the Minnesota case discussed in detail in the following chapters, achieved a satisfactory out-of-court settlement with the defendants despite the legal defeat.[88] Similarly, a California state case found its legal claims all either rejected or mooted, but the decision by the defendant transit authority not to purchase the planned inaccessible buses, which caused the mooting, constituted a considerable political victory for the plaintiffs, if not a legal one.[89]

A stipulated settlement or consent agreement was a very common outcome among the cases. Six more of the federal suits and at least one state suit had ended in settlements by mid-1979.[90] One final federal suit was mooted following an action by the defendants which effectively capitulated to the claims of the plaintiffs.[91]

As the six lawsuits examined in detail will reveal, the successes the disabled plaintiffs won were mostly a result of using the statutory and regulatory law and the courts as leverage against the transit agencies to bring about negotiated agreements. The law itself was too unsettled to provide much hope of definitive court victories, but it provided an entree for remedy-oriented litigation.

Representing the Disabled Population in Court

The disabled litigants in the accessible transit suits took advantage not only of the statutory and regulatory law in bringing their suits but also of the various vehicles for accommodating group interests in a lawsuit. At least fifteen of the twenty-four suits by 1978 were class actions,[92] and all but four had either multiple named plaintiffs, named organizational plaintiffs, or both. Most notably, fully thirteen of the suits included an organization as a named plaintiff, showing their active use of the court's openness to organizational representation. The diversity among disabled people made it difficult to find plaintiffs who were representative in the sense of being in situations most similar to others. As a result, most lawyers chose to work with multiple or group plaintiffs who could represent a variety of situations and different needs for transit.

The point in this litigation where representativeness became most controversial was the debate over the most desirable form of accessible transportation. Disabled people differ among themselves on this question, yet in any given lawsuit the plaintiffs must agree on what remedy to request. The two rival methods for transporting people with mobility handicaps are small, door-to-door, demand-responsive buses or regular route, scheduled buses designed to accommodate all passengers, including those in wheelchairs.

Debate has focused on the short- and long-term costs of each type of service, the likelihood of truly equivalent service with a demand-responsive system in light of the political realities of budget-cutting in services for special populations, and the ability of disabled persons to get to and from bus stops and use regular route service even if the buses themselves were accessible. For many disabled people, however, these considerations are overshadowed at least emotionally by the perceived stigma of special, separate service. In the words of one man with a severe limp from cerebral palsy:

> I don't need to ride a special bus. I don't need to go around with a badge that says I am disabled, you know. It's obvious. And frankly, it hurts, because I can't be part of the regular mainstream and be accepted as a co-equal if I'm rolling around in a special gimp bus.

Not all disabled people agree with this position, however. Some are persuaded by the perceived greater convenience of door-to-door service or point out that some people's disabilities are so severe that only door-to-door service could meet their needs. Among many of the most outspoken, however, their feelings against separate-but-equal service are strong. The same man just quoted continued:

> I thought we had settled the question of separate-but-equal a long time ago. I look at this as a civil rights issue. Those little buses . . . you know, it's a separate service. It's a stigmatizing service. And it sure as hell is not equal. I mean I just do not feel that by virtue of my disability I should have to limit my life to eight-thirty in the morning and six o'clock at night. Now I sure as hell as a taxpayer should not have to get on a waiting list.

The transit industry has tended to favor demand-responsive service at least in part because of technological difficulties both with the lifts added to make conventional buses accessible and with the proposed new Transbus design. Critics of the demand for regular route service have charged that such service is primarily advocated by highly organized, vocal, and politically active "wheelchair independents" who do not represent the true needs for door-to-door service of the fragmented and timid "wheelchair dependents."[93] Because of this controversy, appearing to be representative was particularly important to the plaintiffs in transit litigation. As a lawyer in one case with four individual plaintiffs and three organizational plaintiffs put it:

> With organizations you can speak with the authority of a broader group of people. That has some advantage in this particular area of law in that one of the defenses that you'll often get from transit districts, I understand, is that the handicapped community is divided and some people want demand-responsive service and some want accessible mainline. We thought that there was some advantage in attempting to look like you represent a cross-section of the community rather than a few plaintiffs.

It is very difficult to say whether plaintiff-stacking actually affected the outcome of any case or whether the plaintiffs merely hoped or assumed it would. In the few cases with definitive legal victories or defeats, most of the suits had a very small number of named plaintiffs and no group plaintiffs, while the suits with a large number of plaintiffs were more likely to end with some kind of settlement between the parties. This suggests that perhaps courts themselves are not influenced by numbers, but that large numbers do give the plaintiffs more influence if the case moves into the arena of political bargaining.

The number of accessible transit cases is too small for any aggregate conclusions. Instead, the remaining chapters will look in detail at six lawsuits brought by five groups of plaintiffs to see if their internal dynamics provide insight into their successes and failures. The cases exhibit the characteristics of the new style of social reform litigation in varying degrees. The litigation organizers did engage in considerable plaintiff-stacking. The goals of the suits were generally oriented to remedy rather than precedent. Some of the cases included a great deal of political activity outside the courtrooms that was coordinated with the legal tactics, but others did not.

Notes

1. See George C. Samerotte and Mary B. Harris, "Some Factors Influencing Helping: The Effects of a Handicap, Responsibility, and Requesting Help," *The Journal of Social Psychology* 98 (1976): 39–45; and Jack Horn, "Attitudes: Reactions to the Handicapped—Sweaty Palms and Saccharine Words," *Psychology Today*, November 1975, p. 122.

2. Leon H. Mayhew, *Law and Equal Opportunity: A Study of the Massachusetts Commission Against Discrimination* (Cambridge: Harvard University Press, 1968), pp. 94–101, discusses how difficult and unlikely it is for opponents of statutes that embody the value traditions of a community, such as antidiscrimination laws, to oppose their passage publicly.

3. Because access to public transportation, the issue on which this study focuses, is primarily a problem for people with physical disabilities, the following

presentation of the disability rights movement largely excludes the rise of political activism by and on behalf of persons with mental disabilities. Collective rights consciousness has developed among persons with mental retardation, learning disabilities, and mental illness. These three groups have worked sometimes together and sometimes separately with a complexity equivalent to the relations among persons with physical disabilities.

4. Frank G. Bowe, *Handicapping America: Barriers to Disabled People* (New York: Harper & Row, 1978), pp. 6ff.

5. C. Esco Obermann, *A History of Vocational Rehabilitation in America* (Minneapolis: T. S. Denison & Co., 1965), 336.

6. Ibid., p. 334, and Bert Shaposka, *The N.A.D.—A History of Enlightened Self-Interest* (Silver Spring, Md.: National Association of the Deaf, 1964), p. 10.

7. Obermann, *Vocational Rehabilitiation*, pp. 313–14 and 334–35.

8. 1974 pamphlet published by the Indoor Sports Club, Inc. and undated pamphlet published by the N.A.P.H.

9. *Encyclopedia of Associations*, 11th ed., s.v. "National Congress of Organizations of the Physically Handicapped."

10. U.S., Congress, Senate, *Hearings before a Subcommittee of the Committee on Labor and Public Health, on S. 1066, S. 2273, and S. 3465*, 81st Cong., 2d sess., 1950; as quoted in Obermann, *Vocational Rehabilitation*, p. 303.

11. Alfred H. Katz, *Parents of the Handicapped: Self-Organized Parents' and Relatives' Groups for Treatment of Ill and Handicapped Children* (Springfield, Ill.: Charles C. Thomas, 1961) and Bowe, *Coalition Building*, p. 16.

12. Rita A. Varela, *Self-Help Groups in Rehabilitation* (Washington, D.C.: American Coalition of Citizens with Disabilities, 1979), pp. 2–4.

13. References to previous involvement by disabled activists in other political movements occurred in several interviews.

14. Hale Zukas, "C.I.L. History," Berkeley, n.d. (mimeograph), p. 1. See also the seminal essay by Leonard Kriegel, "Uncle Tom and Tiny Tim: Some Reflections on the Cripple as Negro," *The American Scholar* 38 (1969): 412–30.

15. Rita A. Varela, "Power to the Disabled," *Social Policy* 4 (March/April 1974): 46.

16. Obermann, *Vocational Rehabilitation*, chap. 9.

17. Richard Nixon, "Memorandum of Disapproval of Nine Bills," October 27, 1972, *Public Papers of the Presidents of the United States* (Washington, D.C.: Office of the *Federal Register*, Archives and Records Service, 1953–), p. 377.

18. Varela, *Self-Help Groups*, p. 7.

19. Bowe, *Coalition Building*, p. 3.

20. Ibid., pp. 19–20.

21. Richard C. Handel, "The Role of the Advocate in Securing the Handicapped Child's Right to an Effective Minimal Education," *Ohio State Law Journal* 36 (1975): 350, citing Frederick J. Weintraub and Alan R. Abeson, "Appropriate Education for All Handicapped Children: A Growing Issue," *Syracuse Law Review* 23 (1972): 1038. The Education for All Handicapped Children Act of 1975 (P.L. 94–142), which went into effect 1 October 1977, is now considerably reducing this figure.

22. A thumbnail history of the federal-state vocational rehabilitation program appears in the U.S. Senate Report No. 93-318, 93d Cong., 1st sess., 1973, pp.

8–12. See also Jack Achtenberg, "Law and the Physically Disabled: An Update with Constitutional Implications," *Southwestern University Law Review* 8 (1976): 878–79.

23. Jack Anderson, "A Formidable Alliance of the Elderly and Disabled," *Washington Post,* 1 April 1979, p. B7.

24. James Murphy, quoted in Bowe, *Coalition Building,* p. 6.

25. Bowe, *Handicapping America,* p. 110.

26. Ibid., p. 17.

27. The major exception to this generalization is the political movement among Native Americans.

28. Jeffrey M. Berry discusses some of the problems in forming coalitions among public interest groups in *Lobbying for the People,* p. 261.

29. U.S., General Accounting Office, *Further Action Needed to Make All Public Buildings Accessible to the Physically Handicapped* (1975) and U.S., General Accounting Office, *Mass Transit for Elderly and Handicapped Persons: Urban Mass Transportation Administration's Actions* (1977), especially chap. 3 and chap. 5.

30. Scheingold, *The Politics of Rights.*

31. Bowe, *Handicapping America,* p. xii.

32. Lecture by Christopher Ake, Assistant Professor of Philosophy, Rutgers University, at a Conference on Images of Disability and Law sponsored by the Center on Human Policy, Syracuse University, March 5, 1977.

33. Marcia Pearce Burgdorf and Robert Burgdorf, Jr., "A History of Unequal Treatment: The Qualifications of Handicapped Persons as a 'Suspect Class' under the Equal Protection Clause," *Santa Clara Lawyer* 15 (1975): 858.

34. Ibid., p. 857.

35. U.S., *Code of Federal Regulations,* vol. 45, sec. 84.3(j).

36. Chicago, Ill., Mun. Code 36–34 (1966) (repealed 1974), cited in Burgdorf and Burgdorf, "Unequal Treatment," p. 863.

37. Burgdorf and Burgdorf, "Unequal Treatment," p. 864.

38. U.S., Congress, Senate, *Hearings before the Subcommittee on the Handicapped of the Senate Committee on Labor and Public Welfare on H.R. 8395,* 92nd Cong., 2d sess., 1972, p. 265.

39. U.S., Architectural and Transportation Barriers Compliance Board, *Report on Transportation Needs of Handicapped Individuals* (1975), p. 15.

40. Estimates from the Health Interview Survey, 1970, as reported to U.S., Architectural and Transportation Barriers Compliance Board, *Report to the President and to the Congress of the United States* (1975), p. 145.

41. Bowe, *Handicapping America,* p. 17.

42. Rains et al., "The Labeling Approach to Issues in Deviance," in N. Hobbs, ed., *Issues in the Classification of Children* 1 (1975): 91, as cited by Burgdorf and Burgdorf, "Unequal Treatment," p. 858. See also Robert A. Scott, *The Making of Blind Men: A Study of Adult Socialization* (New York: Russell Sage, 1969).

43. Erving Goffman, *Stigma: Notes on the Management of Spoiled Identity* (Englewood Cliffs, N.J.: Prentice-Hall, 1963), p. 3.

44. Bowe, *Handicapping America,* p. 5.

45. James W. McDaniel, *Physical Disability and Human Behavior* (New York: Pergamon, 1969), p. 23.

46. Bowe, *Handicapping America,* p. 10.

47. One exception to this may be disabled Vietnam veterans, who have occasionally reported comments to the effect that they deserve whatever they got. See Myra MacPherson, "Back: The Vietnam Veterans, Forcing Their Way Into America's Attention," *Washington Post*, 31 May 1979, p. D3. Another indication of the moral blamelessness accorded most disabled persons is the controversy that arose when the Attorney General interpreted Sections 504 and 503, nondiscrimination provisions of the Rehabilitation Act of 1973, to include alcohol and drug abusers. The different moral status given people with these problems led Congress to clarify its intentions in the 1978 amendments to the act. See "New Rehabilitation/Developmental Disabilities Act Amendments Become Law," *Amicus* 3 (November/December 1978): 12.

48. Sometimes programs and benefits for blind persons are administratively separate, perhaps because of their generally earlier origins. See Obermann, *Vocational Rehabilitation*, chap. 10, especially, p. 334.

49. U.S., Congress, House, *The Effectiveness of the Architectural Barriers Act of 1968, Hearings before the Subcommittee on Investigations and Review of the House Committee on Public Works and Transportation*, 94th Cong., 1st sess., 1975, p. 70.

50. *U.S. Code*, vol. 29, sec. 794.

51. *Cherry v. Mathews*, No. 76-0255 (D.C. filed February 13, 1976). On July 19, 1976, District Court Judge John L. Smith ordered HEW to promulgate the regulations without undue delay.

52. Bowe, *Coalition Building*, p. 36.

53. Michael Williams, "This Issue," *The Independent* (quarterly publication of the Center for Independent Living, Berkeley, Calif.), Summer 1977, p. 6.

54. "Alternative Conference Report," White House Conference on Handicapped Individuals, May 23–27, 1977 (mimeograph), p. 14.

55. Ibid., p. 2. The chairperson of the authoring group calling itself Representatives of the Handicapped for an Alternative Conference Report was the current president of the National Federation of the Blind. The traditional separatist position of the NFB may have influenced the Alternative Report, but other members of the group had a variety of other disabilities.

56. Berry, *Lobbying for the People*, pp. 27 and 188, found that of eighty-three Washington, D.C.-based public interest groups, thirty percent had no individual memberships at all and relied upon funding from foundations or church organizations. Fifty-seven percent of the groups that had memberships had no structure to elicit and consider member opinion.

57. The National Center for Law and the Handicapped no longer appeared in the South Bend, Indiana, telephone book in 1982, suggesting it either moved or went out of existence.

58. Nathan Hakman, "Lobbying the Supreme Court—An Appraisal of 'Political Science Folklore'," *Fordham Law Review* 35 (1966): 34, 47, discusses the "egotism" [quotation marks in original] of lawyers in commercial litigation and some criminal defense cases and their belief that their cases are private fights.

59. Interview with Edward Steinfeld, Syracuse University School of Architecture, director of the project to update ANSI accessibility standards, Syracuse, New York, November 23, 1977.

60. A history of the public concern with architectural barriers can be found

in U.S., National Commission on Architectural Barriers, *Design for All Americans* (1968), pp. 1–10.

61. P.L. 90–480; *U.S. Code*, vol. 42, secs. 4151–56.

62. Abt Associates, Inc., *Travel Barriers—Transportation Needs of the Handicapped*, prepared for U.S. Department of Transportation, Office of Economics and Systems Analysis (Cambridge, Mass., 1969).

63. U.S. President, Proclamation 4001, *Weekly Compilation of Presidential Documents* (September 8, 1970).

64. *U.S. Code*, vol. 49, sec. 1612(a).

65. U.S., Congress, House, 93d Cong., 1st sess., September 29, 1970, *Congressional Record* 116: 34180–81.

66. P.L. 93-146; *U.S. Code*, vol. 45, sec. 545(c)

67. P.L. 93–87, sec. 165(b); 87 Stat. 282 (1973).

68. P.L. 93-643; *U.S. Code*, vol. 23, sec. 142.

69. P.L. 93-391, sec. 315; 88 Stat. 781 (1974).

70. U.S., General Accounting Office, *Mass Transit*, p. 28.

71. Ibid.

72. Ibid., p. 29.

73. Civil No. 74-1069-HM (D. Md. October 30, 1974).

74. U.S., *Federal Register*, vol. 41, 18239–41 and 18234 (April 30, 1976) or *Code of Federal Regulations*, vol. 49, secs. 609.1–609.25 and 613.204.49 *C.F.R.* 609.15(a), (b), and (c) were revised effective October 12, 1976. Reported in 41 *F.R.* 45842 on October 18, 1976.

75. Reported in *Amicus* 1 (July 1976): 2–3.

76. U.S., General Accounting Office, *Mass Transit*, p. 69.

77. *Lloyd v. Regional Transportation Authority*, 548 F.2d 1277 (1977).

78. *United Handicapped Federation v. Andre*, 558 F.2d 413 (1977).

79. *Leary v. Crapsey*, 566 F.2d 863 (1977).

80. *Snowden v. Birmingham-Jefferson County Transit Authority*, 551 F.2d 862 (1977), affirming 407 F.Supp. 394 (N.D. Ala. 1975).

81. Eric Peterson, "Legal Challenges to Bureaucratic Discretion: The Influence of Lawsuits on the Implementation of EPSDT," Working Paper No. 27, Health Policy Project Series, Department of Epidemiology and Public Health, Yale University, 1975, p. 44.

82. *Lloyd v. Regional Transportation Authority*, 548 F.2d 1277, 1287 (1977).

83. The Transbus mandate is discussed in chap. 4 below. The HEW guidelines were signed as a result of the demonstrations and sit-in described earlier in this chapter. The Department of Transportation's Section 504 regulations are discussed in chap. 8.

84. *Vanko v. Finley*, 440 F.Supp. 656 (N.D. Ohio 1977), and *Snowden v. Birmingham-Jefferson Transit Authority*.

85. *Bartels v. Biernat*, 427 F.Supp. 226 (E.D. Wisc. 1977), and *Michigan Paralyzed Veterans of America v. Coleman*, 451 F.Supp. 7 (S.D. Mich. 1977).

86. In addition to *Lloyd, United Handicapped Federation*, and *Leary*, above, the other two successful appeals were *Young v. Adams*, No. 77-6056 (2nd Cir. 1977), and *Baker v. Bell*, 630 F.2d 1046 (5th Cir. 1980).

87. *Bagstad v. Orange County Transit District*, No. 79-3426 (9th Cir. 1980), and

Atlantis Community, Inc. v. Adams, 453 F.Supp. 825 (D. Col. 1977), expected to file appeal to 10th Circuit.

88. *United Handicapped Federation v. Andre,* Stipulation of Settlement, May 3, 1978, in consideration for the terms, dates, and conditions set forth in Metropolitan Transit Commission Resolution No. 77-115 of December 21, 1977. The other case which reportedly lost again on remand is *Leary v. Crapsey,* 566 F.2d 863 (1977).

89. *Center for Independent Living v. Alameda-Contra Costa Transit District,* No. 496609-8 (Alameda Co., Calif. Super. Ct., 1977).

90. *Paralyzed Veterans of America v. Washington Metropolitan Area Transit Authority,* Civil Action 776-72 (D.D.C.), settled in October 1978; *Disabled in Action of Baltimore v. Hughes,* Civil No. 74-1069-HM (D. Md.), settled in October 1974; *Abilities Unlimited, Inc. v. Villegas,* Civil No. 75-0001 (D. Hawaii), Settled in April 1978; *M.I.G.H.T. v. Briscoe,* Civil No. A 75 CA 31 (W.D. Tex.), filed April 1975 but settlement date unknown; *Zukas v. Alameda-Contra Costa Transit District,* No. C78-0824 CBR (N.D. Calif.), settled in June 1979; *Rodriguez v. Adams,* Civil No. 76-281 (W.D. Tex.), settled in November 1978; *Hambrick and Ritter v. California Business and Transportation Agency,* No. 180434 (San Bernardino Co., Calif. Super. Ct.), settled in February 1978.

91. *Disabled in Action of Pennsylvania v. Coleman,* No. 76-1913 (E.D. Pa.), mooted in March 1978.

92. Information about class action status was unavailable in two of the twenty-four suits.

93. Neal R. Peirce, "The Great Wheelchair Flap," *Washington Post,* 28 December 1978, p. A23. For a rebuttal, see Frank Bowe, "Civil Rights for the Disabled," *Washington Post,* 9 January 1979, p. A19.

Chapter 4

The Transit Access Cases—The Groups and the Lawyers

Among the twenty-four lawsuits filed in 1972 through 1978 by disabled individuals and organizations against public transit agencies, six cases have been studied in detail. They exemplify variations on the new pattern of litigation made possible by the development since the early Fifties of more statutory and regulatory grounds for suits, more rights-conscious litigating groups, and more legal vehicles for group representation. These cases show how some social reform litigation has evolved from the coordinated constitutional focus of the NAACP to a decentralized style more integrated with other political activities.

The very diversity of the plaintiff groups and their lawyers is strikingly different from the virtual monopoly of the NAACP. The plaintiffs differed in their organizational structures, their ideological orientations, and their degree of political experience. Some of the lawyers were affiliated with law reform groups, others were not; some were paid by the clients, others were not. An introduction to the participants in the six lawsuits and a summary of their facts will provide the background for the subsequent discussion of the "new litigation style" characteristics they demonstrate.

The Plaintiff Groups

The decentralization and diversity of the disability rights movement are evident in the broad range of organizational plaintiffs in the transit access cases. The six suits examined here involved twenty different organizations as named plaintiffs. (Since virtually the same group of plaintiffs brought two suits, the number of cases will be considered to be five

Table 1
Organizational Plaintiffs in Six Transit Access Lawsuits

National Organizations	Paralyzed Veterans of America National Congress of Organizations of the Physically Handicapped American Coalition of Citizens with Disabilities	National Council of Senior Citizens National Caucus on the Black Aged
State or Local Affiliates or Chapters of National Organizations	United Cerebral Palsy of Alameda County (Calif.) United Cerebral Palsy of Pennsylvania National Capitol Area chapter, National Paraplegia Foundation Twin Cities Chapter, National Paraplegia Foundation San Raphael Indoor Sports Club	Washington Urban League
Autonomous State or Local Groups	The Center for Independent Living California Association of the Physically Handicapped United Handicapped Federation Disabled in Action of Pennsylvania Disabled in Action of Baltimore Disabled in Action of New Jersey Disabled in Action of New York Disabled Students Union	Pennsylvania Association of Older Persons

for most purposes.) Sixteen of the organizations were groups of or for disabled people. The other four were senior citizen or black organizations allied with the disabled groups for purposes of the suit. Because the development of senior citizen and black interest groups is historically independent and displays different patterns from the development of disability organizations, the discussion in this chapter will be confined to the latter, although issues arising from litigation coalitions with non-disability groups will be discussed briefly. The twenty organizations are listed in Table 1.

All four historical strands of the disability rights movement are represented among the sixteen participating disability organizations. All eight of the autonomous state or local groups plus the national American

Coalition of Citizens with Disabilities were post-Sixties consumer groups. The Indoor Sports Club, the Paralyzed Veterans of America, and the National Congress of Organizations of the Physically Handicapped were pre-Sixties consumer groups. United Cerebral Palsy Associations were originally and still are officially parent groups, although by the Seventies they were largely provider groups in practice. The National Paraplegia Foundation was predominantly a provider group at the national level, but a consumer group locally.

The pre-Sixties/post-Sixties distinction serves as an ideological classification as well as a chronological one. For the reasons described in chapter 3, the post-Sixties groups tended to be more politically militant than the earlier groups. One area in which this difference is evident is the attitude each group held toward different political strategies. Although all sixteen groups ultimately chose to become plaintiffs in a lawsuit, the ease or difficulty with which they made such a choice and the other political strategies they were willing to undertake reveal the ideological range of the disability rights movement.

Autonomous State or Local Groups

The structure of the groups—whether they were autonomous or are affiliated with a national organization—also reflects the period in which they began. That all of the autonomous state or local groups were of post-Sixties vintage reflects the diffusion of the new militance. Young disabled people, inspired by the civil rights and antiwar movements, generally rejected the existing organizations of disabled persons and formed new ones. One of the groups, the Center for Independent Living, combined service delivery with political action, but the others were all explicitly and exclusively political action organizations.

The Center for Independent Living (CIL) was an ideologically militant self-help organization of and for disabled people. It grew out of a special living unit for severely physically disabled students at the University of California at Berkeley. In 1972 it was independently chartered and funded to provide services for physically disabled persons in the whole community. By obtaining grants from a variety of sources, the center grew until its services included housing and attendant referral, legal advocacy, job development, independent living skills counseling, wheelchair repair, van modification, and special services for blind and deaf persons.[1]

Although formally more a service, educational, and research than a political organization, CIL always had a "philosophy of disability" based on disabled persons' awareness of "the degree to which control over their lives had been taken over by medical and rehabilitation professionals" and of the parallels between the black and student movements and their own.[2] It organized or helped to organize numerous demonstrations on disability issues in the San Francisco area, including the takeover of the HEW building in April 1977 to protest the failure to promulgate regulations for Section 504 of the Rehabilitation Act of 1973 and the blockade of buses in the East Bay Terminal in the summer of 1978 to protest congressional delays of the Transbus program.

While the Center for Independent Living might represent the radical wing of disabled consumer groups in California and the Indoor Sports Club (discussed below) the conservative wing, the California Association of the Physically Handicapped (CAPH) would be called the liberal wing. Organized in 1971, CAPH had thirty-two chapters around the state and approximately 3500 members in 1978. It employed a full-time lobbyist in Sacramento and had eleven state-level issue committees that studied, monitored, and attempted to influence political issues of concern to disabled people. Some years ago the group gave Mason Rose, a disabled Southern California attorney, a blanket permission to file *amicus* briefs in the name of CAPH in appropriate suits.

At the time of this study, the group was suffering from an ideological split, primarily over the use of demonstrations, that was dividing its leaders and discouraging potential new leadership. The state board of directors did not approve of obstructive demonstrations, but local chapters have considerable autonomy and occasionally got involved in activities not condoned by the board. Although some resistance had developed to the cost of lawsuits, litigation was a much less divisive strategy than demonstrations. Members of the more radical Bay Area chapters of CAPH were the most actively involved in the suit in this study in which CAPH was a plaintiff, but the state board did approve the organization's joining.

The United Handicapped Federation (UHF) of Minneapolis/Saint Paul (Minnesota) was a local coalition of organizations on the same general model as the American Coalition of Citizens with Disabilities. It consisted of approximately thirty organizational members since its founding in 1974. Following Saul Alinsky's principles of community organizing, a general social action organization called the Greater Metropolitan Federation assisted in getting UHF started. The original press release announcing the group's formation stated: "Confrontation and pressure tactics—not lobbying—will be the guiding force of the Federation."[3] When the lawsuit was first proposed, there were strong debates about whether litigation was really social action in keeping with their principles.

The four Disabled in Action groups of Pennsylvania, Baltimore, New Jersey, and New York, organized between 1971 and 1974, were autonomous but loosely confederated. After the first group organized under that name in New York City, others began to learn of their new, outspoken style through such communication channels as the annual meetings of the President's Committee on the Employment of the Handicapped and returned to their own communities to organize Disabled in Action groups there. As of mid-1979, seven or eight such groups existed.

The Disabled Students Union (DSU) was a small organization of disabled students at the University of California at Berkeley. There were DSU chapters on other campuses around the country as well, but their ties were of the loosest sort.

Local and State Affiliates of National Organizations

A decentralized organizational pattern is not new among disability groups. Even the older local and state groups affiliated with national organizations possessed considerable autonomy. Specifically, not one of the five such plaintiffs in these cases required permission from its national headquarters to enter a lawsuit, a relatively major organizational commitment.

United Cerebral Palsy (UCP) affiliates are independently incorporated organizations, chartered by the national organization when they meet specified standards in their delivery of services to persons with cerebral palsy and their families. Although UCP was originally a parent group, affiliates generally have a professional staff involved in the service delivery. UCP is a good example of an older organization which experienced the new wave of disabled activism at both local and national levels. A young woman with cerebral palsy who was employed by the Alameda County affiliate characterized her chapter as more liberal than average in getting consumers with cerebral palsy involved in decision making; other affiliates had the attitude of "those poor little CP's—let's help them, but not employ them or put them on the board."

At the national level the United Cerebral Palsy Associations, Inc. put a new emphasis on involving persons with cerebral palsy in planning activities and policies and on taking more explicit political stands, including participation in litigation, through a legal advocacy committee.[4] In the years 1974 to 1976, the Board of Directors of UCP had explicitly discussed whether to engage in litigation. Although the organization had for some time maintained a Governmental Activities Office in Washington which regularly monitored legislation, provided information, and lobbied on issues of concern to people with cerebral palsy, some people felt that litigation was different. They felt it "might get us some bad publicity or generate some ill feeling among members of the public who would otherwise be well disposed toward us," according to the director of UCP's legal department.

The board decided to go ahead, establishing a legal advocacy committee and a set of procedures for deciding to litigate. Through their common work on the law of mental retardation, the chairman of the new committee knew the chief counsel of the public interest law firm handling the transit lawsuit which UCP's Pennsylvania affiliate had joined. The chairman suggested this case as a good first suit for the national organization. Although the board missed the original deadline for joining the suit, the organization did authorize the law firm to represent it. The lawyers prepared papers requesting the court to allow UCP to intervene, but the suit terminated before it did so. The national office still made a financial contribution and participated in later lobbying efforts on the same issue.

The legal director felt that the suit was a positive experience for UCP that would encourage it to litigate again. Transportation was not a controversial issue for the group internally, as the role of medical or rehabilitation professionals might be. "And also there were some meaty issues involved, so those people in the organization who were looking for us to play a significant role and make contributions should be satisfied with what we did." He also pointed out that in their evaluation of the organizational position on litigation, UCP was a year or two ahead of the Easter Seal Society, another national charitable and service organization. Easter Seal had also been invited to participate in the same suit, but only then got embroiled in debating litigation *per se* and was not able to make a decision in time.

The National Spinal Cord Injury Foundation (before 1979, the National Paraplegia Foundation (NPF), as it was known in these suits) was founded in 1948 "to inform and educate the medical profession and the public on paraplegia and allied problems of the spinal cord and column; to make limited grants to medical research; to participate actively in rehabilitation and community services for the paraplegic."[5] The national organization was dominated by research-oriented professionals, while the local chapters had greater participation by paraplegics themselves and greater concern with problems of daily living. Two NPF chapters joined transit lawsuits.

According to a member of the National Capitol Area chapter, the national office decided to organize the local groups in the mid-Sixties "to do the dirty work." In the D.C. case, NPF merged with and superseded an existing local consumer group. The former president of the Twin Cities chapter also referred to tensions between the chapters and national office: a question, in his words, of "Does the national exist for the locals or the locals for the national?" Both chapters discussed joining their respective lawsuits with the national office, but sought neither authorization nor financial backing.

Ideologically, the NPF chapters fell between the earlier and later consumer groups. The D.C. chapter was perhaps the most politically active *local* group in the city, and it was a plaintiff in two of the six lawsuits. A former president of the chapter characterized it as unique because the high proportion of educated, professionally employed members made the group exceptionally politically aware and active. On the other hand, some members had such responsible positions with the federal government that they felt constrained from participating in protests.

The Twin Cities (Minneapolis/Saint Paul) NPF chapter was originally a member of the militant United Handicapped Federation, but it withdrew because of UHF's confrontational style. The NPF chapter president's description of the federation reflects the disagreement about tactics that divides many newer groups from older consumer groups as well as from provider and parent group.[6]

We felt that when they pulled something off, such as a demonstration, and then when it came time to sit down and to talk and negotiate, they never—or were reluctant—to sit down and talk common sense. It always had to be something radical. And a couple of times they had done things that almost blew what we were trying to accomplish. In other words, their actions tended to anger the bureaucrats or the politicians that we had finally got to the bargaining table, and we just decided that they were getting kind of a bad name in the power structure and we didn't want to be associated with that name because they wouldn't change.

The San Raphael Indoor Sports Club was founded in 1950 as a local chapter of the national Indoor Sports Club, Inc., which dates back to 1930. Unlike UCP or NPF, the Indoor Sports Club was always exclusively a consumer group, with an auxiliary called the Good Sports for interested able-bodied people. Although its stated purposes included the "promotion and support of all legislation which gives the physically disabled better opportunities for adequate rehabilitation and employment" and "educating the public" toward the same end, the group was typically more social and recreational than political.[7] The lawyer who worked with the San Raphael chapter characterized it as "primarily a social club where they've been there for a long time; they know each other; they sit around and play cards."

Although personally more politically active and a founding member of CAPH, the area vice president of the region including the San Raphael chapter acknowledged that Indoor Sports is a "very conservative organization." As far as he knew, the San Raphael group was the only chapter ever to bring a lawsuit. He and a past chapter president tried to get the other members more involved and active in the community, but without a great deal of success. At least one reason, according to the past president, is that many members are disabled older people who have little educational or employment experience. Those members who become rehabilitated tend to lose interest in the group and get involved in developing their families and their own interests.

National Organizations

Three national organizations were involved in the five transit cases directly as plaintiffs themselves rather than through their chapters or member groups. Founded in 1947, Paralyzed Veterans of America (PVA) was a membership organization of armed forces veterans who have incurred a paralyzing spinal cord injury through war, disease, or injury. Its $4.5 million 1978 national budget was made up primarily of contributions from the general public, however, and it employed professional staff members scattered around the country to assist veterans with service-related benefit claims, conduct sports activities for disabled people, and conduct public education campaigns about paraplegia.[8]

PVA, too, was following the national trend of greater political involvement by disability groups. In 1978 it added to its existing legislative program a national advocacy program, which addressed the whole range of issues of concern to disabled people, such as discrimination in housing, employment, transportation, and education. In the words of one staff member, the membership realized "relatively early on" that "their day-to-day problems related more to their position as disabled people, as seriously disabled people, as opposed to their status as veterans."

Nevertheless, there were some political divisions within the organization. The board of directors officially approved joining a transit lawsuit as early as 1972, but even six years later the advocacy director commented: "Bringing a lawsuit in our organization is still a rather militant thing to do. I don't view it that way, but I'm not necessarily the mainstream of the organization. . . . Some of our older members are conservative and just don't like the idea of being involved in lawsuits, period."

The other two national organizations involved in the lawsuits were the American Coalition of Citizens with Disabilities and the National Congress of Organizations of the Physically Handicapped (NCOPH). Their coalition structures and their low-key rivalry were described in chapter 3. The older NCOPH was less politicized and was national in little more than name. The group's president reported that over half of its fifty-five member groups were in the state of Illinois.

The lawsuit was the first time that NCOPH and ACCD worked together. The NCOPH president felt that ACCD was basically duplicating what NCOPH had attempted to be for many years longer. In practice, there was little overlap between the organizations' members. The members of NCOPH groups, according to the president, tend to be more severely disabled, more dependent, and less educated. She characterized ACCD leaders as "coming from government jobs or having Ph.D.s."

The Lawyers

The varying sources of legal counsel for the five accessible transit cases, even more than the plaintiff groups, illustrate the ways this litigation differs from the centralized NAACP model. The disability organizations involved in the suits participated as plaintiffs, not as counsel. The principal legal counsel for the five suits came from the following sources: two attorneys in solo private practice, one federally funded legal aid office, one public interest law firm, and one large private firm doing *pro bono* work.[9]

The lawyers' previous experience with disability issues varied considerably, but none had done previous public transportation-related litigation. One of the solo practitioners had been the staff counsel for a state association for mentally retarded persons, which had involved him in a large right-to-education suit for all disabled children in the state. At the time he was approached about the transit access lawsuit, he had recently opened a private practice specializing in rights of disabled persons, handling private cases such as parents' efforts to obtain aid or placements for their disabled children.

The other solo practitioner had done no previous work on disability rights, but he had a local reputation for activist, civil rights-related work and was involved with the community organization that helped to organize the disabled consumers' group. The legal aid lawyers had had some contact with clients with individual problems created by disabilities, but they had not previously worked with organized disabled clients on a public policy issue.

The public interest firm, the Public Interest Law Center of Philadelphia (PILCOP), had had considerable experience with disability issues, although it was primarily focused on mental disabilities. The firm was particularly well known for its success in the right-to-education suit, *Pennsylvania Association for Retarded Children v. Commonwealth of Pennsylvania*.[10] In 1974 it received a grant from a private foundation to research legal means to improve transportation service for persons with disabilities. Thus, at the time the PILCOP lawyers met the local organization that became their client, they had studied the background of the law on transit access and had developed a legal strategy for change.

The *pro bono* lawyers from the private firm were brought into the transit case by a former partner of the firm who was then directing the Institute for Public Interest Representation, a public interest group affiliated with Georgetown University Law School. The institute had done the initial research and laid the strategy for the case, but turned it over to the private attorneys for the trial work. The first private attorney who worked on the suit usually specialized in government contract work and admittedly had "never heard of the National Paraplegia Foundation" before it became one of his clients. Later, a second attorney from the same firm took over most of the work on the case as it stretched out over several years.

Before they became involved in the transit access cases, then, some of the lawyers had a previous substantive commitment to disabled persons and others had general underdog sympathies or whatever combination of motives gets large private firms to do *pro bono* work.[11] In general, they had little background in the issues of accessible transportation since it was a very new public concern, and they also had relatively little communication with each other once the suits did begin. Such a lack of coordination did not have the bad consequences one might expect from the NAACP model of social reform litigation. Because the suits were not attempting to establish constitutional precedents, but sought remedies for rights already stated in the law, decentralized litigation was a plausible approach.

The Cases

While the identity of the plaintiff groups and lawyers alone gives some idea of the diversity of the accessible transit cases, the features of the new style of social reform litigation are most evident in the cases' goals and strategies. Before the remedy-orientation, use of extra-judicial strategies, plaintiff-stacking behavior, and lack of coordination of the cases are examined in detail, a brief introduction of each of the five cases with emphasis on their origins will be presented. The cases are described in chronological order of their filing dates so that they can be related to the general development of the disability rights movement and the legal bases of claims to accessible public transportation discussed in chapter 3. Appendix A summarizes a few facts about each case.

A Typology of Case Origins

The way in which each case originated is one of the most important factors in determining the degree to which the case displays the characteristics of the new style. The origins of the transit access cases differentiate them from one another and also from the classic NAACP model of litigation. The NAACP desegregation litigation was a pure test case model in which lawyers with a previous commitment to the issues and a legal strategy already planned recruit a person or persons willing to become parties.

The plaintiffs in the school desegregation cases, of course, faced an environment very different from the one disabled plaintiffs face today. Blacks who challenged the status quo at that time were likely to face economic reprisals and sometimes physical intimidation. The desegregation litigation predated the mass-involvement phase of the civil rights movement, so initiative fell to those few people in the NAACP national office and local chapters. Again, as Kluger notes, "one couldn't pick and choose one's plaintiffs those days; there were too few willing to risk the fight and possible reprisals."[12]

The religious nonconformists whom Frank Sorauf studies in the church-state litigation were not in so risky a position as the NAACP clients, although Sorauf does document negative consequences experienced by some separationist plaintiffs.[13] Indeed, some of the church-state lawsuits had the sympathy of sizeable groups in a community. As a result, the church-state cases arose in a variety of ways, not just as planned test cases.

Sorauf suggests that the origins of church-state cases fall into three categories: test cases, community conflicts, and "lonely crusades." In the test cases the plaintiffs were recruited by a sponsoring organization with the goal of establishing a legal precedent transcending the particulars of the case, as in the NAACP pattern. In community conflict cases the issue in contention was already dividing the community into opposing groups, and the national litigating organizations were called in by one side for legal support. In "lonely crusades" one individual undertook to pursue an issue and personally recruited a lawyer to assist him or her.[14]

These categories are helpful in examining the origins of the transit access suits, but the latter reveal some overlap in Sorauf's categories. Of the five cases, two were quite pure examples of "lonely crusades." Individuals took the initiative themselves to find a lawyer to help them with the problem and, despite the eventual participation in name by organized groups, remained the only clients intensively involved in the suits. It is no coincidence that the two earliest cases were the two "lonely crusades." The first case in particular and the second case to some extent arose before there was much of an organized disability rights movement.

The other three cases should be called community conflicts in the sense that groups of disabled people had unsuccessfully attempted to pressure a transit agency into providing accessible service before they got involved in litigation. In two of the three, however, the lawyers played a larger role in initiating the suits than simply taking the cases after the plaintiffs had decided to sue. And in one of these, the lawsuit, as finally devised, had goals beyond the confines of the original community conflict and became more like a test case.

The Washington, D.C., Case

The nation's first lawsuit concerning the access of disabled people to public transportation, *Paralyzed Veterans of America v. Washington Metropolitan Area Transit Authority,*[15] was filed in 1972 in Washington, D.C. Richard Heddinger, a Bureau of Labor Statistics statistician who uses a wheelchair, became concerned about the accessibility of the forthcoming Washington area subway system after reading about it in a newspaper article. A group of disabled individuals and the President's Committee on Employment of the Handicapped had worked with subway planners during the Sixties, but no public commitment on accessibility had been made. Through a personal contact with a U.S. Senator, Heddinger worked for passage by Congress of the 1970 amendment to bring Metro under the terms of the 1968 Architectural Barriers Act. He also went to public hearings on Metro station construction, contacted the press, and checked up on Metro officials' cost estimates and claims of Park Service limitations on their alternatives.[16]

When Metro officials insisted they could not install elevators in the stations unless they received additional special appropriations, Heddinger decided to contact a lawyer. With the assistance of a colleague's law student husband, Heddinger contacted Georgetown University's Institute for Public Interest Representation, which agreed to take the case. Very new, the institute was eager to work on cases that could establish its reputation. With little experience and with student help that disappeared during holidays, the institute found it needed to call in assistance for the trial work. The institute's director contacted the large private firm with which he had formerly been a partner, and two attorneys from Arnold & Porter did the bulk of the work on the case at no cost whatsoever to the clients.

Even though the suit was filed in the name of three organizations as well as Heddinger individually, the case remained a "lonely crusade" and only Heddinger met frequently with the attorneys to discuss strategy. When interviewed six years later, the attorney who did most of the work in its early days could not remember ever meeting with anyone besides Heddinger. "Heddinger is really the client in this case. The others were window dressing. We didn't have any real dealings with them."

The legal thrust of the suit was to force the builders of the subway system, the Washington Metropolitan Area Transit Authority (WMATA), to comply with the Architectural Barriers Act of 1968, which required transportation facilities (though not rolling stock) to be accessible to handicapped persons.[17] The 1970 amendment had explicitly extended the Act to cover the Metro construction,[18] but transit officials argued that the law did not apply because of the nature of the interstate compact supporting the construction. The judge ruled in favor of the plaintiffs and issued an injunction that no station could be opened for public use unless it had elevator access in addition to the planned escalators.

Shortly before the first stations were scheduled to open, Metro officials returned to the judge and claimed they could not get the elevators ready in time in three stations. The disabled plaintiffs felt that Metro's reasons were adequate in two of the three cases, but petitioned the judge to keep the Gallery Place station closed until the elevator was installed. The judge agreed and kept the one station closed after the others opened.

This action received a negative reaction in the press and from the neighborhood merchants—the first significant public opposition that the suit had encountered.[19] WMATA and the merchants' association were able to obtain a waiver from the General Services Administration, which had the authority to waive the requirements of the Architectural Barriers Act, and the station opened—slightly more than six months after the others.

The suit still continued, however, because the plaintiffs had also complained that the location of the elevator planned for Gallery Place required persons using it to go so much farther than persons using the escalators that the plan did not constitute "ready access" as required in the court order. The plaintiffs sought a legal interpretation of "ready access" as meaning "substantially equivalent" access "in terms of ease and convenience of use."[20] The original judge retired from the bench without so ruling, however. When a new judge took the case, he pushed very hard for a settlement. Finally, in October 1978 the parties signed a consent order in which the plaintiffs essentially dropped demands for all but minor changes in operating stations in exchange for improvements in the access planned for yet unopened stations.[21]

The Marin County Case

The second case chronologically, *Bohlke v. Golden Gate Bridge, Highway and Transportation District,*[22] was also the second "lonely crusade" case. It occurred in Marin County, California, north of San Francisco. In early 1972 Russell Bohlke, an employee of the Crown Zellerbach Company who became a quadriplegic as a result of a college football injury in the late Forties, began writing letters to the local transit authority, the Golden Gate Bridge, Highway and Transportation District, to complain about the lack of accessible public transportation for disabled persons. Receiving no response, he got permission to use the stationery of the San Raphael Indoor Sports Club, to which he belonged, in hopes that using an organizational name would give his protest more weight.

After two and a half years of trying through both personal and political channels to get a commitment to serve disabled people in Marin County, Bohlke finally retained an attorney in solo practice with previous experience as staff attorney for the California Association for the Retarded. The Indoor Sports Club had the financial means to pay for an attorney, so Bohlke got the organization and three other members to become plaintiffs in the suit.

The attorney met from time to time with the board of the club, but Bohlke played by far the dominant role in the suit. As noted above, the San Raphael Indoor Sports Club was a conservative group with older members. With a college education and full-time professional employment, Bohlke was atypical. In the lawyer's words: "Russ [Bohlke] is such a leadership force in that organization. . . he's so trusted and so relied upon for his advice that if he comes to a conclusion, you're going to find most people going his way."

The lawsuit was filed in November 1974 in the Marin County Superior Court. The plaintiffs charged that the defendants' failure to provide transportation accessible to disabled people violated their obligation under two state statutes, two federal statutes, and the federal Constitution. No purchase of additional inaccessible buses was in sight at the time, unlike the facts of many of the other suits filed. The remedy sought was fully accessible mainline bus service, with special demand-responsive service acceptable on an interim basis.

At a demurrer hearing early the next year, the judge upheld their state causes of action and dismissed the federal ones.[23] This was long before any regulations had been written for the "special efforts" provision of the Urban Mass Transportation Act or for Section 504 of the Rehabilitation Act of 1973, the two federal statutory causes of action. The decision on the state causes of action, however, was very encouraging to the plaintiffs. California Civil Code 54.1 said that handicapped people shall have full and equal access to all public facilities and specifically includes motorbuses. The judge broadly interpreted the statute as obligating the defendants to modify the buses if necessary in addition to simply prohibiting overt discrimination, such as a refusal to stop at a bus stop if a disabled person is waiting.

California Government Code 4500, the other state cause of action, required transit districts to purchase accessible equipment if the equipment was available from two or more manufacturers, unless the equipment was only incidental to the transit district's operation. The judge ruled that the bus service was more than incidental and, therefore, the district must comply with Gov. Code 4500.

With such a favorable legal ruling, the plaintiffs approached the defendants about a settlement. In the course of negotiations, however, it became known that the defendants were planning to order some inaccessible buses in the near future. When the plaintiffs sought a preliminary injunction of the purchase, the judge denied the injunction on the grounds that the equipment was not available, in fact, from two manufacturers.

A hiatus in activities occurred for a while as the plaintiffs considered whether to go into federal court in light of the new regulations in progress at the Urban Mass Transportation Administration. They decided not to, but the attorney later believed the forthcoming regulations might have been responsible for the defendants' contacting them about a settlement again in early 1976. Negotiations broke down, however, over the question of "retrofitting" a few existing buses to provide some immediate service, and the plaintiffs decided to go to trial. Although they put the case on the court calendar in the spring of 1977, a backlog of cases delayed the trial until the spring of 1978.

The trial opened before a judge different from the one who had held the demurrer hearing. On the first day of the trial, the new judge overruled the earlier decision on Civil Code 54.1 and declared that it applied only to overt discrimination and not to discrimination resulting from bus design. Although sixty percent of the evidence they had planned to introduce instantly became irrelevant, the plaintiffs still tried to establish a case because Bohlke had once attempted to get on a regular bus and the driver had refused to help him. They also had to prove that there were two manufacturers of accessible buses back in 1976 when the bus contract was signed, and that there was a danger of the district's buying inaccessible buses in the future.

During the trial a representative of the Golden Gate Transit District testified under oath that the district board had just resolved to buy no more inaccessible buses. The judge declared the issue moot as to the future purchases, and the plaintiffs failed to meet the burden of proof in regard to the 1976 contract. All they substantively gained from the suit was a commitment on the record that the transit company would purchse no further inaccessible buses. Because a California appeals court had construed Civil Code 54.1 to mean the narrow sense of discrimination in a nontransportation case that occurred between their demurrer hearing and trial, the plaintiffs decided not to appeal.

The Minnesota Case

The Minnesota lawsuit, *United Handicapped Federation v. Andre,*[24] was the purest example of a community conflict suit. Soon after its founding in 1974, the United Handicapped Federation chose transportation as one of its top priorities and began a public education campaign and negotiations with the local transit authority to obtain accessible transportation. Making little progress with the Metropolitan Transit Commission (MTC), the group began to consider suing and contacted an attorney recommended by a community organization consultant they employed and by a senior citizens' federation, for which the lawyer had done some work. After acquainting himself with the law, the attorney reported that they seemed to have a good case. They sued MTC Chief Administrator Andre, other MTC officials, federal transportation officials, and AM General Corporation, the company manufacturing the inaccessible buses to be ordered.

The plaintiffs filed under Section 504 of the Rehabilitation Act of 1973,[25] Section 16(a) of the 1970 Urban Mass Transportation Act,[26] and the other similar federal statutes noted in chapter 3. The suit sought an injunction against the completion of a planned purchase of new inaccessible buses and a declaratory judgment ordering a plan drawn up for the provision of public transportation service to disabled people.

The district judge summarily dismissed the suit, and the plaintiffs appealed. The Eighth Circuit Court of Appeals ruled that Section 504 of the Rehabilitation Act of 1973 does create a private cause of action and an affirmative duty on the part of the defendants.[27] It remanded the case for a determination whether the new UMTA regulations were being complied with, but the plaintiffs and the local defendants reached a settlement before trial. Under the terms of the settlement, the MTC agreed to provide transportation service to fifty percent of the disabled population of the metropolitan area by February 1, 1979, to seventy-five percent by February 1, 1980, and to one hundred percent by February 1, 1981. The plaintiffs did not *legally* win the case, however, because the district court judge on remand construed the appeals court decision narrowly and granted the defendants' motion for partial summary judgment.[28] Because of the settlement, the plaintiffs did not appeal again.

The Transbus Case

The lawsuit in Philadelphia, *Disabled in Action of Pennsylvania, Inc. v. Coleman,*[29] was the community conflict that broadened into a test case. When Disabled in Action of Pennsylvania was organized in 1974, it, too, like the United Handicapped Federation in Minnesota, began pressuring the local transit authority to provide accessible transportation. About this same time the Public Interest Law Center of Philadelphia (PILCOP) received a grant from the Levinson Foundation, a philanthropic foundation supported by a Philadelphia family, to explore legal channels for improving transportation for disabled people. The two groups soon discovered each other and began working together. They negotiated with the transit authority until they decided that because of the complexities of transit technology, manufacturers' resistance, and mass transit finances, a federal focus was needed.

According to the primary representative of Paralyzed Veterans of America in the suit and related activities, the transformation of Philadelphia's community dispute with its local transit authority into a test case against the federal Urban Mass Transportation Administration (UMTA) began in 1975 when he, a representative of ACCD, and a PILCOP attorney met while testifying about transportation for disabled people before a congressional committee. The three kept in touch and when in the spring of 1976 it looked as if UMTA was shelving the Transbus project, PILCOP turned again to the Levinson Foundation for funds for a suit. The lawyers and Disabled in Action members began to contact other disability and senior citizen organizations to participate as plaintiffs.

Rather than focusing on the local transit officials, as other transit access suits had done, the Transbus Group (as the plaintiffs called themselves) sued Secretary of Transportation Coleman and the federal Urban Mass Transportation Administration. The plaintiffs' goal was to get them to provide federal funds (which made up 80 percent of the cost of most mass transit equipment) only for buses meeting the specifications of the Transbus. Transbus was a low-floor, wide-door bus accessible to wheelchairs for which UMTA itself had provided research and development funds. All three American bus manufacturers at the time had built prototype models, which were displayed around the country and tested in 1974–75.[30]

In 1976 UMTA was on the verge of deciding not to go ahead with the Transbus design when the suit was filed. The Carter administration reconsidered the issue after it took office, however, and in May 1977 Secretary of Transportation Brock Adams declared that after September 1979 federal funds would be spent only for buses meeting the Transbus specifications. With its purposes essentially accomplished, the judge dismissed the lawsuit as moot. The activities of the plaintiffs continued, however, shepherding the Transbus mandate through subsequent political thickets to be described in chapter 5.[31]

The East Bay Case

The fifth case comprised both the state and federal suits brought in Alameda County, California, which embraces Oakland and Berkeley (thus, the "East Bay case"). These suits arose from a community conflict, too, because the organizational plaintiffs were all involved in pressuring local or state transportation officials for service for disabled persons before they began to litigate.

Initiative for the first lawsuit, however, came from legal aid attorneys, who read about a transit suit in Rochester, New York, in a publication for legal services lawyers. The attorneys contacted the Center for Independent Living, whose activities on behalf of disabled persons were well known in the area. CIL members had been attending transit board meetings, knew of the planned purchase of inaccessible buses, and were very interested in legal action.

The state case, *Center for Independent Living v. Alameda-Contra Costa Transit District,*[32] was filed in June 1977 to enjoin an imminent purchase of inaccessible buses, as in Minnesota. At the hearing for preliminary and permanent injunctive relief, the judge denied all the plaintiffs' requests. They filed an appeal with the state Court of Appeals and shortly thereafter requested a stay against any activity toward obtaining the buses, pending the appeal. The stay was denied, but an appeal of the stay to the state Supreme Court was successful, and the case went back to the Court of Appeals on the merits. At that point the defendants assigned their rights to buy the buses to another transit district, so the court declared the case moot. In hopes of still obtaining an interpretation of state law that would bind any future purchases as well, the plaintiffs appealed again to the Supreme Court, which denied the appeal, thus ending the state case except for a petition for attorney's fees.

The federal suit, *Zukas v. Alameda-Contra Costa Transit District,*[33] was filed in April 1978. When it appeared that the defendants were delaying putting out bids for accessible buses and had no real plans to furnish accessible transportation, the plaintiffs charged them with violating the federal requirement that "special efforts" be made to provide such transportation. Plaintiffs and defendants filed cross motions for summary judgment. The judge asked both sides to submit plans for interim relief until accessible full-sized buses would be integrated into the system under the terms of the Transbus mandate.

In June 1979 the parties to the federal suit settled, with the defendants committing themselves to buy more than 300 accessible buses over the next five-year period. An order for the first 160 was made that summer. The buses were to be full-sized and lift-equipped, an available design that was accessible to persons in wheelchairs but less desirable for several reasons than the still-embattled low-floor Transbus design. Even without a court ruling, the plaintiffs said they were happy with the settlement.

Given these basic factual events, we will now be able to see exactly what besides the participants made the accessible transit cases different from the classic NAACP model of litigation and products, instead, of the changes in the political environment since the time of *Brown v. Board of Education*. The principal differences are that the transit cases focused on remedy rather than constitutional development. This enabled the disabled plaintiffs to work toward the same material goals outside and inside the court simultaneously. With litigation merged so thoroughly with other political activities, the recruitment of plaintiffs came to take on the flavor of mobilizing a political coalition, including some of the attendant problems of coalition efforts. Since remedy was the goal, the suits were also able to be much more decentralized and less coordinated with each other than the NAACP's constitutional campaign needed to be. The next chapter will consider each of these features as they appeared in the five case studies.

Notes

1. Zukas, "C.I.L. History."
2. Ibid., pp. 1–2.
3. Press release, September 9, 1974.
4. United Cerebral Palsy Associations, Inc., *1976 Annual Report* (New York: United Cerebral Palsy Associations, Inc., 1976), p. 4.
5. *Encyclopedia of Associations*, 1981, 11th ed., s.v. "National Paraplegia Foundation."

6. In a study of private interest groups, Donald Hall also found groups wary of joining coalitions with other groups that had a bad image. See Hall, *Cooperative Lobbying—The Power of Pressure* (Tucson: University of Arizona Press, 1969).

7. Pamphlet, Indoor Sports Club, Inc., 1974.

8. Paralyzed Veterans of America, *1978 Annual Report* (Washington, D.C.: Paralyzed Veterans of America, 1978).

9. The modifier "principal" is used because of the situation in the Washington, D.C. case, where a public interest firm originally took the case and then turned it over to the private firm.

10. 334 F.Supp. 1257 (E.D. Pa. 1971). PILCOP chief counsel, Thomas Gilhool, also appeared in *Pennhurst State School and Hospital v. Halderman*, 451 U.S. 1 (1981).

11. See discussion of the roots of *pro bono* work in Joel F. Handler, Ellen Jane Hollingsworth, and Howard S. Erlanger, *Lawyers and the Pursuit of Legal Rights* (New York: Academic Press, 1978), chap. 2, and F. Raymond Marks, *The Lawyer, the Public, and Professional Responsibility* (Chicago: American Bar Foundation, 1972), chap. 1.

12. Kluger, *Simple Justice*, p. 156.

13. Sorauf, *Wall of Separation*, pp. 151–52.

14. Ibid., p. 240.

15. Civil Action No. 776-72 (D. D.C. 1972). The suit was originally titled *Washington Urban League v. Washington Metropolitan Area Transit Authority* until the Urban League withdrew.

16. Richard W. Heddinger, "The Twelve Year Battle for a Barrier-Free Metro," *American Rehabilitation*, May/June 1976, p. 7. Interviews with Mr. Heddinger provided additional information about the lawsuit.

17. P.L. 90-480; *U.S. Code*, vol. 49, secs. 4151–56.

18. P.L. 91-205; *U.S. Code*, vol. 49, sec. 4151.

19. For example, Walter T. Ridder, "Minority Tyrannies," *New York Times*, 29 July 1976, p. 31, and Richard Cohen, "Merchants at 9th and G Stood Up By Subway," *Washington Post*, 6 June 1976, p. B1.

20. Plaintiffs' Brief on the Legal Standards Governing Adequacy of Facilities for the Handicapped under the Court's Order of October 24, 1973, *Washington Urban League v. Washington Metropolitan Area Transit Authority*, Civil Action No. 776–72 (D. D.C. 1972), p. 2.

21. Douglas B. Feaver, "Metro Bows to Demands of Handicapped," *Washington Post*, 13 October 1978, p. C5.

22. No. 73362 (Marin Co., Calif. Super. Ct., 1974).

23. At a demurrer hearing the defendants admit, for the purpose of this motion only, all facts properly pleaded. The defendants assert that even if the facts are correct, the plaintiffs have no valid cause of action or legal grounds to proceed.

24. 558 F.2d 413 (8th Cir. 1977), remanding 409 F.Supp. 1297 (D. Minn. 1975).

25. *U.S. Code*, vol. 29, sec. 794.

26. *U.S. Code*, vol. 49, sec. 1612(a).

27. 558 F.2d 413 (8th Cir., 1977).

28. The judge held that the regulations did not apply to projects approved prior to their effective date.

29. No. 76-1913 (E.D. Pa. 1976).

30. David Young, "The Transbus Compromise," *Mass Transit*, January/Feburary 1979, pp. 12–15, provides background on the development of the Transbus design.

31. David C. Hackney, "Elderly, Disabled See Transbus as Last Hope," *Mass Transit*, January/February 1979, p. 16.

32. No. 496609-8 (Alameda Co., Calif. Super. Ct., 1977).

33. No. C78-0824 CBR (N.D. Calif. 1978).

Chapter 5

The Transit Access Cases as the New Style of Social Reform Litigation

In varying degrees the five accessible transportation cases illustrate the characteristics of the new style of social reform litigation made possible by the developments in statutory and regulatory law, collective rights consciousness, and vehicles for group representation in the judicial process. While all the cases were basically remedy-oriented rather than focused on setting precedents in constitutional or statutory interpretation, some confined themselves much more to courtroom efforts than others did. The groups consciously intended their use of organizational and/or multiple individual plaintiffs to affect the outcomes of their cases. Although most of the groups achieved some success with their suits, it did not come without problems. The cases illustrate the features of politicized social reform litigation, including its possible problems.

Remedy Over Principle

The statutes under which most of the federal litigants brought their cases were very vague and were not backed up with specific regulations for some time after their passage. To many disabled people, however, the legislation meant that they had a *right* to public transportation. When some of them went to court, then, they did not focus on establishing a principle, such as the right to travel, but on enforcing what they believed to be an existing right. Although a few also included arguments for a constitutional right to travel based on the Fifth and Fourteenth Amendments, the suits were based primarily on statutory arguments.

The distinction between principle and remedy is not exactly the same as the distinction between establishing a constitutional precedent and enforcing statutory rights, of course. The principle/remedy distinction can exist in either realm. Even in relation to the NAACP's equal protection litigation, Derrick Bell writes of the gap between the belief of the civil rights lawyers in the principle of school integration and the desire of the children's parents for an emphasis on better education, regardless of integration or segregation.[1]

On the other hand, where statutory rights already exist, there can also be a conflict between remedy and principle. The question in the transit access suits was whether it was more important to get the remedy—the transportation service—or to get a court ruling that the transit agencies were legally obligated to provide such services. In most cases the plaintiffs were aware of the desirability of the latter as protection against later changes in policy, but were quite willing to settle for the former alone.

The emphasis of lawyers' legal training on appellate court decisions and orderly development of legal doctrines, in addition to the likelihood that they are not personally experiencing the injury, can create an inclination toward broad principles over tangible solutions.[2] One of the lawyers in the transit cases expressed some regret at not being able to pursue the issue for an appellate interpretation of the law. Nevertheless, lawyers, including this one, generally agree that clients have the last word on a settlement decision—when to settle a suit in exchange for what.[3]

Lawyers are not likely to be passive in the settlement decision process, of course, but the disabled clients in these suits were not reticent about expressing their opinions nor dependent on the lawyers to tell them what they wanted. Nor was there much communication among the various litigants around the country to establish a coordinated strategy that might require agreement on principles, so tangible remedy remained the focus of the suits. This is not to say that the clients had no interest at all in principles, and small elements of pursuing principle appear in most of the cases. The measure of their pragmatism, however, is that in all five cases, if they were successful at all, the plaintiffs settled for less than a definitive court ruling.

In the most traditional of the suits in its legalistic goals and strategies, the Washington, D.C., plaintiffs won the most clear-cut court victory when the federal judge enjoined the D.C. subway system from opening until elevators were installed in addition to the planned escalators. Richard Heddinger, the single individual plaintiff and the person most involved in the suit, was fully aware of the difference between a court ruling and a settlement without one. He observed that if the transit authority had obtained the extra appropriation from Congress to make the stations accessible that it originally requested, it probably would never have been told by a judge that it must make the system accessible *with or without* additional money.

The suit was also traditional in that the lawyers advised Heddinger to structure the suit purely as a matter of rights under the relevant statute. While Heddinger said he originally wanted to challenge the defendants' claim of how much elevators would cost, the lawyers persuaded him it was better not to get involved in debating costs or potential ridership, merely rights and duties.

That Heddinger, as well as the lawyers, was interested in establishing principles is witnessed by his keeping the suit alive for five years after the judge's injunction. The judge's order was that the stations must be constructed so that disabled people have "ready access" to them. When one station was built (and others planned) with the elevators located such that people using them would have to travel considerably greater distances than people using the escalators, Heddinger attempted to obtain a clarification from the judge on what constituted "ready access." Urged to a settlement by the new judge, Heddinger hated to abandon the struggle for a legal mandate, but finally settled for some modifications in existing stations and an advisory role in the design of yet unopened stations.

The East Bay plaintiffs used two different lawsuits to press for accessible service. The first suit, in state court, demanded accessible regular route buses and sought to enjoin the purchase of inaccessible ones. When the defendants assigned their rights to buy the immediate buses in question to another district, most of the case was mooted. The plaintiffs had been working with the state attorney general's office on a companion suit which also hoped to get a definitive interpretation of the state law, so they kept their suit alive to get such a ruling vis-à-vis any future purchases. The case died when the state supreme court refused to hear their appeal on that issue, but neither the East Bay plaintiffs nor their lawyers cared much about it. They felt that halting the purchase of the inaccessible buses had been a victory.

Although the transit agency had agreed not to purchase inaccessible buses in the future, it was taking no immediate steps toward providing transit service for disabled people. Consequently, much the same group of plaintiffs filed a federal suit. The plaintiffs, again, did not get a definitive court ruling, and their own lawyer admitted that the transit agency did not agree to much more than they were planning to do anyway. Nevertheless, the plaintiffs felt they had succeeded by obtaining a commitment for service regardless of what happened to the Transbus or to other federal regulations setting national standards.

The Minnesota plaintiffs were perhaps the most pragmatic on both the issue of agreeing to a settlement without a court ruling on the law and the issue of the type of service to be provided. Although the lawyer in the case urged the plaintiffs to see the potential significance of their case as a national precedent, the goal of the lawsuit was always first and foremost to obtain service. They originally demanded accessible regular route service, while the transit commission argued that demand-responsive service was more feasible. After the Court of Appeals overturned the district court's dismissal of the plaintiffs' case, the parties reached a settlement before trial.

Under the terms of the settlement, the plaintiffs dropped their demands for any particular kind of service and agreed to leave it to the transit commission to determine what kind of service should be provided as long as certain percentages of the handicapped population were served by certain dates. With this approach they felt they were forcing the transit commission to implement the policy it had earlier been advocating as a way of avoiding the original demands. According to the lawyer, "We just conned them into believing that we didn't really want this but we'd take it only reluctantly and that they were really taking our pants off. And by God, we had drafted the whole thing, every word of it and wanted it, and that was our strategy from the very beginning." A staff member of one of the plaintiff organizations saw the same shift in terms of the maturity of the organization—hardly an ideological perspective:

> When you think about it, UHF [the United Handicapped Federation] came from "Well, we're suing for 338 accessible vehicles," to a policy of "We won't define for you what delivery system to use. Just get it on the street; we'll go from there." I think that we did a lot of changing. And that's a compliment to the organization that it felt strong enough, that the leadership felt strong enough that they could pull it off by actually changing and reevaluating how they perceive delivery systems to be.

The Transbus plaintiffs were the most adamantly against separate-but-equal service, which is why they chose to sue the federal government to get it to back the development of a new full-size bus rather than suing a local agency to get any service at all. Some of the people involved in this suit were quite impatient with disabled persons who favor demand-responsive service. As one woman said from her wheelchair:

> I think that disabled people are very spoiled in that they haven't had to sit out in the rain or go through the snow or sweat at a bus stop or whatever. But quite frankly I think they need to do that. And I think we have a right to be uncomfortable. . . It's much more important to be able to do things independently than to have to depend on others, and to be pampered, and driven back and forth.

Despite its ideological overtones, the emphasis on regular route service is still an orientation to remedy over legal principle. The Transbus plaintiffs were delighted to win without a court ruling when Secretary of Transportation Brock Adams mandated that the Department of Transportation would provide federal funds only for the Transbus model. The Transbus lawyers made a modest effort to argue that the courts should require the Transbus model anyway since subsequent secretaries of transportation would not necessarily be bound by Adams' decision. Nevertheless, when the judge ruled that the case was moot because Adams' regulations "fulfill plaintiffs' objective" and "have the full force and effect of the law," the plaintiffs hailed it as a victory.[4]

The Marin county suit was much less successful than the others, but this was not because the plaintiffs put principle over remedy. Indeed, when Russ Bohlke first began complaining to the transit district, his original goal was merely to have Golden Gate Bridge tolls lowered for handicapped drivers because they had no alternative to driving. By the time a lawsuit was filed, the goals had been broadened to accessible buses on the regular route system. As the lawyer put it: "We didn't want separate facilities. We wanted integrated full access to what travels down the road—to be able to board at any bus stop on any bus, a bus just like everybody else." In reality, however, he said they would have been very happy to settle for "something less" in the interim. In fact, they got neither.

Extra-Judicial Strategies

As the specifics of these five cases show, the plaintiffs were generally more oriented to remedy—obtaining accessible transit service—than they were to establishing a constitutional principle or a definitive statutory interpretation. Because this was so, there were other actors besides the courts who could give them what they wanted. Indeed, in some of the cases their success was due in part to their coordination of litigation with some of the other tactics Jeffrey Berry noted among public interest groups, such as political protests, administrative intervention, and personal lobbying. Some of the plaintiffs were quite conscious of using litigation as much to force the transit officials to the bargaining table as to win in court. As one of the Minnesota plaintiffs said:

> We knew it would look better and we'd have more commitment by the [Metropolitan Transit Commission] if they would agree to a negotiated settlement, because then we could say, "Look, you agreed to this; you weren't mandated by a court." Which a lot of people in government—a court tells them what to do and they say, "Screw it. We don't have to do that."...I think the lawsuit had enough of an impact to apply pressure.

One of the litigants in the East Bay suit put it very similarly:

> Basically it [the lawsuit] was a tool for pushing them as far as we could, but we didn't expect that the ultimate results would all be in the courtroom. You know, we knew that we would be able to use the suit to go to the public and to put pressure on [Alameda-Contra Costa] Transit and to force them into a more cooperative posture, which, I think, is what came out of it.

There were greater differences among the five cases in their use of extra-judicial strategies than there were in their emphasis on remedy over principle. The main determinant of the use of multiple strategies seems to have been the number of people available to share the work of many activities, which is related to the origins of the suits. The ideological orientation of the clients and, independently, of the lawyers seems to have been a secondary determinant.

The litigation with the least extra-judicial activity was the Washington, D.C., case. The actively involved plaintiff first tried many avenues, including an acquaintance with a member of Congress, to persuade the transit authorities to include elevators in the new subway system, but to no avail. After he initiated the lawsuit, however, his lawyers cautioned him against other activities. Specifically, when a congressional hearing was held on the Metro access question shortly after the first court hearing, the lawyers advised him not to comment on any legal aspect of the situation because it might affect further court proceedings. These were the only lawyers who gave this type of advice, and these were also the only large corporate firm lawyers involved in the five cases.

Despite their lack of extra-judicial activities, the D.C. plaintiffs won the most definititve court ruling of any of these cases, when the judge enjoined the transit officials from opening any stations until the system was made accessible. Undoubtedly the major reason for this degree of success is that these plaintiffs had the strongest law on their side. The statute requiring accessibility of the D.C. subway system was specific to it, and it was considerably less ambiguous than the statutes under which the suits on bus access were brought.[5]

The Marin County plaintiffs attempted no coordinated political activities either, but their lawyer attributes this largely to the lack of time and resources for them, since only he and one individual plaintiff were much involved. Because they were paying for the litigation on a fee-for-service basis, the plaintiffs did approach two other groups for contributions, but their letter writing efforts to recruit other support were unsuccessful. The lawyer commented in retrospect that perhaps they should have done more in the way of demonstrating and mobilizing external support. The lawyer and the one active client did finally organize a demonstration for accessible transit at the Marin County Civic Center, which was the first demonstration that most of the members of the plaintiff group had ever joined, but it was not organized until the lawsuit was over and lost.

One of the few positive things the Marin County plaintiffs got from the suit was a commitment in open court from a representative of the transit authority that in the future it would buy only accessible buses. Since this was a reversal of the transit officials' position as recently as the start of the trial, it is quite possible that the reversal was a response to pressure created by the suit. This suggests that if the plaintiffs had drawn more attention to the suit through extra-judicial strategies, they might possibly have gotten some service from the defendants soon rather than only a vague promise for the future.

The Minnesota and East Bay cases were quite similar in their use of multiple strategies. It was the failure of direct pressure on the transit agencies through meetings and publicity that led to the litigation, which the plaintiffs hoped would improve their bargaining position. A Minnesota plaintiff put it this way:

> I saw it [the lawsuit] as one, albeit a large component, effort to get accessible buses. . .I saw it as our way of saying to the transit commission, "You gotta stop shitting on us." And, you know, "We have the right to go into court, and this is the way we will do it. When we get into court, we'll be equals." We definitely felt that we were not bargaining from equal positions. In fact, we knew we weren't bargaining from equal positions with them.

The Minnesota plaintiffs planned to continue political activities on other fronts during the lawsuit. The district judge's summary dismissal was so discouraging, however, that most activities were suspended until the successful appeal to the Eighth Circuit provided renewed enthusiasm and bargaining leverage. While going on with the preparations for trial, the plaintiffs began intensive negotiations with the Metropolitan Transit Commission, which culminated with MTC's resolution to provide service, and with state legislators about funding for the service. Senator Hubert Humphrey and other notables were enlisted to express their support for the plaintiffs' demands.

The East Bay plaintiffs, who had also been involved in transportation lobbying activities before the lawsuit, continued them during the suit. With the attorneys sometimes accompanying the clients to transit meetings and the clients frequently consulting with the attorneys about the suit, they worked along parallel tracks toward the same goal.

With the help of their partial court victories described above, the plaintiffs in both of these suits reached consent agreements with the defendants which gave them at least some of the additional transit service they were seeking. Since the statutes under which these litigants were suing were much the same as those in the unsuccessful Marin

County suit, it is likely that their more political approach helped them achieve what they did. They were able to do this because there were many people available to go to meetings, contact the press, organize rallies, and raise funds. Also, such activities were much more a part of the regular activities than was the case for the Indoor Sports Club.

Furthermore, their lawyers at least did not oppose such activities. The Minnesota plaintiffs were represented by a private practitioner with a local reputation for being flamboyant and for previous involvement in controversial litigation. The East Bay lawyers were Legal Services Corporation lawyers, who presumably had absorbed from the poverty law tradition the sense of litigation as an organizing and consciousness-raising tool.

The Transbus case was by far the most self-conscious integration of litigation and other political activities. Lobbying in legislative and executive circles began before and continued long after the lawsuit. Thomas Gilhool, the Chief Counsel of the Public Interest Law Center of Philadelphia (PILCOP), which brought the suit, had even authored an article that presents this strategy at length.

> The courts are not a magically different instrument of change; like each of the other instruments there are tasks and times to which they are especially well fitted. But in no case will singleminded use of the courts be effective. The use of litigation along with lobbying and bargaining promises to be effective. Our task is to use the courts not only for their own yield, but also for their effect in other arenas.[6]

When the suit was filed in June 1976 and the plaintiffs had their first strategy meeting, the sentiment was, in their attorney's words: "It's not just a lawsuit. It's more. We have to lobby; we have to go to the public; we have to go to the presidential candidates; we have to go to Congress; we have to really proselytize this thing in terms of how right Transbus is." And they did all those things, including amassing testimony for a hearing on Transbus, which Secretary Adams himself told them was impressive.

The legal activity stopped soon after the Adams mandate, but a delaying action in Congress led by General Motors required intensive lobbying and coordinated rallies and demonstrations around the country in support of the Transbus in the summer of 1978 to kill the unwanted amendment. Several more organizations that had not been plaintiffs in the suit joined the supporting activities, and the groups won the congressional battle.

Stacking the Plaintiffs

The strategy of pressuring the defendants in many arenas requires that a number of people be involved in the undertaking. This may be a reason for naming multiple plaintiffs in a lawsuit. Persons or groups other than named plaintiffs can and do contribute to the litigation campaign, however, and persons or groups who are named plaintiffs do not always take an active part. It seems that the number of people actually involved depends more on the origins of the suit, whether it is a lonely crusade, community conflict, or test case. This suggests that there are other reasons for naming multiple plaintiffs—namely, what I have called "stacking the plaintiffs."

Stacking the plaintiffs is the practice of selecting plaintiffs in line with the assumption that the larger the number of people who can be shown to be affected by the problem, the greater the chances are of winning. It may also involve naming plaintiffs who are personally influential or who represent variations on the common interest, so that one can claim to represent a cross-section of the relevant population. Judges are assumed to weigh the costs of a decision to the defendant against the benefits to the assembled plaintiffs. Some of the participants in the transit access cases held such assumptions quite explicity.

> I don't care what you say, litigation is still a political process and a lot of funny pressures can be brought to bear on the judges. Judges are people and in many cases if it's not a federal judge, they're elected. Even if it is a federal judge, he often has political aspirations. He obviously has a social conscience and in terms of justice, in terms of doing his job he's just going to be more apt to listen to your side of the coin on a situation like this if the organization is to represent all these people as opposed to three or four people. You know, you can't sit up there and say you're going to make multimillion dollar modifications to this system and you're going to cost the taxpayers all that money just because three people say it's their legal and civil right. To my mind it probably should be done if you can prove the legal and civil rights of those people. But the point is, in reality...

The considerations made in choosing plaintiffs in these cases reveal a variety of ways of meeting the need to appear representative. All five cases had at least one organizational plaintiff.[7] They all had at least one individual named plaintiff as well. Some of the lawyers mentioned including individual plaintiffs largely to ensure standing in case there was any question about the organization's standing, though no such challenges actually arose.

In general the process for selecting plaintiffs involved consultation between the lawyer and the individual or group representatives who first initiated the suit. Choosing individuals whose personal situations would evoke the appropriate sympathy was probably the most common reason for choosing individual plaintiffs, but there were others. Although it was not necessary here to find individuals who were insulated from public retaliation for participating in these suits, as it was for the

NAACP and some First Amendment litigation, some did give consideration to individuals' lack of personal resources in case the court happened to charge them for court costs.

Others resorted to naming whoever would volunteer. It was not always easy to find individuals who were willing to get up in court and discuss their personal problems. In one suit, which involved organizations with a range of ideological orientations, one individual plaintiff was included as a "peacemaking measure" between two sometimes rival factions, according to one of the lawyers.

Class action suits were not usually the vehicle selected to demonstrate representativeness. Only two of the five cases involved class actions, a much lower proportion than in the whole twenty-four cases. In two of the three non-class actions, the lawyers mentioned the complexities involved with class actions as deterrents to their use. In one case the lawyers noted that the declaratory and injunctive relief they were seeking, in contrast to a suit for monetary damages, would inherently include all disabled people. The other lawyers who commented felt that having organizational plaintiffs served equally well to indicate the broad group of people concerned with the suit, revealing that those using class actions as well as organizational standing sometimes assume that the weight of numbers influences the court. Another sign that class actions and organizational plaintiffs are seen as alternative indicators of representativeness is that one of the two class actions was the only suit which had only one organizational plaintiff, the Marin County suit. There the lawyer noted that it "shows that the class is an established group."

A much more common representational device was to name multiple organizational plaintiffs. Only one case had but one group plaintiff. One case had two group plaintiffs, two had three, and one had twelve. There was a distinct emphasis on recruiting supporters in these suits, especially in the Transbus case with its twelve named group plaintiffs. One final indication that the plaintiffs believed their numbers would influence the court is that at least three suits (four, if both East Bay suits are counted) mentioned in their original complaints the number of members each organizational plaintiff had.

The Marin County case exhibited the least plaintiff-stacking behavior, although the lawyer and Bohlke, the one active client, did consider the emotional impact possible witnesses would have. They had some difficulty persuading other members of the Indoor Sports Club to become involved, but finally signed up as plaintiffs three other club members who were "best on this with their story." Describing one plaintiff, Bohlke commented approvingly: "If she had gotten on the stand, why . . . she would have been bawling all over the place." The reason the lawyers cited for joining the club as a plaintiff, in addition to support for the request for certification as a class, was to be able to call on the group for financial backing and guidance in determining litigation strategy. A group could be involved in these ways without being a named plaintiff, however.

The two group plaintiffs in the Minnesota case were the United Handicapped Federation (UHF) and the Twin Cities Chapter of the National Paraplegia Foundation (NPF). This suit was actually as "numbers-conscious" as any of the rest because UHF is an umbrella coalition with thirty-six member organizations. The structure of this group and its very reason for being emphasize a belief in strength through numbers.

At the time the suit began, the NPF was a member of UHF. Concerned about maintaining its own identity, NPF was the only organization that joined the suit in its own name as well as through UHF. During the course of the suit, however, under circumstances to be described shortly, NPF left the federation. It remained a plaintiff in the suit, however, and the split had relatively little effect on the lawsuit.

Some of the suits also demonstrate the belief that the identity of the parties as well as their numbers will influence the court. Some undertook intentional "ticket balancing" or representation of various points of view among the plaintiffs. One reason is the controversy noted in chapter 3 about the different types of accessible transportation.

In the East Bay case and the Transbus case, there were explicit attempts to represent the ideological spectrum among disabled people. The three group plaintiffs in the East Bay federal suit were the Center for Independent Living, California Association of the Physically Handicapped, and United Cerebral Palsy of Alameda-Contra Costa Counties, which are relatively militant, moderate, and conservative organizations respectively. The representative of United Cerebral Palsy in the litigation activities even commented that she supposed they had been asked to join the suit because of their established reputation.[8]

The twelve organizations in the Transbus case also represent an ideological spectrum. The twelve named plaintiffs were: Disabled in Action of Pennsylvania and its sibling groups in New York, New Jersey, and Baltimore, Paralyzed Veterans of America, the National Capitol Area Chapter of the National Paraplegia Foundation, American Coalition of Citizens with Disabilities, United Cerebral Palsy of Pennsylvania, National Congress of Organizations of the Physically Handicapped, National Caucus on the Black Aged, National Council of Senior Citizens, and Pennsylvania Association of Older Persons. The four Disabled in Action groups are militant consumer organizations, the National Congress of Organizations of the Physically Handicapped a more conservative consumer organization, and the others somewhere in between. One of the organizers of this suit felt it was a "coup" to involve the NCOPH because it had not previously joined with the more radical group in any activities.

Representatives of the plaintiff groups, which called themselves the "Transbus Twelve" or the "Transbus Group," met regularly with the lawyers to plan strategy for the suit and the coordinated lobbying activities. Some of the organizational plaintiffs were more active than others; at least six were very active. Some, such as the Disabled in Action groups of New York and New Jersey, were too far from the centers of activity in Philadelphia and Washington to participate heavily. The National Council of Senior Citizens was highly involved, but the other two senior citizen groups much less so. The National Caucus on the Black Aged withdrew from active participation after the most interested member died, and the participation of the Pennsylvania Association of Older Persons was always nominal.

Senior citizen groups were included in the Transbus suit and also in the Washington, D.C., suit in the interest of appearing representative of a broader population. Elderly persons are disproportionately dependent on public transportation, and many of them have greater or lesser physical limitations which would be minimized by a bus so accessible that even persons in wheelchairs could ride it.

The named plaintiffs in the D.C. suit were Heddinger, the National Capitol Area Chapter of the National Paraplegia Foundation (NPF), the Paralyzed Veterans of America (PVA), and the Washington Urban League. Heddinger was a member of the board of the NPF chapter at the time, and he asked them to join. He also contacted PVA because he was acquainted with its executive director through their joint participation in the local NPF chapter and knew of his involvement with the subway access issue through the President's Committee on the Employment of the Handicapped in the Sixties.

The third group plaintiff, the Washington Urban League, is a social reform organization of long-standing, but it is not normally associated with disability rights issues. According to the Arnold & Porter lawyers, the Urban League was brought in to represent the interest of low-income urban elderly in accessible transit, but they could not remember working with any particular individual from the group. The director of the Institute for Public Interest Representation thought he had probably approached the Urban League himself because he had worked with them before on other issues and "they would lend their name for any suit if it wouldn't cost them anything."

The comment of one of the lawyers that Heddinger was the real client and that the group plaintiffs were just "window dressing" suggests the presence of plaintiff-stacking. The NPF group was involved only by way of Heddinger's regular reports at chapter meetings. The participation of the Urban League was minimal. A lawyer on the staff of PVA was consulted occasionally. He was satisfied with the degree to which he was kept informed, and he had confidence in Heddinger to represent his group's interest. As negotiations for a consent order reached a final phase, he formally authorized Heddinger to speak for his organization.

Decentralized Litigation: Communication Without Coordination

The diversity among the five cases should make it apparent that the transit access litigation did not have the central planning and coordination of the NAACP desegregation litigation. The variety of sponsoring groups and attorneys involved in these cases testifies to their decentralization. Each group set its own goals and devised its own strategies. Nevertheless, there was some communication and mutual assistance among the parties, which should be described.

The informal social links among disabled people in a given locale, which create a communication grapevine, were noted in chapter 3. Bureaucratic creations, such as the President's Committee on the Employment of the Handicapped and the advisory committees of vocational rehabilitation departments, and, recently, some transit authorities have opened opportunities for communication about many subjects besides those for which the committees were specifically created. Through these channels and by organizations' sending their internal newsletters to other groups, news of a lawsuit in one community would spread to another. Specific coordination of legal strategy is another matter, however.

When Richard Heddinger began his suit in 1972, the only accessibility lawsuit he had ever heard of was in Cleveland, Ohio, where a man sued on constitutional grounds because he could not get into a courthouse.[9] The D.C. subway suit itself did not provide much precedent for other transportation litigation because it concerned fixed facilities rather than rolling stock and was covered under different legislation. The Architectural Barriers Act of 1968 and its 1970 amendment aimed at the D.C. subway construction do not apply to buses. Also, the *pro bono* attorneys for the case were not part of the informal communication network that developed among attorneys doing the transit litigation, nor did they follow the others' subsequent litigation.

Word of Heddinger's success in getting an injunction spread, however, and by 1974 the tempo of activities began to pick up on the question of accessible transportation, as well as other disability rights issues. The attorney in the Marin County case had heard of an earlier suit in Baltimore, which had been quickly settled out of court, but he virtually started from scratch in preparing his case.[10] That same year, the Public Interest Law Center of Philadelphia (PILCOP) received its grant from the Levinson Foundation to research legal approaches to improving transportation for disabled people. After the results of its study were published and disseminated the next year by the President's Committee on Employment of the Handicapped, PILCOP became an informal consultant to lawyers around the country interested in transit access litigation.[11] Both the Minnesota attorney and one of the East Bay attorneys talked to PILCOP while planning their cases.

The closest things to actual coordination among the attorneys in the suits around the country were two conferences on accessible public transportation sponsored by the National Center for Law and the Handicapped (NCLH) in the fall of 1975 and again in the fall of 1977. At least one attorney from each of the four bus cases attended one or both of these conferences. The Marin County lawyer, for example, found the first one helpful in acquainting him with developments in federal law so that he could decide whether to file a second suit in federal court. The conferences did not attempt to force a unified legal strategy to be followed nationwide, however, and there was disagreement among the attorneys about whether some of the others' cases should be brought. In the words of one of the PILCOP lawyers:

> It wasn't very structured. They just brought people together without any real plan in terms of what they were going to do there, and there was no plan for what they were going to do when they left there. It was a good opportunity for people who were involved in the area to interact.

Further controversy surrounded the second conference, when NCLH invited a representative of UMTA to the conference. The plaintiffs' attorneys felt that they could not comfortably discuss confidential matters of strategy with a representative of the "enemy" present. Furthermore, they did not wish to reveal the disagreements among themselves about the use of lifts versus ramps to make buses accessible to wheelchairs.

Disagreements also persisted about the acceptability of demand-responsive service rather than accessible regular route service. The advocates of the Transbus design reportedly attempted to discourage the filing of suits that did not emphasize Transbus, and it was a perception of the lack of coordination and long-range vision among the lawsuits that prompted PILCOP to focus its suit at the federal level. A PILCOP lawyer complained of the other suits:

> There were twelve other lawsuits that were filed and all of them failed. And one of the reasons was that they were never—well, we think they had the wrong target. They were all after local transit authorities which we learned through our negotiations with SEPTA really did not have that control over the market. But none of them was able to develop a factual record... The initial suits, I would really say, were more suits of outrage. I mean they were not really thought through in terms of what we wanted to achieve; I mean just more suits saying, "Stop everything! We want service!" but not really thinking through what that service looks like.

On the other hand, some lawyers prided themselves on obtaining service of some kind for their clients long before Transbus could become a reality. According to one lawyer, "the people in Philadelphia probably felt they were playing the role of the NAACP, but they weren't." As the director of legal services at NCLH describes the conference: "People shared information and then went their own ways."

Clearly there has been no NAACP in disability rights litigation. The lack of coordinated legal strategy has not been devastating to the cause of accessible public transportation, however. A new style of litigation evolved to serve a different cause in different times.

Problems of the New Style

The choice of remedy over principle and the use of multiple strategies and multiple plaintiffs are no guarantee of victory, of course. In fact, they also tend to bring some new problems. While some conflicts were avoided by not trying to forge a nationwide litigating strategy, the use of multiple plaintiffs on the local level gave rise to some similar conflicts. Moreover, the adoption of some tactics besides litigation caused some of these conflicts.

Plaintiff coalitions are susceptible to all the problems of any coalition. In his study of public interest groups, Jeffrey Berry found that the major force working against coalition efforts was the typical desire of members or staff to enhance their own group's reputation.[12] This goal may be frustrated when identity is shared among coalition partners in the event of either success or failure. Concomitantly, groups may be cautious about entering into coalitions with groups with questionable reputations.[13]

Problems of organizational jealousy, different priorities, protection of one's reputation against being tainted by disreputable groups, and disagreements over strategy all occurred among the transit plaintiff coalitions. For instance, desire for a share in the publicity caused some friction in two cases. A representative of the National Congress of Organizations of the Physically Handicapped mentioned several occasions when the group's name had been omitted in the list of Transbus plaintiffs in news stories released from Philadelphia, which annoyed some of its members. In the Minnesota suit the smaller National Paraplegia Foundation chapter felt its role in the suit had been slighted in comparison to that of the larger United Handicapped Federation.

It is probably no coincidence that the two least active groups were senior citizen rather than disability groups.[14] Even a representative of the National Council of Senior Citizens (NCSC), which was active in the Transbus activities throughout, said it was "not a top priority of NCSC at any time. It was an important issue, but don't forget that it's a much more important issue for the handicapped than it is for the elderly." The same person, however, noted that cementing relationships between the elderly and the handicapped was one very good thing that came out of the Transbus issue, and that they have continued to work together on other issues, such as architectural barriers and Social Security. One other problem this speaker observed was that the disabled groups, which tend to be more recently organized than senior citizens, were naive about some aspects of Washington lobbying. Around the country, successful experiences working with senior citizen groups were reported by the disability groups in Minnesota, but persons in California and New York mentioned unsuccessful efforts.

The coalition which came closest to disaster was the one in the Washington, D.C., case. In 1977, the Urban League withdrew as plaintiffs. Among the five suits, this was the only major split over the substance of a suit, but it shows that even three plaintiffs are enough for conflict. The disagreement developed after the General Services Administration (GSA) issued the waiver allowing the inaccessible Gallery Place station to open. The disabled plaintiffs wanted to get a judicial review of the GSA action, and it was at that point that the Urban League withdrew.

No present or past Urban League official would admit to knowing enough about the situation at the time to discuss their withdrawal. The attorneys' description of the situation was that the Urban League "had a different constituency than the other groups, so they represented people who might be more interested in advantages of having the stations open than maybe interested in particular rights of the handicapped." The remaining plaintiffs were lucky that their opposition did not exploit this break in the ranks. The departure of the Urban League was not mentioned in the press, nor did it have any noticeable effect on the suit.

The situations which caused the most tension among the plaintiff groups did not arise from the lawsuits themselves, but occurred when some groups wanted to engage in strategies other than litigation. Demonstrations tend to be perceived as more radical than litigation and can cause rifts among plaintiffs. The possibility of conflict between broad-based participation sought for plaintiff-stacking, on the one hand, and extra-judicial tactics, on the other, was illustrated in the controversy surrounding the post-litigation activities in the Transbus campaign. When a series of rallies and demonstrations around the country was scheduled to keep the Transbus alive in Congress, the groups could not agree on whether the demonstrations should have a positive tone of support for the Transbus or a negative tone of protest.

The nationwide Transbus controversy even affected some of the other cases. The East Bay suit itself did not involve any tactics with which the more conservative plaintiffs disagreed. During the course of the suit, however, some of the plaintiffs became involved in the Transbus-related activities, and this did create tension. The protest strategy adopted in the Bay Area involved blocking the Bay Bridge during rush hour. While some of the plaintiffs in the East Bay suit joined the demonstration, others felt it was much too radical. Although this did not affect their working together on their own suit, it illustrates the possible limitations of combining litigation with other strategies and maintaining a diverse plaintiff coalition.

Similarly, in the course of the Minnesota suit, the local chapter of the National Paraplegia Foundation (NPF) split off from the United Handicapped Federation (UHF), the umbrella coalition of which it had been a member. Among other disagreements, the NPF leaders felt that UHF leaders tended to prefer confrontation to negotiation and that "they were getting kind of a bad name in the power structure and we didn't want to be associated." Since NPF had been an independently named plaintiff along with UHF from the beginning of the suit, they did not withdraw from the litigation, but the conflict again illustrates the possible risks of a multi-strategy approach.

The issues dividing the transit access litigants, then, were similar to those dividing nonlitigating political coalitions. This is not surprising since so much of their struggle occurred outside the courtroom. The choice of litigation as a strategy has some characteristic dangers, however, and the next chapter explores whether groups which use the new style of litigation encounter the same risks as groups involved in the old style and whether they respond in the same way.

Notes

1. Bell, Jr., "Integration Ideals and Client Interests."

2. Ibid.; Sorauf, *Wall of Separation*, pp. 86–88. See also Scheingold, *Politics of Rights*, especially chap. 10; Shklar, *Legalism*; Brill, "Uses and Abuses of Legal Assistance."

3. Rosenthal, *Lawyer and Client*, p. 113.

4. Letter, James J. Raggio to Kent Hull, March 23, 1978.

5. 1970 Amendment to the Architectural Barriers Act of 1968, *U.S. Code*, vol. 49, sec. 4151.

6. Gilhool, "Uses of Courts," p. 155.

7. This was a principal criterion for selecting the cases because of my interest in the impact of litigation on ongoing community groups. See chap. 6.

8. In the East Bay state case, the Disabled Students Union was the third organizational plaintiff, rather than the California Association of the Physically Handicapped.

9. Heddinger probably was referring to *Friedman v. County of Cuyahoga*, No. 895961 (Cuyahoga, Ohio 1972). The case is discusssed in Achtenberg, "Law and the Physically Disabled," pp. 859–60.

10. *Disabled in Action of Baltimore v. Hughes*, Civil No. 74-1069-HM (D. Md.

1974). Achtenberg, "Law and the Physically Disabled," p. 873, also discusses this case.

11. James J. Raggio et al., *The Disabled and the Elderly: Equal Access to Public Transportation*. (Washington, D.C.: The President's Committee on Employment of the Handicapped, 1975).

12. Berry, *Lobbying for the People*, p. 261.

13. Ibid., p. 260.

14. The participation of two of the senior citizen groups in the strategy session and lobbying activities surrounding the Transbus suit was so nominal that I was not able to locate an individual to speak to from these groups.

Chapter 6

The Risks of Litigating Revisited

Chapter 2 identified several dangers for community groups of choosing litigation as a political strategy. These were commitments of money and time which crippled the organizations, deception of the groups by symbolic court victories which made them believe their war was won when it was really only a battle, the slow pace of litigation which let external events resolve the situation in fact before the court could rule on the principle, and domination of the litigation by lawyers in both the short and long run.

The accessible transit cases experienced some of these difficulties, but in no case were they fatal for an organization. The characteristics of the new style did help meliorate some of the potential problems. Specifically, the orientation of the plaintiffs to remedy rather than principle almost by definition helped avoid the danger of deception by symbolic victories, and it may have helped to reduce the financial strain of litigation by making the clients less anxious to carry their suits on through appeals if they could get what they wanted through a settlement. The use of multiple strategies in different forums served to fill in the time during the slow pace and in some cases helped plaintiffs influence the external events affecting the issue. The use of alternative strategies that could be carried out by nonlawyers, the presence of multiple plaintiffs, and the decentralization of the cases all helped to avoid the suits' being dominated by lawyers.

The great cost of a style of litigation which involves active client participation is the toll such participation takes in human energy, individual or collective. Individuals face the risk of "burnout," of simply not having the energy left to pursue the case to ultimate victory. Organizations can reduce this problem by dividing tasks among several members, but may find themselves divided over the allocation of group resources to the lawsuit at the expense of other priorities. This chapter will examine how the groups in the transit access cases experienced this problem and the other four risks of litigation.

The Financial Costs of Litigating

The financial costs to the groups varied tremendously, depending largely on the source of their counsel. Two groups paid no money at all. In the Washington, D.C. case, all costs of the suit were underwritten by a commercial law firm *pro bono publico* and by the Institute for Public Interest Representation. In the East Bay cases, the Legal Aid Society of Alameda County provided lawyers and assumed all costs. The latter lawyers remarked that it was an inexpensive suit with no depositions or extensive factual findings.

In the Transbus case financial costs of the lawsuit did not have a major impact on any of the group plaintiffs because the $25,000 grant from the Levinson Foundation paid a large part of the costs, underwriting the work of the Public Interest Law Center of Philadelphia. The client groups did contribute, however. Some of the big national organizations, such as United Cerebral Palsy Associations and Paralyzed Veterans of America, gave several thousand dollars. Three of the small Disabled in Action groups managed to give a few hundred dollars each. Others contributed no cash, but donated office space or staff help. And all the active participants paid their own travel expenses for the frequent meetings of the Transbus Coalition.

The two cases using private counsel, Marin County and Minnesota, did experience some difficulty with lawyers' fees and litigation costs which could have proven fatal except for particular circumstances in each case, an unusual source of income in the former and an eventual court award in the latter case.

For a group of its type, the San Raphael Indoor Sports Club was extraordinary in having the financial resources to hire a lawyer on an hourly basis to conduct a major lawsuit. Investments from the proceeds of a piece of property donated to the group years ago had created standing assets of roughly thirty thousand dollars at the time the suit began. Furthermore, a weekly bingo game continually brought in seven thousand dollars a year, by one person's estimate, and two or three hundred dollars per week, according to another estimate. Bohlke was turned down by a San Francisco public interest law firm on the grounds that the organization had enough money for a private attorney when he approached it first about the transit case. The public interest firm then referred him to the solo practice lawyer he retained.

The lawsuit ultimately cost enough—$20-$25,000—that the club sought other sources of support. The California Association of the Physically Handicapped allocated it $10,000, of which approximately $5,000 was spent. The district office of Indoor Sports contributed another few thousand dollars. The lawyer noted that the court could have charged them as losing plaintiffs with another $500 to $700 in court costs, as the defendants requested, but the judge was "compassionate" on that point. As it was, Bohlke estimated that even after all the costs, the Indoor Sports Club had about as much in its treasury at the end of the suit as it had started with.

In the Minnesota case, the financing of the lawsuit was complex and was the source of some confusion among the parties. According to the lawyer, the plaintiffs agreed to pay all the direct expenses of the suit and to pay him at his then prevailing rate of fifty dollars per hour, with any payments to be applied first to the direct expenses. When the suit first began, the United Handicapped Federation set out enthusiastically to raise funds for it through special appeals to churches and civic groups and by selling a button proclaiming "We Will Ride." As the suit dragged on through the courts, the enthusiasm waned and UHF began to pay the costs from its main organizational budget. In time it signed a note for an eight thousand dollar loan from a church group to help with the costs.

UHF was able to pay for all the eight to ten thousand dollars of direct costs, such as depositions, travel, and transcripts. Toward the secondary costs of the lawyer's office overhead and the salary of his assistant, it raised another twelve thousand dollars, according to the lawyer, and at least another twenty thousand dollars, according to UHF staff and officers. The lawyer believed he spent approximately thirty-five thousand dollars in unreimbursed personal cash in the case, without considering the value of the hours he worked.

Although the lawyer believed that the named plaintiffs—UHF, the National Paraplegia Foundation chapter, and six individuals—were legally liable to him for the costs, the president of the NPF chapter, who was also an individual plaintiff and who did not have much contact with the fund raising after NPF withdrew from UHF, was under the impression that they were not liable. Apparently, the initial understanding was not clear to all the parties.

The confusion that existed on the point eased in 1980 when the Eighth Circuit Court of Appeals overturned the district court and awarded the plaintiffs attorney's fees in the case.[1] The transit commission paid $15,000, which the clients gave entirely to the lawyer. UHF was still trying to make some arrangement about the church loan in 1981.

These cases show that the need for low-cost counsel is not eliminated by the new style of litigation. Thus, it must continue to be a source of concern, as many writers on social litigation have noted.[2] Nevertheless, the emphasis on extra-judicial strategies in coordination with the litigation reduces the relative importance of tasks which can be performed only by lawyers rather than by the clients themselves.

Deception by Symbolic Court Victory

There was virtually no problem at all in these cases of the plaintiffs' abandoning their efforts too soon because they succumbed to the "myth of rights" and believed that a court victory would ensure them the benefits they sought. With their strong orientation to obtaining accessible transportation service more than establishing a legal principle, the disabled litigants knew that they had not won until they were riding. In some cases the clients persevered and did the follow-up necessary to achieve their ultimate goal after a legal victory, and in others they did not win anything from the court itself which they could mistake as an ultimate victory.

In the East Bay case, for example, the plaintiffs scarcely won anything outright. In their first lawsuit, they did win a stay from the Supreme Court of activities by the defendant toward purchasing a group of new inaccessible buses, pending an appeal of the trial court's denial of their claims, but the state suit was ultimately found moot. The federal suit ended with a consent agreement, and the clients remained active on the transit agency's consumer advisory panel to monitor the implementation of the agreement.

The Marin County plaintiffs' success at the demurrer hearing is a good example of a court victory followed by ultimate failure, but it was not due to the plaintiffs' being deceived about its significance. The legal ruling induced the parties to begin settlement negotiations, but these collapsed. The plaintiffs eventually pushed the case to trial, where they lost on all counts because of unfavorable higher court interpretations of the law between the time of the demurrer hearing and the trial.

The D.C. suit also involved no problems of a symbolic court victory lulling the plaintiffs into inactivity. The preventive injunction the judge ordered, keeping the subway stations from opening to the public until elevators were installed, was sufficient to provoke action from the transit officials, and the court retained supervision over the case to see that its order was carried out. Also Heddinger, the individual plaintiff, did much more than minimal follow-up. He not only continued the suit until elevators were installed, but also pursued the additional issue of exactly where the elevators should be located and how the stations should be designed to provide truly ready access.

The Minnesota plaintiffs' first victory at the Court of Appeals could have been symbolic because it was merely procedural rather than substantive, but, like the Marin demurrer hearing, it gave them leverage to negotiate a settlement. Unlike the Marin case, these negotiations were successful, and the plaintiffs won a major substantive victory when the defendant Metropolitan Transit Commission (MTC) passed the resolution specifying percentages of the disabled population to be served by certain target dates over the next four years.

Nevertheless, this case shows that political victories can be as symbolic as legal victories if they are not carefully monitored. The MTC resolution was a quantified remedy. According to Handler it should have been relatively easy to monitor, but the clients lost momentum for supervising the implementation.[3] In the words of one member of a plaintiff group: "The issue kind of fell apart to some degree because there was no more issue; everyone had agreed to it." Although a few members continued to go to meetings of the advisory board set up by MTC, they felt that the community at large believed the problem had been completely solved.

The Transbus case also illustrates the point that court victories are not the only ones which can turn out to be largely symbolic. Adams' mandate seemed a complete victory at the time, but the plaintiffs had to keep fighting to see it implemented. The coalition held together to protect the fruits of its litigation in battle in Congress with the manufacturers. Nevertheless, the coalition was finally stymied when manufacturers simply refused to bid on orders for a Transbus-style bus.

In none of these cases were the plaintiffs lulled into inactivity by a court victory that later failed to have practical results. Where there were legal victories, they stimulated negotiations between the parties or, in the D.C. case, were supervised by the court itself. The need for continuing vigilance by the plaintiffs in the event of political victories as well as court victories is clear.

The Slow Pace of Litigation and the Impact of External Developments

The length of time between filing and final court action in the six suits varied greatly—from fourteen months in the East Bay federal suit to six years in the D.C. suit. In some instances, however, the delay was due to the plaintiffs' own choices, rather than their being victims of legal foot-dragging by the defendants. Moreover, the external events occurring during several suits proved to be more positive for the plaintiffs than negative. Nevertheless, the slow pace of litigation did cause a problem in two of the cases.

The Washington, D.C., case lasted from 1972 until 1978, even though the judge's injunction requiring the installation of elevators was issued in 1973. Three years passed while work on the subway proceeded. The conflict over the Gallery Place station occurred in 1976. For the final two years the principal plaintiff chose to keep the suit going by pursuing the ready access issue beyond the mere installation of elevators. On the other hand, the defendants also did all they could through introducing complicating motions to keep the ready access issue from reaching a decision.

The Marin County case lasted from 1974 to 1978. Some of the delay during the four years was the work of the plaintiffs. It had a bad effect ultimately because of the unfavorable changes in judicial interpretations of the statutes under which they had filed during the time between the demurrer hearing and the trial. It is always hard to tell if a delay will have positive or negative effects, of course. At one point in 1975 the plaintiffs chose to postpone action on the suit because it appeared that federal law was becoming more favorable to their position. The lawyer suggested later that events at the federal level probably did encourage the defendants to initiate the second round of settlement negotiations in 1976, but these also collapsed as the first ones had. When the plaintiffs decided to go to trial, there was another delay of nearly a year waiting for a date on the trial calendar. The only group to go to trial was the one which gained the least from its suit.

As the Marin case shows, external events during the course of a lawsuit may be either positive or negative. In most of the cases, they were actually more positive than negative, in contrast to the warnings of di Suvero and Horowitz.[4] In general, during the mid-Seventies public awareness of the rights of disabled people and of legislation to meet their needs increased, creating a more favorable climate for the suits.

More specifically, in the D.C. case, between the judge's first denial of a preliminary injunction against construction of the subway and his declaratory judgment in the plaintiffs' favor a year later, congressional hearings were held at which several members of Congress were highly critical of the transit authority's failure to follow the law requiring accessibility. The parties in the case did not infer that this was a direct influence on the judge, but felt that he became better educated on the issue through the full briefs submitted the second time and through the general public airing of the issue.

The East Bay suits, the latest and the shortest of the six, particularly benefited from the improving political climate. During the summer of 1978 the congressional battle over the Transbus was receiving national attention. Some of the East Bay litigants brought the protest home by blocking the Bay Bridge during rush hour. The participants felt that public reaction to their cause was supportive, despite the inconvenience created. It is perhaps no coincidence that it was just at that time that the transit company sued by the East Bay litigants assigned away its rights to buy the buses in contention. This action mooted the lawsuit in state court, but it met the plaintiffs' objective of halting the purchase of inaccessible buses and was considered more a victory than a frustration of their goal.

In the Minnesota suit, too, the signing of the Section 504 regulations and the Transbus mandate created a positive national climate for the plaintiffs. Specifically, MTC's decision to settle may have been influenced by its being transferred to more direct state control during that period because of a variety of other political problems.

Another type of external political development which influenced a few of the cases was changes in personnel. A new general manager took over the Washington Metropolitan Area Transit Authority soon after the subway system opened, and Heddinger noted a "difference between night and day" in the attitudes of the two men. This new manager, the new judge who replaced the first one upon his retirement, and the drift of federal Transportation Department policy in favor of the disabled population encouraged the final settlement in the D.C. case.

In a broader sense of personnel change, a participant in the Transbus case believed that it was the transition from the Ford to the Carter administration which turned the tide in that case and brought about its resolution. The lawsuit itself was not very long—twenty-one months from filing to final action, and the executive order of transportation secretary Adams, which effectively ended the suit, came only eleven months after filing. This, too, was an external political development which mooted the suit, but it seemed as good as or better than winning in court.

The Transbus and the East Bay events demonstrate that clients actively involved in parallel activities during litigation can help make the political developments that affect the lawsuits favorable to their interests rather than unfavorable. The administrative mandate by Secretary of Transportation Adams that mooted the Transbus lawsuit was at least partially a product of vigorous lobbying by the plaintiffs while the suit was in progress. In the East Bay case, too, the litigants continued to press their cause in all available political arenas while the lawsuit went forward.

This is not to say that the slow pace of litigation is inevitably or even frequently an advantage. It is probably only where the litigants can keep up their enthusiasm by engaging in alternative political activities that the slow pace is not a problem. In the Marin County case, for example, which involved virtually no extra-judicial activity, the numerous delays did result in losing the interest of most of the Indoor Sports Club members. Bohlke would report on any developments at their meetings, but he noted later: "You can see pretty soon that their eyes are getting glazed and they're thinking about other things."

The Minnesota suit especially suffered from the problem of maintaining organizational impetus. The suit was filed in 1975 and lasted until 1978, not counting the petition for attorney's fees. During that time money-raising efforts diminished; group members got tired, bored, or wrapped up in jobs or other activities. The group found it hard to get much publicity value from the suit between the few big decisions. The problem of interim defeats in litigation was almost fatal here.[5] As the UHF staff organizer described it:

> If there was a low point, that was it, when [Judge] Alsop slapped us with the first rejection. And then [the lawyer] came to the officers and talked about appealing to St. Louis and stuff like that. . . And it was not an easy decision for the officers to make because the results of the first attempt at litigating it had proven so disastrous. I think that was the low point. That was tough to get through because it seemed like everything had gone against us—politically and within the courts.

Indeed, one consequence of the trial court defeat was that people lost their original enthusiasm for concurrent political pressures until the court of appeals victory revived the plaintiffs and spurred negotiations with the transit commission.

The slow pace of litigation can indeed be a problem, particularly if the situation is not of the plaintiffs' making or if they are unable to stay active on other fronts and use that time to try to influence external events in their favor. Groups which do adopt a multi-strategy approach to their goal seem to be more able to weather the slow pace, but even they need periodic successes to maintain their enthusiasm.

The Risk of Lawyer Domination

The danger of litigation actually undermining community organization and thus the clients' ability to engage in long-term political struggle was not nearly as evident in these cases as in the gloomy observations of the antipoverty litigating and organizing efforts. In none of the five cases was the litigation taken over entirely by the lawyers. This was prevented by the presence of at least one active client in each case to inject the clients' point of view.

In two of the five cases, the D.C. case and the Marin County case, there was only one active client, but in both of these that one person was strong enough to direct the lawyers' efforts to some extent. In Washington, D.C., the one active client, Richard Heddinger, was involved in all phases and decisions of the suit. He not only got copies of all legal documents in the case, but he actually suggested legal arguments to the lawyers, action rare in any of the other cases. On the other hand, the lawyers noted that he "always took our advice." Heddinger did have one clash with a young lawyer from the Institute for Public Interest Representation in the early days of the suit. Heddinger felt the lawyer was accepting too much of the defendants' argument about why they could not install elevators, and the lawyer responded with an attitude that "I'm the lawyer and I know better," according to Heddinger. Ultimately, Heddinger convinced the senior lawyers on the case of the correctness of his position, and the young lawyer soon left the case.

Heddinger was also heavily involved in working out the resolution of the suit. The judge appointed him and a transit authority architect as a Solutions Committee to propose an acceptable settlement. Heddinger made the final decision to accept the transit authority's compromise and give up his quest to get a legal definition of ready access. Furthermore, his personal persistence was the only monitoring mechanism for assuring that the promised changes in new stations were made. As one of his lawyers put it: "I exacted a promise from him. . . that he would be reasonable and give them something like the time limits that were specified in the order as being reasonable before he started getting on their back." In other words, this client showed an extraordinary commitment to the problem and perseverance in seeing it through.

The other clients were satisfied with their much more minor roles in the suit. The representative of Paralyzed Veterans of America felt he was "kept well informed throughout." He had confidence in Heddinger and in the final stages officially authorized him to represent PVA in the negotiations. Heddinger did make some effort to involve other persons in the NPF chapter, of which he was a member, but mostly got a reaction he characterized as "Keep up the good work, Dick." He remembers only one meeting with the lawyers and the executive director of PVA and the president of the NPF chapter. That Heddinger did not even know who spoke for the Urban League when the lawyers consulted them occasionally indicates how absent they were.

In the Marin County case Bohlke and the lawyer made efforts to involve the rest of the members of the Indoor Sports Club, but did not have a great deal of success. The lawyer phrased issues in the form of recommendations among which the clients should choose. He met with the whole club at least four times, though mostly he kept in touch with and explained things to Bohlke, who then reported to the group. According to Bohlke, many of the club members never really understood what was going on with the suit because of the legal terminology. A number of the Indoor Sports Club's members were severely disabled and had little education.

Bohlke himself played a much larger role. He collected data on lift technology, wrote letters trying to raise money and support for the suit, and eventually testified at the trial (the only plaintiff who did so). Occasionally Bohlke instructed the lawyer to write memoranda explaining a legal point or development or to write letters commenting on political developments at the national level.

The East Bay case avoided lawyer domination, too, but through the active involvement of several clients from several different organizations rather than through such intense involvement by one individual as in the first two cases. Overall, the East Bay lawyers and clients felt they achieved a satisfactory division of labor. Through meetings and phone conversations, the clients discussed the issues of selecting plaintiffs, deciding when to file, choosing between state and federal court, and preparing the interim relief proposal in the federal suit. The clients were responsible for contacts with the press about the cases, and they attended meetings with the transit agency.

On major issues, such as the decisions to appeal and to settle, the boards of the organizational plaintiffs took official votes. Most of the contact with the lawyers, however, was carried on by one staff member of the United Cerebral Palsy Association (who has cerebral palsy herself), a few local members of the California Association of the Physically Handicapped and several members of the Center for Independent Living. These individuals were for the most part very satisfied with their role in the suits. "We had the knowledge," said one, explaining the clients' role. "Our reactions have been invaluable to the attorneys" said another. For their part, the attorneys recognized the help they were getting from the clients—particularly in contrast to their typical experience with legal aid clients: "They are a political movement on their own. . . They're doing the work."

On the other hand, the clients were not so involved in every detail as Heddinger or Bohlke was. Some of the clients were not clear about all of the facts about the suits, even a rather major point like whether there had been a full trial in the state case. "We let the attorneys advise us on the legal stuff," one put it. Another said the lawyers generally prepared the proposals and "ran them by us," an arrangement he found satisfactory.

There was a hint of dissatisfaction over the final settlement reached in the federal suit, in which the defendants agreed to buy only accessible buses during the next five years. The lawyer acknowledged that "it doesn't really do anything more than AC Transit was going to do anyway, but certainly the details are more definite and it protects them against a reversion in AC Transit's policy." The lawyer believed the clients were satisfied with the agreement, but they were perhaps somewhat less so than she thought. The expectations of one client were clearly higher; she hoped for some retrofitting of existing buses. Another felt that the lawyer had to some extent encouraged them to accept this proposal because she was soon leaving the Legal Aid Society for another job. The second lawyer who had been heavily involved with the earlier state case had already left the agency. Overall, however, in the words of one client, they had a "very good marriage with the attorneys," if not a perfect one.

Among all the five cases, the parties in the Transbus case were the most aware of the potential of lawyer domination of social reform litigation and tried the most consciously to avoid it. The sensitivity of both the lawyers and the clients to this issue also resulted in some clashes over the proper division of labor and decision-making responsibility between them.

The client groups' role in the initiation of the suit and its transformation from a community conflict to a test case were related in chapter 4. Once the suit was launched, the mechanism for client participation was periodic meetings of representatives of the plaintiff groups, first in Philadelphia and later in Washington, D.C. as well. Communication to the groups from the active members in the coalition undoubtedly varied from group to group, as the coalition came to function semi-autonomously.[6] This was no problem for the larger, more bureaucratized groups used to a division of labor, such as PVA, ACCD, or the National Council of Senior Citizens (NCSC). Some of the members of the small Disabled in Action of Pennsylvania, however, felt somewhat excluded after the suit changed from being their local battle to the coalition's national effort.

The group representatives actively involved encountered some problems in realizing the participatory lawyer–client relationship for which they were striving. In theory, all the participants agreed that the lawyers' role is to carry out the will of the clients and that a distinction could be made between policy decisions and the legal expertise necessary to carry them out.[7] In practice, there were no disagreements reported by either clients or lawyers about the substantive content of the lawsuit, but there were occasional clashes about their respective roles.

One lawyer described the division of labor as "We prepare them and they do the work." Indeed, the clients did most of the testifying, lobbying, meeting with government and business officials (including the president of General Motors). One client's perception of the division of labor was somewhat different, however:

> The attorneys did most of the bulk work. We were there primarily, I think, as directors and advisors. They were to carry out our will, but what happened is that in most instances they told us what they felt our will should be. And after we discussed it, we agreed one hundred percent of the time, usually. Because as I said earlier, PILCOP was extremely thorough in really investigating all of the different possibilities.

One instance of conflict occurred at the time of the hearing called by Secretary Adams to reconsider the Transbus shortly after he became

Secretary of Transportation. The lawyers had written testimony on various aspects of the issue for the clients to present, and the clients saw the testimony for the first time just before they were to read it. Until they learned that such a practice is quite common, they felt that able-bodied people were once again telling disabled people what they ought to do and say. As this incident illustrates, the collaboration of a group of clients trying so consciously to become independent with lawyers accustomed to using their legal skills resulted in sometimes volatile relations.

Some perceptive clients recognized, at least in retrospect, several reasons for the difficulties. While some of the clients were used to working with or as professionals, others were unused to being in the position of employers annd trusting the lawyers to do work for them.[8] Their lack of experience and assertiveness and the "crazy hours" the lawyers kept sometimes made it hard for them to keep up with the PILCOP lawyers. Additionally, tension surfaced occasionally because the lawyers were making a living from the problems of disabled people, while the disabled people themselves were expected to volunteer their time to work for their rights. Over time, however, satisfactory roles were worked out.

Because the Transbus campaign included a variety of activities, there were opportunities for many more people to be involved than litigation alone would have provided. One of the legally trained clients echoed Stephen Wexler of the National Welfare Rights Organization as she described the way lawyers could and should teach their clients a range of negotiating skills rather than "leaning" on litigation.[9] Indeed, negotiating skills became particularly important after the suit ended and the focus of the efforts shifted completely to lobbying. As a result, control of the activities moved more to the client groups based in Washington, some of whom were experienced lobbyists.

On top of all its other difficulties with financial costs and slow pace, the Minnesota case also came the closest of the five to being dominated by the lawyer. These difficulties partially derailed the roles of the lawyer and clients established in the early days of the suit. The initial litigation strategy was laid in meetings of the lawyer with the officers of UHF and later with its Transportation Task Force. Major decisions, such as whether to sue in the first place and whether to appeal, were made by UHF's governing Delegate Assembly. When the smaller group met, many of the open choices of the suit were discussed: who should be named plaintiffs and defendants, which judge to try to get, how to keep the issue before the public. Members turned out to attend court hearings or meetings with transit officials. One individual involved primarily in the early stages of the suit remembered the lawyer as encouraging the clients to speak out and in no way stifling debate or information exchange with a patronizing attitude.

As the case dragged on, especially after the district court defeat, subtle changes occurred. In the words of one client: "It's clear to me that it became his [the lawyer's] issue...as opposed to the organization's....He was completely immersed in it....He began to be our expert." A number of factors contributed to this. One UHF officer suggested that the normal turnover in leadership was frustrating for the lawyer. The lawyer would have to explain things again to new people, who themselves were very uncertain of how much they could instruct him. Clients also had difficulty carrying out their role of informing the community about the suit when members of the press would gravitate to the lawyer either because the lawyer knew a number of them from previous lawsuits and cultivated such relationships or, as one client observed, because the media prefer persons who speak in "bellshaped tones" and some UHF officers had speech impairments.

Complaints about the lawyer began to arise. He allegedly announced to the press that they were going to drop the local defendants from the suit after the Metropolitan Transit Commission's resolution, before the delegate assembly had officially voted to do so. There were complaints that trying to reach the lawyer was "like trying to get a hold of God." There were occasionally explicit conflicts over who was supposed to make certain decisions. In contrast to the impression of the client involved in the early stages, one who became involved later felt that the lawyer's attitude was more "I can handle this; leave things up to me"—the traditional rather than participatory style, in Rosenthal's terms. The lawyer and representatives of the MTC drafted the settlement resolution, though it was later approved by the plaintiffs. Even when the activities shifted from litigation to lobbying state legislators for additional funding to support the service agreed upon, the lawyer continued to play the largest role.

Time and Energy Costs

Although active client participation that can persevere regardless of interim setbacks is the best protection against lawyer control of social reform litigation, such participation is certainly not without its costs. The cost of active client participation is in human time and energy. For the individual "lonely crusaders" the cost may be tremendous, but whether it is worthwhile seems to depend heavily on whether the final outcome is success or failure. Russ Bohlke stuck with the losing Marin County suit to the bitter end, but in retrospect he "wonder[s] if I'd want to be a Don Quixote again....It takes so darn long. The legality goes at its own speed." Richard Heddinger, on the other hand, complained of the personal toll on family and other interests of his intense involvement in the D.C. suit, but then soon after a final consent agreement was reached, he volunteered his services to the transit authority to test some new accessible buses it was receiving.

With such an intensely active individual as Heddinger, his organizational coplaintiffs had to invest scarcely any time in the litigation at all. In light of the resulting accessible subway system, the suit was for them, in the words of a PVA representative, "one of the most cost-effective type things we were ever involved in." The benefits for PVA were similar to those seen by Handler for "funded social movements" when they work with law reformers:

> The leaders [of the social reform group] have a free resource, an opportunity to gain publicity for themselves and the organization, and the opportunity to accomplish some of their goals through the legal system. The lawsuit may not be a high priority item on their agenda, but the leaders are willing to go along because of the free or low-cost gains.[10]

That the experience had no negative effects on PVA or the NPF chapter is suggested by their both joining as plaintiffs in the Transbus suit in 1976.

When an organizational plaintiff takes a more active role than did those in the D.C. case, the presence of a number of group members to share responsibilities helps to diffuse the personal impact felt by "lonely crusade" plaintiffs. The relevant cost of active involvement for a group is more the time and other resources diverted from competing organizational goals. For example, the representative of the United Cerebral Palsy Associations in the Transbus activities reported some conflict between the New York UCPA office, which supported its involvement, and the Washington office staff, which had other priorities than the Transbus issue.

The problem can be especially great for small or young groups. Because it was the first group involved and was in some ways the "host" organization in Philadelphia, Disabled in Action of Pennsylvania invested nearly its total organizational energy in the Transbus issue. As a result, it received criticism from some members for sacrificing more immediate local problems for such a long-range, national-level target.

For other organizations their transit lawsuit was only one of many activities they pursued simultaneously, and thus they felt the impact of their involvement less. This was generally true of the organizations in the East Bay case. The California Association of the Physically Handicapped, which felt financially burned by its contribution to the losing Marin County suit, declined to participate when the state suit began. By the time the federal suit was filed, however, the leadership had become more liberal and there was 95 percent support for joining, by one estimate. A statewide group, the organization as a whole was little involved in the details of the suit and felt little impact from it, since it cost no money and was focused solely on two counties.

Even the Center for Independent Living, which had several members actively involved in both suits, felt that they did not have much impact on the organization per se. When clients are already militant activists, as with CIL, a lawsuit serves no consciousness-raising functions. It was just one more activity among the many going on at CIL. Despite being actively involved in getting people to be plaintiffs or witnesses, to go to hearings, or to speak at press conferences, one woman noted: "It's something that in reality we do a lot less work on than we do on practically anything else that we're working on, because the lawyers handle so much of it."

Summary and Conclusions

The impact of the litigation on the organizational plaintiffs in the transit access cases included some good and some bad effects, but the impact was not as negative overall as some of the literature on litigation and community organizing would lead one to expect. Although few of the groups were seeking organizational benefits for their own sake, some of them got such benefits regardless. On the other hand, the dangers were real, but none of the groups was overcome by them.

In the first place, these suits involved scarcely any primary consciousness raising and community organizing because they were all brought by fairly well established organizations. This was, of course, a criterion of the case selection. The kinds of organizational and ideological gains from litigation that Sorauf found some First Amendment litigators seeking were also not prominent motives among the transit access plaintiffs. The goal of the suits was primarily to obtain the transit service.

In the two "lonely crusade" cases and the East Bay case, there were hardly any efforts to use the suits to attract attention to or support for the organizations in themselves, although some groups may have had the minimal sense that joining the suit would be good public relations among their constituents. The United Cerebral Palsy Association of Alameda County was the most conservative of the organizational plaintiffs in the East Bay suits, and it was cautious about joining. It had lawyer members of its board investigate before signing on. The woman representing the group in the litigation activities, however, said that they received no negative reactions to their participation and that their "constituents looked up to us" for the suit.

It was undoubtedly the fear of negative public relations that prompted the Urban League to withdraw from the D.C. suit in the face of the public criticism of the lawsuit when the Gallery Place station was kept closed after the rest of the stations then constructed were opened. Even though none of the group plaintiffs was mentioned in the newspaper stories or editorials about the situation, the Urban League director decided: "We had gone as far as we could with the case."

Several of the Transbus plaintiffs consciously and successfully aided other organizational goals with their participation in the lawsuit. The national UCPA was intentionally trying to increase its political activities. Recalling his group's debate over getting involved in litigation, the representative of the group noted that Transbus was a "good first suit to get involved in" because "those people in the organization who are looking for us to play a significant role and make contributions should be satisfied with what we did." For other groups, the Transbus activities contributed to their general long-range goals, such as cross-disability cooperation for the American Coalition of Citizens with Disabilities and disabled–elderly cooperation for the National Council of Senior Citizens.

Even if they had not intentionally sought it, several groups received at least temporary boosts of membership interest or public recognition from their involvement in the litigation. This was notably the case for Disabled in Action of Pennsylvania, despite the concern of some members that the Transbus activities were too militant or took too much time and money away from other priorities. The president of DIA in 1979 believed that while they may have lost a few members over the issue, the group grew from 180 to 300 members during the time the suit took place. Overall, the impact was positive. Local publicity brought in "activist-minded" people. "DIA really became established in the public's mind as *the* organization fighting for civil rights for the handicapped—at least in this area. And it certainly got a national reputation, also," the DIA president continued. Disabled in Action groups were established in Syracuse, New York, and Kentucky and one or two other places between 1976 and 1979. Further evidence that DIA of Pennsylvania viewed its litigation experience positively is its subsequently joining two more lawsuits unrelated to transit accessibility.

For the San Raphael Indoor Sports Club Bohlke felt that the suit had a cohesive effect on the group at first, raising member interest, but that this was lost when it dragged on. The lawyer believed the suit politically sensitized the group somewhat. After they lost the suit, Bohlke and the lawyer attempted some political organizing in the form of a demonstration at the Marin County Civic Center, which was the first demonstration most club members had ever participated in.

Bohlke felt that it was at least good to be "part of the whole wave that came about." He hoped they had contributed a little to the suits filed after theirs, especially since the favorable demurrer ruling on the equal access law stood as an encouraging decision for three years and was reported in law reviews at that time.[11] In mid-1979 the club was doing a little lobbying with county officials, "getting a little more recognition and a little more direction, but nothing outstanding," in Bohlke's words. Mostly the Indoor Sports Club went on as it always had, as a largely recreational and social outlet for relatively severely disabled adults. Apparently, this was an appropriate role for it, for the organization was gaining new chapters in isolated parts of California where there had not previously been any organizations of disabled persons at all.

In Minnesota both the organizational plaintiffs felt the effect of their involvement in litigation. The former president of the National Paraplegia Foundation chapter noted that the suit led to a larger turnout at meetings. It made "things a little more exciting and people feel more involved." He felt the suit got NPF members more involved in other political activities, such as "buttonholing MTC commissioners on the side and things like that."

The United Handicapped Federation (UHF), perhaps because it was so new at the time the suit began and because of its Alinsky orientation, tried more consciously than any other group to use the suit as an organizing device. UHF did experience a surge in both internal and external interest for a time, but it had difficulty sustaining that interest. The suit certainly had some positive effects. As one member put it:

> It gave the organization focus; it gave the organization an issue; it gave people something to coalesce around. For a lot of people it was what UHF was designed to be: just get an issue and grab it hard and go with it and make sure you win, doing it using reasonable tactics. Use cooperation when that's going to work; use confrontation if only that will work. It helped the organization learn to devise strategy, and appropriate strategy.

On the other hand, the suit was an emotional "high" which left an "organizational hangover":

> Some people look at that as being *the* UHF. This was UHF at its highest. This was the most emotional point for some people. This was the most involved point. It was the most important aspect of the organization. . . . And when the organization changes its focus on another issue, or uses different tactics, some people wonder, you know, "Why aren't you the aggressive organization you used to be?"

After the lawsuit UHF had difficulty getting the MTC to implement its resolution on schedule, regaining its financial stability, and moving on to other issues. Its biggest crisis was a schism in 1979 when several officers and past officers left the organization, but that dispute was primarily over the appropriate role of staff members in the organization and should not be attributed to the lawsuit. UHF has survived, but it never was able to capitalize fully on its litigation-initiated victory.

Overall, the group won a large victory in getting the MTC to agree to provide accessible service, but the staff organizer believed that the officers and members did not give themselves enough credit for it. The slow pace and the interim stages created "confusion, grey areas." The organizer offered a good analysis of how a victory can get lost organizationally.

There's no black and there's no white. There's no clear-cut victory. I think the resolution of December was a clear-cut victory, but it didn't come off that way, because it was very hazy, very gray. Because we got the commitment, but did they have the wherewithal to follow through with it?. . . Secondly, the issue did not die. As a matter of fact, if anything, it then went up another notch in intensity after the December meeting because we had to get the appropriations from the state legislature as well as we had to get MTC orientated staff-wise and programatically-wise to carry through on their commitment. And so people have not—I mean it didn't produce accessible transit overnight on the street; therefore, the significance of that commitment has been lost. Or people didn't really let it kind of get into their whole system and say, "Hey, we really did something and it took an organized effort."

The Minnesota case came the closest of the five to illustrating the detrimental effects of litigation on community organizations predicted by some observers. Nevertheless, a number of factors helped the Minnesota groups and the others avoid the full impact of the negative possibilities of litigating. Most obviously, as Handler predicts, outside financial support in the form of subsidized legal assistance and/or external contributions to litigation costs protected most of the groups from a severe financial burden.[12] The time costs were eased in some of the suits by having a number of individuals involved to share the work. The heavy personal toll borne by the two "lonely crusaders" emphasizes one advantage of widespread client participation.

The problem of being lulled into inactivity by a court decision which turns out to be more symbolic than substantive is greater for precedent-oriented than remedy-oriented litigation since remedy-oriented clients know that they have not won until they have obtained the desired service or benefit. Nevertheless, all these cases are a reminder that any success, be it a court order or an out-of-court settlement, requires follow-up to see that is is implemented.

The transit access cases did experience some problems with delay. Occasionally the causes were completely external to the particular lawsuit, such as the year's wait for a court date in the Marin County case, but more often the delay was due to decisions by one or both parties to the suit. In general, a willingness on both sides to compromise hastened a suit, as in the East Bay federal case. In contrast, Heddinger's interest in obtaining a legal definition of ready access and the Marin County plaintiffs' delay to watch the developments in federal law contributed to making both cases last a long time. The defendants in both cases contributed, too, of course. The length of the Minnesota case reflects the long time it takes to appeal cases in federal court.

A multi-strategy approach to an issue minimizes some of the problems caused by the slow pace of litigation, because the plaintiffs are not just waiting for the court to decide, but are actively participating in and actively manipulating the political forces outside the courtroom. The absence of extra-judicial activities in the Marin County case may have speeded the loss of interest of the Indoor Sports Club members in the suit. Also, when the Minnesota plaintiffs lost their enthusiasm for a multi-faceted campaign after their district court defeat, they had a hard time keeping up interest in the lawsuit as well. By providing roles for more people to be involved in political action, a multi-strategy approach helps to protect the organization not only against atrophy but also against the feeling of complete dependence on the lawyer.

The transit access cases generally escaped lawyer domination because at least one client in each case was sufficiently active to avoid having the suit completely shaped by the lawyer. To give the lawyers their due, some were very sensitive themselves to the issue of client participation, particularly in the Marin County and Transbus cases. Others simply did not have agendas of their own which they were tempted to urge on the clients, because they did not work primarily in the field of disability rights and had no great stake in the issue. Neither, however, did they try to impose a legalistic preference for an ultimate appellate court victory rather than a consent agreement, although one lawyer admitted he wished his clients had been willing to go further in court.

The negative impact of litigation on organizations comes largely from focusing solely on the lawsuit without involving members directly in the litigation. To some extent, carrying on other nonrelated activities can have the same preservative effect on the organization as engaging in multiple political pressures toward the one goal. This can be true for both small groups with bingo games, like the San Raphael Indoor Sports Club, or large organizations with many activities, like PVA, ACCD, or NCSC. Only active participation in the litigation itself, however, can ensure both that the substance of the suits is controlled by client preferences and that the organization does not atrophy. In short, lawyer domination was and is a real possibility, but these groups managed to maintain enough client involvement to avoid it. At the same time they were able to have the advantage of lawyers doing a considerable amount of the work.

Active client participation proves to have been important in these five cases for providing the manpower for extra-judicial activities, shaping the content of the lawsuits to the clients' preferences, and monitoring the implementation of the gains from the litigation. All the client groups survived the hazards of litigation, and those clients who shared in the decision making in the lawsuits generally remained active in trying to ensure that the commitments were fulfilled. Since the experience of these disability rights groups with litigating was largely different from Handler's conclusions that client groups tend to be incapable of long-term follow-up and from the dire predictions of several observers of past attempts to combine litigation and community organizing, it is necessary to explore further what factors influenced the likelihood and the amount of client participation in these suits.

Notes

1. *U.H.F. v. Andre*, 622 F. 2d 342 (8th Cir. 1980). The district judge's decision was announced in Dan Wascoe, Jr., "Lawyers Don't Get Fees from MTC Suit," *Minneapolis Tribune*, 12 June 1979, p. 1B.

2. Rabin, "Lawyers for Social Change," pp. 255–61; Cahn and Cahn, "Power to the People"; Borosage et al., "New Public Interest Lawyers," pp. 1148–51; Scheingold, *Politics of Rights*, pp. 185–99; Handler, Hollingsworth, and Erlanger, *Lawyers and the Pursuit of Legal Rights*, pp. 189–94; Russell F. Settle and Burton A. Weisbrod, "Financing Public Interest Law: An Evaluation of Alternative Financing Arrangements," in Weisbrod, Handler, and Neil K. Komesar, *Public Interest Law: An Economic and Institutional Analysis* (Los Angeles: University of California Press, 1978), pp. 532–49.

3. Handler, *Social Movements and the Legal System*, p. 56.

4. di Suvero, "The Movement and the Legal System," pp. 67–68; Horowitz, *Courts and Social Policy*, chap. 3.

5. di Suvero, "The Movement and the Legal System," pp. 67–68.

6. In the terms of Berry's typology of coalitions—dependent, participatory, and independent—the Transbus coalition fell somewhere between a participatory and an independent coalition. Although it never had any staff of its own, the Transbus coalition did print stationery in its collective name to use for its litigation and lobbying activities. See Berry, *Lobbying for the People*, pp. 256–60.

7. Gilhool, "Uses of Courts," p. 174. Gilhool is Chief Counsel at PILCOP.

8. In fact, three of the most actively involved client group representatives were lawyers themselves, and some other lawyers from client groups participated from time to time.

9. See Wexler, "Practicing Law for Poor People," pp. 1057–58.

10. Handler, *Social Movements and the Legal System*, pp. 31–32.

11. E.g., Achtenberg, "Law and the Physically Disabled," p. 869.

12. Handler, *Social Movements and the Legal System*, p. 13.

Chapter 7

Client Participation: Who, When, Where, and Why

What are the conditions under which clients participate more or less in litigation decision making? Despite the differences which client participation made in the transit access cases, this question has not been directly examined for social reform litigation. It has scarcely been examined in any litigation context. Some light can be shed on client participation in other collective activities, such as voluntary associations, political action, social movements, and interest groups. Some of the reasons for the participation of the accessible transit clients, stated by them or observed from their behavior, are consistent with reasons for participation found in the literature on these other activities. Other reasons for client participation are unique to litigation.

Studies of participation in voluntary associations, social movements, and interest groups usually focus on why people join more than on how actively involved they are once they are members. This question is not directly relevant to these cases because the individual clients were already members of the disability organizations when they became involved in the lawsuits. Here the concern is not so much why the individuals came to join the disability organization or how each group as a whole came to be involved in litigation, which has already been considered, as it is why the individual group members, either as named plaintiffs themselves or as representatives of a named group plaintiff, took a more or less active role in the conduct of the lawsuits. Nevertheless, there are similarities between reasons for joining and reasons for being active, once a member.

The literature reveals three basic types of explanations of individuals' participation in group activities: demographic, psychological, and economic. The demographic type actually offers not so much an explanation as a set of correlations of group membership with various demographic variables. The study of voluntary associations and political participation has emphasized demographic correlates of joiners compared to nonjoiners, although attention is also given to differences on personal attitudinal dimensions.[1]

Psychological explanations have predominated in studies of social movements, which could roughly be defined as change-oriented voluntary activities more or less formally organized. This approach has been particularly popular in relation to minimally organized mob actions[2] and extreme right-wing political movements,[3] but others have presented psychological explanations of the 1960s student movement and the black civil rights movement.[4] Typical of the more general, less explicitly value-laden attempts to theorize about social movements is the conclusion of Gian Sarup's work linking social movements to reference group theory: "By restoring a set of normative anchorages to the alienated individual, social movements give him a scheme of meaning, a measure of stability, and a feeling of personal worth."[5]

The economic model of participation originated with Mancur Olson's challenge to traditional interest group theory, represented by David Truman, which posited that interest groups came about because people rationally join together to pursue interests they have in common.[6] Olson argued, instead, that rationality would not lead people to join groups pursuing collective goods because collective goods, by definition, are those which benefit people in common and cannot be limited to those who directly contribute. In a group large enough that one's individual contribution would not be crucial for obtaining the good, the most rational strategy would be to be a "free rider," one who benefits from collective goods without contributing to them.[7]

The solution to this dilemma attempted by most groups is to offer members some selective incentive in exchange for their contribution in addition to the collective good acquired by the group's resources. Selective incentives can take a variety of forms. Joel Handler, applying this explanation to membership in social reform movements, divides selective incentives available to potential group members into material, solidary, and purposive incentives.[8] Material incentives are individual, tangible, economic benefits such as publications, services, discounts, etc. Solidary incentives include friendship, loyalty, sociability. Purposive incentives are good feelings acquired from contributing to the accomplishment of a goal; such incentives are most like Truman's assumption that people join organizations in order to pursue common goals.

These three types of explanations for participation in organized activities—demographic, psychological, and economic—all appear among the reasons for client participation in litigation. The demographic characteristics of the clients, their personalities, and a normative system which made the opportunity to participate in itself a selective incentive all help to explain how much the disabled clients participated.

An additional factor in explaining participation in litigation, as opposed to other group activities, is that client participation involves a relationship to a professional. The participation is not like that among equals in a collective activity, but always occurs in relation to a lawyer, whose participation is not problematic.[9]

Litigation involves several factors that influence the degree of client participation besides the clients' own demographic and psychological characteristics and responses to incentives. One such factor is the clients' perceptions of the special expertise required to participate in the decisions of a lawsuit. The perceptions of the clients may or may not relate to objective differences in the difficulty of the law in different areas.

Another factor is the individual characteristics of the lawyers. Just as with the clients, the demographic and personality characteristics of the lawyers and the norms they hold influence the participation of the clients. Finally, structural characteristics of the lawyer–client relationship affect the clients' participation, specifically, the social organization of lawyer–client contact and the organizational status of the clients themselves.

This chapter explores the various influences on client participation observed in the transit access cases and, where possible, compares these cases with findings in the literature on participation in other contexts. The demographic and psychological explanations of participation are discussed first as they pertain to the clients and then to the lawyers. Next the norms of lawyers and of clients about client participation and the incentives the clients' norms create are discussed. Finally, the perceived significance of legal expertise, the social organization of the relationship between lawyer and the client, and the degree of client organization are examined for their influence on client participation.

Clients' Demographic Characteristics

Studies of participation in many different contexts have focused on the correlation of participation with a variety of demographic variables, including race, sex, age, religion. The variable which often appears as the most significant in influencing participation, however, is socioeconomic status (or education, which correlates closely with socioeconomic status).

That the relationship between lawyers and the clients varies according to the socioeconomic status of the client is a frequent observation in the literature on lawyer–client relations. Joel Handler puts it most pithily: "Strong, rich, and confident clients direct their lawyers; on the other hand, lawyers dominate the relationship when clients are poor, or deviant, or unsophisticated."[10] The low level of involvement by poor clients is one of the reasons some commentators reject the use of litigation as a strategy for organizing poor people.[11]

Another area in which the passivity of lower-class clients has been noted is in the plea bargaining of criminal charges. Lawyers frequently initiate and control plea bargaining decisions.[12] This has been noted in other countries as well as the United States.[13] Criminal justice studies, however, rarely permit meaningful comparison across socioeconomic levels because the majority of criminal defendants come from a limited group of the population. One study which does compare plea bargaining practices in white collar and common crime prosecutions reveals no differences in client role between the two.[14]

Another indirect indicator of client passivity among lower socioeconomic clients is evidence that such clients feel as if their lawyers take less interest in their problems. A survey of people's experiences with lawyers in New South Wales, for example, found that clients from lower status occupations consistently rated their solicitors lower than did clients from higher status occupations on such matters as "paying attention to what you had to say," "keeping you informed on progress," and "interest and concern about your problems."[15] This suggests that these clients are less successful at pressing their concerns upon their lawyers, implicating perhaps the clients' ability to communicate and take part as well as the lawyers' initial attitudes.

Direct tests of differential participation by different classes of clients are nonexistent. In one of the few explicit studies of client participation, Rosenthal presumes that higher status clients would be more active than lower status clients and consequently biases his sample in favor of clients from wealthier census tracts in order to assure himself of a sufficient number of active clients.[16]

Sorauf's study of church–state litigation reveals the difference between participation in the form of taking an active part in litigation decisions and participation in the form of merely becoming a plaintiff. Although a high proportion of the plaintiffs were of high socioeconomic status, these clients were no more active in the suits than were the low status clients, and perhaps even less active. Many more of the plaintiffs chosen by the attorneys (83.3 percent) were of a high or medium socioeconomic status than were those plaintiffs who initiated their own cases (65.5 percent).[17] Sorauf does not directly compare his data on socioeconomic status with the roles plaintiffs played in decision making during the litigation, but he notes that most of the plaintiffs, plaintiff-originators as well as lawyer-chosen plaintiffs, assumed a more passive role once the national litigating organizations entered the cases.[18]

The more common finding of greater activity from higher status clients is consistent with studies of political participation and voluntary associations. Payne, Payne and Reddy summarize decades of research finding that higher status persons, as measured by income, education, occupation, home ownership, family lineage, and combined measures, have a higher rate of involvement in voluntary organizations than lower status persons[19] Similarly, Milbrath and Goel summarize research finding that political participation, including unconventional politics such as protests, is greater among higher status persons, also as measured by income, education, occupation, etc.[20]

The accessible transit studies add further unsystematic evidence that higher socioeconomic clients are more active participants in litigation than lower socioeconomic clients. The data are unsystematic because detailed information about individuals' characteristics which would determine their socioeconomic level was not gathered, since organizational plaintiffs were the primary focus of the study.

Even if data had been gathered, a methodological problem arises in determining the status of disabled persons. Two of the typical indicators of socioeconomic status are education and employment. Disabled persons have had limited access to these two areas of social attainment until very recent years. As a result, a disabled person's education or employment or income may not accurately reflect other characteristics often associated with class status, such as attitudes and values and sense of political efficacy. In cases of nonhereditary impairments, father's education or employment might be a more accurate measure of the class of a disabled person. A staff member of one of the organizational plaintiffs rejected a characterization of the membership as middle class because so many members existed on public assistance programs rather than earned income, but his inference should be questioned. People with disabilities may be middle class in many important respects even though they receive public assistance.

Notwithstanding these methodological limitations, the cases do give some support to the usual hypothesis about higher status clients. The most obvious example is the Marin County case, where the one active client was both well educated (a college graduate) and professionally employed. He was unusual among the members of the Indoor Sports Club, most of whom were less educated, less mobile, and considerably more passive. Notably, the other lonely crusader was also professionally employed as a government statistician.

The lawyers who had the most experience working with clients of lower socioeconomic status were the Legal Aid Society lawyers in the East Bay case. By the standards they were accustomed to, the disabled clients were very highly involved. As one put it: "I thought there was so much more [client participation] than any other lawsuit. Maybe not as much as there is in these cases where you have much more highly educated clients. These are the most politically aware and educated clients that Legal Aid ever has to deal with."

A final supportive finding comes from the Transbus case, in which a number of the active clients held professional positions with national organizations. Three of the intensely involved clients and two other moderately involved clients were themselves lawyers. This high status of the Transbus clients may partially explain the very high level of client participation in this case. Many other factors conducive to client participation were also present in this case, however.

There are, of course, demographic variables other than socioeconomic status, such as religion, sex and age. Rosenthal entertains the possibility of religion as a determinant of participation in his study of New York City personal injury victims, on the basis of a stereotype that Jewish clients might be more assertive. He explicitly tested his sample for this and found no relation between religion and level of participation.[21] Many studies have found Jews to be relatively more involved in political activities and voluntary associations than Catholics and Protestants, though the data are often not controlled for socioeconomic status.[22] Religion did not appear as a relevant variable at all among the clients in the disability rights cases.

Studies of people who join political activities or voluntary associations also find sex to be an important variable, with women generally found to participate less than men. In litigation, Sorauf found men to predominate (77 percent) among the separationist plaintiffs, but then many of those plaintiffs were selected by the lawyers.[23] As with socioeconomic class, Rosenthal assumes that men will participate more than women and biases his sample to include mostly men.[24] Nevertheless, Rosenthal does find a number of examples of actively participating women.[25] In the transit access cases the two lonely crusader plaintiffs were men, but in the other three cases where more than one person was actively involved, the number of men and women participating was fairly equal.

The transit access cases divide similarly on the variable of age. While the two lonely crusaders were middle-aged men in their forties at the time the suits were filed, the active clients in the other suits tended to be considerably younger. This reflects the tendency for younger persons to be more involved in the newer, more militant disability rights groups which were lead plaintiffs in the East Bay and Minnesota suits especially. This is consistent with the literature on age and political participation. While participation in mainstream political activities peaks in middle age and is low among the young, participation in militant political activities is predominantly the field of the young.[26] In the disability rights movement, age is strongly related to organizational ideology, a variable which will be examined as an independent determinant of participation later in this chapter.

One final client characteristic, unique to the disability rights movement, which might also be a determinant of client participation is age of onset of a person's disability. Empirical research is scarce and contradictory on the effect of differences in age of onset of disability, and perceptions of disabled people on the question vary.[27] Some members of the disability rights movement see a tendency for leadership to come more from persons disabled later in life, but there are far too many counter examples of leaders who were disabled at birth or in infancy for a firm generalization. If there are such differences in group leadership, then it is reasonable to suspect that the same differences might appear in more or less assertive behavior toward lawyers.

Client Personality

Any difference in behavior due to the age at which one was disabled no doubt is one facet of client personality, another likely determinant of client participation. People who are more outgoing in other areas of their lives will probably be more active clients in a lawsuit. Rosenthal adopts this hypothesis and tries to measure client personality to explain the differences between the active and passive clients. He is unable to establish any relationship between personality and litigation behavior, but he attributes the failure more to his inexperience in measuring personality than to counter evidence which would refute the hypothesis.[28]

Some studies of participation in voluntary associations have examined the personality differences between more and less active members. Characteristics found to correlate with active participation include extraversion, self-sufficiency, optimism, dominance, subjective political competence, achievement orientation, and positive community identification.[29] These are very much the same characteristics that distinguish members from nonmembers[30] as well as political "gladiators" from political "apathetics."[31]

Personality differences between disabled activists and nonactivists have occasionally been implied. A political columnist critical of the drive to make regular mass transit facilities accessible rather than adopting specialized services alleged that the former was promoted by "wheelchair independents" who are "highly organized, vocal, articulate and politically active" at the expense of "wheelchair dependents," who need specialized services but are "fragmented, lack any organized advocates and remain withdrawn and timid."[32]

In the transit access cases client personality appeared to be a major force in only one of the five cases. Several people in the Washington,

D.C., case implied that the lonely crusader carried the suit by the weight of his personality. One of his own lawyers described him as "as difficult a man as I've ever worked with—very strong personality and way above average intelligence." This client may be quite an exception because the perception is much more common that, in general, people with disabilities tend not to be very assertive. Three of the disabled clients themselves from three different cases, including two who were very active in their suits, made such an observation.

Despite this popular impression, the scholarly literature does not support any such generalization about a "personality of disability." "Disabilities produce no firm and definable effects in any predictable way," according to one authority on disability.[33] Indeed, evidence points in contradictory directions. On the one hand, an impression of nonassertiveness could be created by the "inhibited and over-controlled" quality of much interaction between persons with disabilities and those without them.[34] On the other hand, an application to disabled persons of Allport's analysis of ego-defenses of individuals discriminated against suggests that militancy or aggressiveness toward nondisabled persons is one of many possible reactions of disabled persons.[35]

In any event, any attempt to discuss the personality of disabled persons in general rather than personality that distinguishes any one individual from another quickly blends into the issue of political ideology or norms about how active or assertive one *should* be rather than how one is involuntarily. This is indeed a major issue within the disability rights movement. Not coincidentally, the clients from one of the most militant organizations were perceived by both their lawyers and one of their fellow clients from another organization as being aggressive. The significance of norms encouraging participation will be discussed later in this chapter.

Lawyers' Demographic Characteristics

It is inappropriate to look only at the characteristics of the clients as the determinant of client participation in litigation. Participation is relational, and the lawyer is the other half of the relation. Characteristics of the lawyer, as well as the clients, influence the degree and kind of client participation. As Rosenthal found, "there are. . . limits to the effectiveness of [client] participation. It is always in the lawyer's power—intentionally or unintentionally—to evade requests, disregard client concerns, and fail to bring to the client's attention considerations that greatly matter to him."[36]

The lawyer may play the main role in setting expectations of participation or nonparticipation by the client. Two lawyers in the transit access cases expressed such an opinion, one the attorney-of-record in one case and the other a client who was also a lawyer. The latter commented: "If the lawyer is sending out nonverbal messages to the clients that they really think that they should make those decisions themselves, then clients will be feeling comfortable in making them."

Scholars have examined both demographic and personality characteristics of lawyers for their impact on the lawyer–client relationship, but not on client participation per se. Jerome Carlin's studies of lawyers in Chicago and New York are the classic investigations of the social strata of the metropolitan bar. Carlin finds, in short, that lawyers from lower socioeconomic backgrounds go into individual or small-firm practices, where they serve predominantly clients who also have lower socioeconomic backgrounds. Lawyers from higher-class backgrounds tend to practice in large firms and have primarily large businesses or wealthy individuals as clients.[37] As a result, it would be difficult to separate the effects of the lawyer's class from the effects of the client's class on client participation.

The nature of the lawyer–client relationship differs greatly in these two strata. Lower-class clients are more likely to be one-shot business, so that commitment to the client and his or her problem is less than commitment to the source of referral of that and future clients. A higher status clientele tends to be more stable, sometimes to the point that lawyers get so intimately involved with their clients' business interests and ventures that they lose the proper disinterestedness of a fiduciary relationship.

Carlin collects no direct evidence about the degree of client participation with lower and higher status lawyers. His primary concern is lawyers' violations of ethical norms of the profession, which did not directly address the issue of client participation at the time of his studies.[38]

Even Rosenthal, who is explicitly interested in client participation, does not directly compare lawyer status with client participation and, as a result, reaches some possibly misleading conclusions. He finds both that more active clients obtain better case results[39] and that clients with attorneys from larger firms (thus higher status lawyers, following Carlin) obtain better case results.[40] Since in neither case does he control for the third variable, it may be that higher status clients both retain higher status lawyers and take a more active role in their lawsuits. If so, Rosenthal fails to isolate client participation as the determinant of success, as he thinks he has.

Similarity of lawyer and client characteristics might itself be conducive to greater client participation because the client would simply feel more comfortable about getting involved. This may hold true for characteristics other than social status, too. For example, one accessible transit client suggested that the similarity in ages of the clients and lawyers—both quite young, in their twenties and thirties—made the clients in his suit feel more able to take an active part.

I think one thing that really helped us in our relationship with the lawyers was that we were basically at the same age level and we had a lot in general in common. And after rapping for a while, we really became more friends than professional versus client kind of atmosphere. . . . With all the time that we spent down at their offices, we just became one of the gang, and never very formal.

Similarities of race or sex would seem to be other characteristics which would facilitate lawyer–client compatibility and thus client involvement, although I know of no research on this. In the transit access cases none of the lawyers were themselves disabled, so there was no opportunity to check this out (although the Transbus clients included disabled lawyers, who tended to be actively involved). It is necessary to note the possibility, on the other hand, that great compatibility between lawyer and client could lead instead to such complete trust by the client in the lawyer that the client is completely passive, confident that the lawyer will pursue his or her true interests.[41]

Lawyer Personality

Another facet of compatibility is sheer personality—the "working so well together" to which one disabled client attributed his participation and satisfaction with his lawyers. And lawyer personality is just as important as client personality in shaping a relationship. Rosenthal acknowledges that lawyer personality is half of a dominance–submissiveness relationship, but he does not even attempt to measure lawyer personality and is unsuccessful in measuring client personality.

A good deal of literature exists which advises lawyers about the psychological aspects of client interviewing and counseling.[42] A much smaller body of literature looks at the ways in which attorneys' personalities affect their handling of cases[43] or recognizes the interactional dynamics between lawyers and clients.[44]

Lawyer personality appeared to be a significant factor in client participation in the transit access cases. Although there were certainly other factors involved, in the one case where the clients came closest to losing all control of the lawsuit, Minnesota, the principal lawyer handling the case had a particularly dominant personality. One of the participants in that suit generalized from their situation: "The kind of lawyer you tend to get is an ego maniac," noting the lawyer's need for "political moxie" to be able to face thirteen lawyers for the defense.

The lawyers expressed a range of feelings about working with clients.

One lawyer admitted to going into public interest law at least partly because he saw it as an opportunity to get away from as much contact with clients as he had had in corporate practice. In the East Bay suit, where two or more lawyers shared the case most of the time, two of them divided their work so that one handled more of the contact with the opposing parties and the other handled more of the contact with their own clients. The former acknowledged that she does not enjoy the work involved in keeping clients in touch with a case, such as meetings and letter writing. She even seemed a little surprised that the clients generally expressed satisfaction with their participation in the suit.

In general, the clients were satisfied with their lawyers and frequently offered compliments about the lawyers' patience and efforts to explain difficult subjects. How much this is due to individual personalities and how much to professional norms is difficult to tell because even more than for clients, attorney personality blurs with norms about how lawyers are *supposed* to behave. For example, one lawyer frequently referred to his clients as "colleagues," but the choice of terms could be a reflection of either a congenial personality or his high ideological commitment to client participation for its own sake.

Legal Norms

Lawyers' opinions about the proper role of lawyers and clients are likely to be strongly influenced—and their behavior largely controlled—by professional standards. Those standards, however, address only lawyer behavior and are somewhat ambiguous. On the one hand, the old Canon of Ethics and the current Code of Professional Responsibility limit advertising and proscribe soliciting clients and encouraging litigation.[45] On the other hand, the code encourages lawyers to be active in "zealously" representing their clients' interests.[46]

The 1969 revision of the Code of Professional Responsibility for the first time added a statement of the client's ultimate decision-making authority, though as a part of the Ethical Considerations of the code, the provisions are aspirational rather than obligatory.

> In certain areas of legal representation not affecting the merits of the case or substantially prejudicing the rights of the client, a lawyer is entitled to make decisions on his own. But otherwise, the authority to make decisions is exclusively that of the client and, if made within the framework of the law, such decisions are binding on his lawyer.[47]
>
> A lawyer should exert his best efforts to insure that decisions of his client are made only after the client has been informed of relevant considerations. A lawyer ought to initiate this decision-making process if the client does not do so. Advice of a lawyer to his client need not be confined to purely legal considerations. A lawyer should advise his client of the possible effect of each legal alterna-

tive. . . . In the final analysis, however, the lawyer should always remember that the decision whether to forego legally available objectives or methods because of non-legal factors is ultimately for the client and not for himself.[48]

This ideal—that clients are ultimately to determine their own interests and to direct their litigation—is what students learn in law school, but the line between interpreting the law and suggesting alternative courses of action, on the one hand, and choosing the proper alternative, on the other, blurs in practice. As one of the disabled clients who is a lawyer put it: "Decisions about what way to go, the thrust of the suit, what's being asked for, the policy-type decisions are client decisions. Lawyers really, as I was taught in law school, oughtn't to be making those decisions in the first place—although they often do."

Other norms and assumptions of the profession work to undermine the ethical considerations just quoted. According to Richard Wasserstrom, the very assumption that clients know their own best interests is challenged. "Because the matters for which professional assistance is sought usually involve things of great personal concern to the client, it is the received wisdom within the professions that the client lacks the perspective necessary to pursue in a satisfactory way his or her own best interests."[49] This factor, in combination with the professional training and language possessed by the lawyer, results in the client's not being "treated with the respect and dignity that he or she deserves."[50] Because he believes that "there are important and distinctive competencies that are at the heart of the legal profession," Wasserstrom does not go far toward proposing a solution for what he sees as a moral dilemma.[51]

William Simon's critique of the legal profession goes much farther. He, too, believes that the norms of legal advocacy inhibit client autonomy and responsibility by imposing the authority of a supposedly neutral expert on the client and by subverting substantive issues with procedural issues. Furthermore, when the lawyer assumes the responsibility of acting for the client's interests, he or she is encouraged by existing law to impute stylized ends to the client rather than discerning the true, personal ends of the individual client. It is the particular stylized ends imputed to all clients which make the law so compatible with a capitalist system, according to Simon.[52]

Empirical research has found that lawyers' views of their role are related to their assumptions about the proper ends of law. Jonathan Casper's research on lawyers arguing civil rights and civil liberties cases finds a relationship between a belief that the principal ends of law are to bring about social change and preserve democratic processes and the belief in an active role for lawyers in facilitating those ends.[53] Conversely, those lawyers subscribing to more traditional views that the ends of law

Table 2
Casper's Legal Types[58]

The End of Law As:	*The Lawyer As:* Passive	Active
Conflict resolution/social control	Traditionalist	Activist
Democracy/change	Theoretician	Reformer

are social control or dispute settlement also tend to take the more traditional view that a lawyer should wait for clients to come to him or her. Casper calls these lawyers Reformers and Traditionalists, respectively. Other studies of public interest lawyers discuss the nontraditional, more active role played by these lawyers compared to those in traditional private litigation.[54] The lawyers are likely to be involved in at least indirectly initiating the litigation, setting its goals, and determining its strategy.

Since the time of *NAACP v. Button*[55] (and reiterated more recently in *In re Primus*[56]), the interpretation of solicitation and barratry has been more relaxed for lawyers engaged in litigation as a form of political expression and association rather than pecuniary gain. The more active role permitted these lawyers may have contributed to the passive client situations seen in some social reform litigation. In contrast, in business-related law, where the traditional norms are still strong, corporate clients play a more assertive role.[57]

Because the norms relating to lawyer role and the ends of law are conceptually distinct, the combinations of Traditionalist and Reformer are not the only ones possible, although they are the most common. Casper identifies some lawyers who subscribe to the other combinations: "Theoreticians," who believe in change-oriented ends of law but a passive lawyer role, and "Activists," who believe in traditional ends of law but an active lawyer role. (See Table 2.)

Interestingly, Casper finds the Activist perspective most common among lawyers in areas requiring vigorous competition for clients, such as divorce and personal injury. This is one indication that the pattern of lawyer–client interaction that Rosenthal labels the traditional model, on the basis of personal injury cases, may be less ubiquitous than he thinks and the product of some forces he does not consider.

Theoreticians may appear in social reform litigation in the form of lawyers who work for large commercial firms and do some social reform work on a *pro bono* basis. Such lawyers may take active clients for granted and cue their *pro bono* clients that such behavior is acceptable and even expected. This may have been another factor reinforcing the client activity in the Washington, D.C., transit case.

The legal norms discussed thus far concern client participation only as an indirect consequence of lawyer behavior. The Traditionalist-Reformer-Theoretician-Activist typology does not encompass a new development—lawyers who believe that they should actively facilitate social change and who also have an ideological commitment to client participation as a positive good in itself. The pattern that emerges is a partnership of sorts between the lawyer and clients, similar to the participatory model advocated by Rosenthal.

An active lawyer–client partnership is feasible if both parties share the same ideological commitments and goals for the litigation. If lawyer and clients actively pursue different goals, however, the potential for conflict is great. In general, the lawyers committed to client participation will cede the final decision to the client in such situations.[59] Thomas Gilhool puts it thus:

> The client's role is to be assertive and the lawyer's role is to be responsive. Roles such as initiator, listener, idea man (or woman), prober, insister, and so on will be shared, sometimes weighted on one side and—from issue to issue, from matter to matter, from function to function, from struggle to struggle—sometimes weighted on the other, but the gestalt of the relationship will show clearly that decision making is the role of the client.[60]

This position is closely related to Casper's Theoretician, but it differs in focusing on the client's activity rather than the lawyer's passivity. It is remarkably similar to the passages from the Ethical Considerations of the Code of Professional Responsibility quoted above.

The idea that clients can and should take an active role in litigation decision making is thus a relative newcomer among legal norms. Perhaps it is somewhat surprising then that so many lawyers in the transit access cases held explicit commitments to client participation. At least one case is no surprise, because the public interest law firm that handled the Transbus case was headed by Thomas Gilhool himself. The Marin County lawyer seemed equally committed to the value of client participation for its own sake. He was very aware of the tendency of class action plaintiffs to passivity and of the potential harm this can cause to the organization and the suit.

> Something that organizations have to be careful of is that they often just let it go to the attorneys and forget about it and don't do anything and don't follow up or put pressure on the attorneys. And if that's not done, you're going to find the attorneys making important strategy decisions that may not be what's

good for the group or what the group actually wants. And that's one of the real dangers in the whole area of law reform litigation—that in class action lawsuits you get removed from the people themselves. And that's very harmful. It's harmful for the organization because the organization develops that powerlessness feeling, and that the attorney's doing it all. And the attorney develops a lack of interest because he doesn't see it really as a personal issue anymore; he sees it as an academic problem. And once that happens he loses a lot of motivation if he's a libertarian-based law reform attorney.

The legal services lawyers who handled the East Bay case did at one point refer to lawyers as a "tool" for clients to use, but they were generally unaccustomed to active involvement by their clients and did not expect it. As one of the lawyers commented about herself in contrast to the lawyer representing the transit interests: "I mean it would never occur to me to seek an authorization from any of our clients on a decision like that, you know, to join a third party or not to join a third party." Others might see such a decision as one with important ramifications in which clients should be involved.

Client Norms

Lawyers are not the only ones who have ideas about the proper behavior of lawyers and clients. Clients certainly do, too, although they are not formally codified, as are the lawyers' norms. In Rosenthal's presentation of the traditional and participatory models of lawyer–client relations, he describes traditionalists as "convinced in fact that people would reject an active problem-solving role even if it were offered to them by an unusually self-sacrificing and foolhardy professional."[61] Participationists, on the other hand, retort that if so, clients have been socialized by the traditional model to believe that wanting to be involved reveals a lack of trust in the professional.

Even if the clients might subscribe in the abstract to the traditional view of what constitutes proper behavior of a legal client, there are other forces which can create norms running counter to traditional "passive client" expectations. A social movement, for instance, may put a positive value on participation or assertiveness for its own sake. Saul Alinsky's community organizing movement, the mass movement phase of the civil rights movement, and the women's liberation movement all encourage their participants to express their own views of their situations and take affirmative actions to improve the situations.

To the extent that social movements emphasize individual repsonsibility to try to improve one's lot, they resemble another type of social organization, self-help groups. Self-help groups and social movements are not synonomous. In fact, at one level they are likely to be contradictory. Persons who join self-help groups do so to achieve immediate concrete benefits for themselves, while members of social movements are often expected to defer personal gratifications in the interest of changing society.[62] On the other hand, one of the forces that can join these two is belief in the therapeutic value of action to bring about change. Among the considerations noted by Katz and Bender in comparing social movements and self-help groups, at least two concern the importance of individual participation:

> The extent to which a social movement stresses socialization and interpersonal interaction among its members, to the minimization of the movement's overall goals, aids in its classification as a self-help group.
>
> To the extent that a social movement permits and enhances ongoing face-to-face relationships on an egalitarian basis, with continuous participation in decision making, the social movement approximates a self-help organization.[63]

The same group may combine more than one function. Indeed, Michael Barkun has noted the development of groups in contemporary America

> that combine the functions once separately parcelled out to utopian communities, self-help groups, and interest groups. These functions are, respectively, the creation of a social microcosm based upon some conception of perfect human relationships; the renovation of personal identity in a social setting; and the assertion and vindication of claims for legal rights and public resources.[64]

He notes further that the geographical isolation, which formerly created boundaries within which utopian communities could perform their self-transforming functions, is no longer possible in urbanized modern life. Instead, groups are defining boundaries according to

> those criteria that defined groups in the pre-industrial past: criteria of birth and biology. These criteria include race, ethnicity, gender, sexual orientation, position in the life-cycle, and physical handicaps; precisely those criteria regarded as least politically and legally relevant during the long march of individualism.[65]

These characteristics provide strong boundaries because, in Barkun's words, "they are peculiarly impervious to homogenizing tendencies."[66] These groups also have in common what Erving Goffman has called a "spoiled identity"—membership in a group that has suffered some degree of social stigma and corresponding personal shame.[67] Social movements based on devalued personal identity, then, may have a greater cohesiveness than those based on commitment to an external cause.[68]

Barkun continues: "When the sources of spoiled identity become the foundation for group membership, the group is likely to be engaged not only in attempts to change the perceptions and behavior of outsiders, but in the psychic remolding of its own members."[69] Encouraging active participation may be part of this psychic remolding of the members of groups that have been denied a role in mainstream society and made to feel dependent and worthless. This definitely appears to be true among disabled people.

Many disabled people feel that social and environmental barriers have excluded them from many experiences that able-bodied persons share. As a result, they may be especially eager to participate actively in a social reform organization or interest group, which, in turn, puts a positive ideological value on participation. The right to be independent of constant reliance on other people and the right to participate in the activities of the larger society are common themes in the disability rights movement.

In the presence of such normative support for participation, opportunities for active involvement in an organization may be a positive, selective incentive for joining or remaining in the group. For some people, then, participation opportunities work as "glue" to help hold together an organization seeking collective goods. Terry Moe observes:

> The individual may become an active participant for solidary reasons, placing a high value on the social relationship that can be developed and maintained through his performance of such roles. . . . Aside from these incentives, which are essentially independent of group goals, the individual may also perform services for purposive reasons—because he believes in the groups' policy positions, for instance, and feels a responsibility to do his part.[70]

In self-help groups more than other organizations, participation by professionals is likely to be de-emphasized or even discouraged. Katz and Bender note that in self-help groups, "The climate, the structure, the formal and informal patterning of social statuses along with rules for participation *minimizes* [sic] *the playing of professional roles*" (original emphasis).[71]

The disability rights movement, more than any other of the identity-based social movements, has reason to be ideologically antiprofessional. Disabled persons have the dubious distinction of having a large number of professionals who specialize in *their* problems, such as rehabilitation counselors and some doctors and social workers. Many disabled persons suspect that professionals have more to gain from maintaining specialized institutions and programs for people with disabilities than from assisting them to become fully independent citizens, not needing sheltered workshops or institutional residences.[72] "Independent Living Centers," where disabled people provide each other both material and psychological support for living outside institutions, are an extension of self-help philosophy.

Although certainly many enlightened professionals are now working closely with disabled consumer groups, tension between professionals and consumers has often been overt in the disability rights movement. One dissatisfied group of disabled participants at the White House Conference on Handicapped Individuals in 1977 issued an unofficial "alternative report" that complained about the attitude of professionals:

> Inherent in attitudinal barriers faced by the handicapped is the assumption of intrinsic inferiority, reinforced by continual association with the medical, psychological, rehabilitation, and special education industries/institutions; and by continual representation of and segregation of such individuals in sterile, stereotyped social contexts.[73]

The negative feelings of many disabled persons toward these professionals does not necessarily carry over to negative attitudes toward lawyers. In fact, at no time did any client in the transit access cases make a direct or even indirect connection between the attitudes or behavior of lawyers and those of medical or rehabilitation professionals. Nevertheless, it is not surprising that there seems to be a link between level of commitment to participation itself and level of political militance, including consciousness of oppression by professionals.

The most politically militant groups also tended to be those with the strongest sense that they—the group members—should be making the decisions rather than the lawyers. The clients in the Transbus, Minnesota, and East Bay cases approached the lawyer–client relationship as one more area where they should exercise independence and assertiveness. Sometimes the clients sensed that they should be making the decisions even when they were not sure how, as when new officers took charge of a plaintiff group and began to work with the lawyer who had been involved with the case for several years.

Client norms about participation, of course, determine actual participation no more than do many of the other factors considered in this chapter. In fact, the two most personally involved clients were the lonely crusaders in the D.C. and Marin County cases, neither of whom expressed self-conscious concern that he *should* participate. Normative commitment to participation seems to be a product of group ideology.

Objective Complexity of the Law

One of the things which can intervene between intended participation and actual participation is the client's perception of professional expertise. The mystique of professionalism depends to a large extent on some sense of exclusive knowledge—a "unique scientific body of knowledge."[74] To the extent such exclusive knowledge really exists, the clients may be deterred from participating because they lack the necessary information or understanding to do so. To the extent the clients *believe* that it exists, they may also be deterred by awe or intimidation.

Even clients who reject the claims of medical and rehabilitation professionals to special knowledge may still feel in awe of the legal profession. Indeed, a number of the transit access clients mentioned being confused by legal terminology. Some of the more self-consciously active clients made an effort to distinguish legal decisions from policy decisions, leaving the former to the lawyers and assuming the latter to be their province. This approach circumscribes the professional mystique of law without completely denying it. Drawing the line between legal and policy questions is rarely easy, however.

One of the characteristics of law as a body of knowledge is that it crosscuts a vast range of substantive areas. Clients' belief in legal expertise tends not to differentiate one legal subfield from another. In spite of this, the actual ability of clients to understand the law may vary according to knowledge they have about the substantive issues involved. Similarly, if some areas of law are inherently more complex or arcane than others, then the ability of any given client to understand may be dependent on the degree of difficulty of the law. Available studies in which lawyers themselves identify some types or parts of law as more complex or intellectually challenging than others permit us to examine the latter possibility that client participation may be a function of the objective complexity of the law.

In their study of the Chicago bar, Laumann and Heinz surveyed lawyers in twenty-three different legal specialties.[75] The lawyers evaluated the field or fields in which they practice on the basis of "professional expertise," by describing their legal practice in one of the follow ways: "The type and content of my practice is such that even an educated layman couldn't really understand or prepare the documents"; or "A paraprofessional could be trained to handle many of the procedures and documents in my area of the law."

The percentage of lawyers who rated their specialty as requiring considerable professional expertise ranges from a high of 90 percent for securities law to a low of 29 percent for general family law. High ranking fields (60 percent or above) besides securities law are patents, general corporate, tax, municipal, labor (management), and civil rights/liberties. Others ranking low (45 percent or below) are antitrust, public utilities, personal injury (defendants and plaintiffs), criminal (defense), and divorce.

The same study separately rates the freedom of action held by lawyers in the different specialties, defined as the degree to which the lawyer is "free to pursue whatever strategic course of action his own professional judgment may suggest" as opposed to being "more highly constrained by *knowledgeable clients* or by organizational superiors, who supervise and guide his decisions" (emphasis added). This rating was done not by the lawyers who specialize in the various fields, as was the professional expertise index, but by an expert panel of nineteen law professors and researchers from Northwestern University and the American Bar Foundation.[76]

The standardized scores for freedom of action range from a high of 70 for civil rights/liberties to a low of 35 for banking. Other specialties rated 60 or above in freedom of action are antitrust (plaintiffs), environmental (plaintiffs), personal injury (plaintiffs), criminal (defense), consumer (debtor), and general family (poverty). The great freedom of action experienced by lawyers of civil rights and liberties, environmental, and poverty plaintiffs appears to corroborate the observation that social reform litigation tends to be lawyer-dominated. Those areas rated 45 or below are securities, antitrust (defendants), public utilities, general utilities, general corporate, municipal, labor (management), labor (unions), environmental (defendants), and consumer (creditor).

If the complexity of a field of law were a significant determinant of client participation in those cases, as the definition of a professional suggests, then one could expect those fields ranking high in professional expertise to be rated high in freedom of action as well and those low in one to be low in the other. This is not the predominant pattern—it is true only for civil rights/liberties (high on both) and public utilities and antitrust (defendants) (low on both). A more common pattern is an inverse relationship. Those high on expertise and low on freedom of action are securities, general corporate, municipal, and labor (management). Those low on expertise and high on freedom of action are personal injury (plaintiffs), criminal (defense), and family (poverty).[77]

In general, this comparison suggests that complexity of the law is less important than other factors in determining the degree of client involvement. Furthermore, it does not help at all in differentiating active and passive clients within a single legal issue like the law of transit accessibility.

The Social Organization of Legal Services

As well as requiring different amounts of professional expertise, legal practice in different areas of law also tends to take different organizational patterns. The prototypical professional–client relationship is that of an individual client hiring an individual professional and paying on a fee-for-service basis. Today this pattern is undoubtedly more the exception than the rule for legal as well as many other professional services. Legal services are delivered through a vast number of different organizational patterns. Two facets of organizational pattern are relevant to client participation: the institutional setting of the lawyer's practice and the structure of the client's relationship to the lawyer's practice.

Laumann and Heinz's "freedom of action" variable combines both of these facets by including constraints imposed by knowledgeable clients and by organizational superiors. It would appear that lawyers in the low freedom areas—banking, securities, antitrust (defendants), public utilities, general corporate, municipal, labor (management), labor (unions), environmental (defendants), and consumer (creditor)—work *in* and *for* public or private bureaucratic organizations. In the high freedom areas—civil rights/liberties, antitrust (plaintiffs), environmental (plaintiffs), criminal (defense), consumer (debtor), and general family (poverty)—the lawyers generally work in solo practices or relatively small organizations for individual or loosely organized clients.

Lawyers' Ties with Each Other

Many studies have found that professionals of all types are increasingly employed in large organizations rather than in private practices.[78] Professionals working in institutional settings have other professional colleagues or administrative superiors or both exerting some degree of supervision and control over their work more than do professionals in individual practice. They may make the professional either more or less responsible in advancing the client's interests, depending on the standards and policies of the institution. At the very least the structure adds an alternative reference group other than the client which is closer at hand than the professional reference group is for solo practice professionals.

Both Carlin's early study of lawyers' conformity to professional ethics and Zemans' recent study of lawyers' more general conceptualization of professional responsibility find that the attitudes and behavior of lawyers toward these matters vary according to firm size and internal organization (hierarchical or peer-group).[79] If such organizational factors influence legal ethics, it is reasonable to explore them as contributing determinants of client participation, too. Indeed, Zemans discusses the relationship between professional responsibility and the ethics involved in interpersonal relationships, which for lawyers includes returning telephone calls from clients, keeping them abreast of the progress of their cases, and providing them a reasonable amount of attention.[80]

Brakel's study of the satisfaction of low-income clients using an experimental Judicare program compared to similar clients using a staffed-office legal services program also suggests the importance of the organizational patterns of legal services.[81] The Judicare clients expressed notably higher satisfaction with the service they received than the clients of the staffed office did, but Brakel did not investigate the degree of personal involvement of clients in the two programs.

Even organizational ties among lawyers that are much looser than the ties among lawyers practicing in the same office may affect the lawyer–client relationship, too. If they are in contact with each other, lawyers involved in similar litigation have the possibility of coordinating their lawsuits by agreeing on goals and strategies, accelerating or slowing one case in the interest of another, and sharing supportive legal research or expert witnesses. Both the cooperating attorneys of the NAACP and the lawyers in the Legal Services Corporation have had the organizational ties and the communication vehicles, such as the *Clearinghouse Review*, to facilitate coordination.[82]

When lawyers plan a litigation strategy across several cases, it may be tempting for them to try to persuade the clients in each case to go along with the existing plans rather than set their own goals and strategies. Lawyer ties, then, lay the groundwork for lawyer dominance.

Communication among the lawyers in the accessible bus cases was very limited and it was nonexistent between them and the lawyers in the D.C. case. Lawyers in three of the five cases did attend a legal conference on accessible transportation sponsored by the National Center for Law and the Handicapped in 1975, but no coordinated strategy emerged from the conference. Indeed, there was considerable disagreement about such fundamental issues as whether to focus on the national level, as the Transbus suit did, or on the local level, as the others in this study did. Even the lawyers in the two cases on different sides of the bay in the San Francisco metropolitan area communicated very little, although both relied on the same state statutes.

Lack of ties among the lawyers in no way guarantees active clients, of course, but decentralized litigation may be conducive to client participation by leaving more decisions open to be shared with the clients in individual suits. The more closely that lawyers work together, the more they may be inclined to rely on each other for advice and consultation rather than on their clients.

Clients' Ties with the Lawyers

More than the organizational structure of the lawyers' practice, the factor which some observers have suggested is the major determinant of the client's ability to take an active part in decision making in the legal process is the financial nexus between client and lawyer. When an individual client hires an individual professional and pays on a fee-for-service basis, the client is simultaneously employer and recipient of the service. On a large institutional scale, the government also stands in the same dual relationship to the lawyers it employs.

Judith May argues that as long as the client is in the position of the overall employer, as with a person who hires either an individual lawyer or a law firm, the client retains some control over the professional's work.[83] If the professional is instead supported by public or private funds to provide service to the clients, then the clients become consumers of the professional service rather than employers of the professionals. The consumer-clients lose all market control that is available to those who can pick and choose among professionals, negotiate fees, and terminate one relationship in favor of another if the first is unsatisfactory.

May's contention that employer–clients have more control over professionals than do consumer–clients finds support in numerous studies of the legal profession. For example, the lawyers having high "freedom of action" on Laumann and Heinz's scale typically provide service for clients that is paid for either wholly or in part by third parties (public interest law firms, public defenders, Legal Services Corporation) or by court-awarded attorney's fees (environmental or antitrust plaintiffs). Others have noted the potential conflicts created for lawyers whose funding (and often moral support as well) comes from "constituents" or "clientele groups" different from their direct clients.[84]

Edgar and Jean Cahn are particularly critical of government-funded antipoverty lawyers who "seem to feel freer to discard this fundamental relationship [the client determining the client's best interest]—perhaps because they are not paid by the client, perhaps because they perceive the client as powerless to do anything about it.... Private law firms tend to honor the lawyer-client relationship more scrupulously than poverty lawyers."[85] A similar criticism has been made of public defenders in the criminal arena.[86]

The transit access cases included considerable variation in the financial arrangements existing between the lawyers and clients: salaried legal aid lawyers, private lawyers paid a fee-for-service, public interest law firm lawyers with foundation funding, and private lawyers working *pro bono publico*. Because all five cases had significant client participation, there is no obvious support for May's generalization, and the number of cases is far too small to support any finer distinctions of degrees of participation compared to financial arrangement. Those lawyers who had had experience with both paying and nonpaying clients were asked about differences among them, however, so there is a little anecdotal evidence to add about the importance of the financial nexus as a determinant of client participation.

Two of the lawyers now working exclusively with nonpaying clients presumed that paying clients get better service or at least more deference than non-paying clients. One of these was a legal services lawyer who just did not expect much involvement by clients. The relatively high level of participation by the disabled clients was atypical for her. Her expectations about client participation and the significance of the financial nexus were captured by a comment that "it would never occur to me to seek an authorization from any of our clients on a decision like that—to join a third party or not to join a third party. I suppose when you're spending somenone else's money, it's a different thing."

The other lawyer, formerly in private practice and now with a public interest law firm, frankly admitted that clients would not get the same service if they were not paying for it. "Money talks," he noted, unless the lawyer is young, naive, and altruistic. In addition to the financial difference, he suggested that public interest clients tend to be less "able" than private clients and often ask the lawyer what to do, whereas paying clients tell the lawyers what to do.

The private attorneys doing one of the cases on a *pro bono* basis held a contrary postion: "I would say in our experience the clients in *pro bono* actions are at least as involved as those in commercial actions. They are people that come in here with their hearts on their sleeves and have a principle that goes far beyond their own personal interests very often." Clearly there is no consensus about the effects of client payment on client participation. These quotations do, however, reinforce the earlier suggestion that the lawyer's expectations of client behavior are a significant influence.

The most important qualification of May's generalization as it applies to lawyers is that even for employer–clients who do pay fees the market conditions May assumes often do not exist. Rosenthal and Ladinsky have both studied the problem that arises when clients do not have the necessary information about prospective lawyers to make a rational market choice.[87] Lack of officially recognized specialization among lawyers, bar association constraints on advertising, and lack of appropriate and familiar appraisal criteria all contribute to client ignorance about choosing lawyers. In sum, Rosenthal finds that rather than shopping around for a lawyer as in a free market model, the clients tend to choose the "first lawyer they know who comes to mind, the first lawyer recommended to them, or the first lawyer they meet."[88]

The transit access cases, too, sustain this conclusion. In the two cases in which clients assumed the full responsibility of the litigation costs, Marin County and Minnesota, there was no evidence that the clients "picked and chose" among professionals or felt free to terminate the relationship even though in one case it was not entirely smooth. The Marin County plaintiffs had some difficulty finding a lawyer who would take their case and were finally referred to their lawyer by a public interest firm that rejected them for having too much money. The Minnesota clients hired the lawyer who was recommended to them by a consultant.

Another problem with May's generalization is that consumer–clients and employer–clients are not pure types. A number of financial arrangements can exist between lawyers and clients other than the clients paying all or nothing. For example, in prepaid legal service plans clients contribute to the general support of the lawyers but do not individually pay them fees for services rendered. (Some clients may not even contribute, if the legal service is an employment benefit.)

Marks' study of the Shreveport Plan, the first prepaid legal service program, found a high quality of lawyer–client interaction:

Both lawyers and clients reported that they were more satisfied with one another; there was greater trust; clients thought that the lawyers gave them more attention and more service; lawyers thought that they gave better service and that *clients participated more in their own affairs*. The certainty—on both sides—that reasonable fees would be charged and paid seemed to shift the relationship from paternalism to mutuality (emphasis added).[89]

Another ambiguous type of financial arrangement from the perspective of May's theory is the contingent fee. While Marks' prepaid clients are more like May's employer–clients than consumer–clients, the contingent fee clients Rosenthal studied are more like consumer–clients, since the size of the personal injury damage award or settlement won by the lawyer determines how much he or she makes more than the client does. As Rosenthal notes, frequently the lawyer's interest lies in a quick settlement, whereas the client's interest would be best served by going to trial.[90] The lawyer is thus not inclined to encourage client participation. Mazor also notes the tendency of a lawyer to "treat the litigation as if it were his own" in contingent fee cases.[91] Casper's finding that personal injury lawyers are likely to be Activists seems to reflect the same tendency.[92]

In addition to financial variations the transit access cases provided a few examples of unanticipated problems that can arise in situations where the clients pay part of the costs, but not all of them. In the Transbus case the public interest lawyers were salaried by the firm's externally supported operating budget, but the Transbus clients contributed differing amounts to the litigation expenses. One client reported that they sometimes felt disgruntled when they were expected to volunteer their time for activities such as writing press releases while the law center staff was getting paid and they were not. "A lot of work, rightly or wrongly, was slumped off on the Disabled in Action members. . . . And we felt that maybe some more of the work should have been borne by the staff at PILCOP or the secretarial people, instead of us ourselves having to put in eighteen hours a day."

An entirely different kind of problem arose in the Minnesota case. There the clients were supposed to pay fee-for-service-plus-costs, but were not able to raise sufficient money, so that the lawyer found himself carrying the case at considerable personal financial sacrifice. This may be one reason why the lawyer grew increasingly dominant in the case, to the point that one client noted that it gradually became "his" case. Ironically, some of the clients in this case felt that they had the same problem with their own staff person when the organization was unable to pay his salary and he worked awhile without pay.

In short, it appears clear that the financial nexus between lawyer and client plays a large role in determining the balance of paternalism and mutuality, in Marks' terms, though the relationship is not so simple as May suggests. One final aspect of the social organization of the lawyer–client relation, which is considerably more intangible than the financial aspect, deserves brief comment.

The prevailing view in the literature is that *continuing* access to legal services that are broadly defined rather than narrowly focused is most conducive to the successful use of litigation for social change. Marc Galanter, for instance, sees this as a matter of the lawyers' willingness and ability to identify with their clients:

> The contribution of the lawyer to redistributive social change, then, depends upon the organization and culture of the legal profession. . . . The more that lawyers view themselves exclusively as courtroom advocates, the less their willingness to undertake new tasks and form enduring alliances with clients and operate in forums other than courts, the less likely they are to serve as agents of redistributive change.[93]

Galanter's concern with success, however, does not consider client participation as important in itself. The advocates of litigation as a community organizing strategy, on the other hand, consciously look to contact with lawyers to improve the ability of clients to solve problems themselves.[94] Indeed, Marks' empirical study of prepaid legal services reaches the conclusion

> that the sense of entitlement to legal services will in many instances be as important to the client as the actual fact of representation. The study suggests that the availability of legal services made individuals more willing to assert themselves in situations where legal services were potentially useful. This increased assertiveness led to more satisfactory outcomes without any need for legal assistance.[95]

If this empirical finding is borne out in other situations, so much the better. In general, however, the same persons whose expectations about the consciousness-raising powers of legal services have been the highest are also the most sensitive to and concerned about the problem of creating client dependence on lawyers.[96] One possibility which should be investigated is that continuing and diversified access to legal services could contribute to dependence in a way that is less likely when lawyer–client contact is more sporadic and limited.[97]

This proposition is highly speculative, of course. Nevertheless, the major concern about creating client dependency on lawyers arose in antipoverty litigation, where the relationship between lawyers and the poor was recurring and institutionalized through the OEO Neighborhood Legal Services (later Legal Services Corporation). In contrast, the lawyers helping disabled groups were usually involved with them for only one discrete lawsuit and were rarely involved in the groups' other affairs. Indeed, in the transit access cases, the strain characteristic of dependence and resistance to dependence—feelings of inferiority, resentment about who gets the glory, and accusations of paternalism—was greater in relation to the group's full-time staff member than in relation to the lawyer in the case of one plaintiff organization.

Handler suggests that organizational ties between lawyers and social reform groups tend to give the groups more control over the lawyers and to reduce the lawyers' litigation bias and their need to hold the limelight.[98] The examples he considers, however, are strong national organizations, such as the Sierra Club or Consumers Union, which are clearly experienced in setting their own policies. This is very different from the structural ties linking NAACP or Legal Services lawyers and clients, and it reflects more on the next factor to be considered: the organizational status of the clients.

Dependence may require the opportunity for extended contact. This does not mean, of course, that such contact necessarily will produce client dependence, nor that minimal contact will ensure client participation. Many other factors in this chapter may differentiate poor clients from disabled clients more than this aspect of the social organization of their legal assistance does, but the possibility seems worth exploring.

Organizational Status of Clients

This study has asserted that organized clients can be crucial in monitoring a court victory and ensuring long-term success. Organization for this purpose presumably could develop as a by-product of the litigation itself. It is also possible, however, that organization among clients affects their ability to participate in the litigation processes, so that already-organized clients might participate in litigation decision making more than unorganized clients.

Returning to Laumann and Heinz's freedom of action scale among different areas of legal practice, we see that the clients of the lawyers in the low freedom areas—banking, securities, antitrust (defendants), public utilities, general corporate, municipal, labor (management), labor (unions), environmental (defendants), and consumer (creditor)—are invariably public or private organizations. In some of the high freedom areas—general family (poverty), consumer (debtor), and criminal (defense)—the clients are almost as invariably individuals.

In other high freedom areas, however—civil rights/liberties, antitrust (plaintiffs), and environmental (plaintiffs)—clients may well be organized. These clients are also likely to be consumer–clients in that they receive subsidized legal services, but their organization may help to offset the dependence created by the financial relationship.

May describes a trend for consumer–clients of other kinds of professional services to organize themselves in an attempt to equalize their role vis-à-vis the professionals.[99] Some of the examples she cites are welfare recipients demanding hearings before their grants are cut off; public housing tenants, before they are evicted; and students, before they are disciplined. Furthermore, clients are demanding to be represented on the governing boards of institutions to share with professionals the responsibility of determining how scarce resources are allocated. Access to decision making does not guarantee changes in the substance of decisions, of course, but it may make changes more likely than they would be in the absence of any client participation.

Client organizing activities like those May describes have occurred among legal clients in several different ways. One example is an organization, such as a union, hiring a lawyer to assist members with disability or workmen's compensation claims. Prepaid legal insurance plans, such as legal services for college students supported by a student activity fee, are another example, although the organizational ties among members of such a plan may be very loose. In recent years, organizations as clients themselves have become more common, especially in social reform litigation which addresses problems people have collectively.

Merely having clients organized in one of these ways, however, does not ensure that they will play a more active roles vis-à-vis the lawyer. One of the principal theoretical studies of the advantages of organizing clients, Marc Galanter's proposal to turn one-shot players into repeat players examines the advantages of organizing for increasing the chances of successful litigation.[100] Galanter himself does not examine client participation in the litigation, but an empirical study using Galanter's concepts suggests that the organizational status of the clients does directly affect the lawyer–client relationship.

In a study of the extent to which British solicitors either accept their clients' objectives as their own before translating them into legal terms or reject or transform the clients' objectives, Maureen Cain found that the results differed for repeat and one-shot clients. None of the recurring clients, who were generally businesses or landlords, had his or her objective rejected, while one out of six of the one-shot clients, who were private individuals, did.[101] Furthermore, loose, informal organizational links among the one-shot individual clients of one solicitor protected them against having their objectives rejected or transformed. This solicitor was a solo practitioner in an urban immigrant community and was dependent on maintaining a good reputation within the neighborhood.[102]

Organization among clients can help strengthen their position vis-à-vis the lawyer even when the lawyer is not financially dependent on the clients. Jeffrey Fitzgerald's study of the Contract Buyers League in Chicago shows how this may come about.[103] The most important thing about organizing the Contract Buyers League was the moral support and the sense of community it gave the formerly isolated individual home buyers. As a manifestation and reinforcement of their solidarity, the group organized a payment strike, although this was against the advice of their volunteer lawyers. The organized clients became more active participants, even if not exactly in the lawsuits.

In addition to collective financial clout or psychological reinforcement, there are other reasons why organization can contribute to client participation. The transit access cases illustrate some of these reasons, although they also illustrate some of the limitations or countervailing forces involved. The main point is that having organized clients is more likely to ensure some client participation, but it by no means implies that all clients will then be involved in the litigation decision making.

In the first place, an organization is likely to have designated leaders who are accustomed to articulating the concerns of the members, taking the initiative to advance the interests of the members, and making decisions to implement policies and programs of the organization. People with such leadership experience may well continue to exercise those capacities and become actively involved in the decision making of a lawsuit.

One limitation to this generalization was experienced in the Minnesota case. There the suit lasted so long that there was turnover of the group leadership, and the new officers lacked familiarity and confidence with the issue. This frustrated both them and the lawyer and perhaps contributed to client deference to the lawyer. This was less of a problem in the other cases with broad group participation. The East Bay cases simply did not last as long. The active Transbus clients were more likely to be persons expressly chosen to represent the group plaintiffs in the litigation deliberations than to be the regular officers of the group, so there was less turnover.

Secondly, active participation in a lawsuit is very time-consuming. Different members of an organizational client can share the responsibilities of gathering evidence for the case, keeping in touch with the lawyer, and maintaining group interest. Together they can do more work than even a very dedicated individual client can do. Many participants were involved in the East Bay and Transbus cases, in contrast to the D.C. and Marin County cases.

Most groups do have some kind of division of labor, however, so that not all members will be equally involved. The division may be formal, as in the Minnesota case, where the paid staff member handled a good deal of the contact with the lawyer. It may be informal, as in the East Bay case where member involvement seemed to be mostly a function of individual interest and geographical proximity. In the Transbus case, one organization was represented by a paid staff member whose sense of distinct professional functions was so clear that he, considering himself a lobbyist, sounded more deferential to the lawyers on anything he deemed legal matters than were the nonprofessional group representatives.

A final problem occurring in groups is a version of the free rider problem with which this chapter began. Individual members of a named group plaintiff may assume that other group members are taking care of the suit. This was the case in the Marin County and the D.C. cases, where one person in each carried virtually the full responsibility of representing the clients, despite efforts to involve others more. The attorney in the Marin County case observed that in his experience class action clients tend to be less actively involved than his private clients, such as parents of disabled children seeking appropriate education for them. This situation simply demonstrates that the free rider problem for public goods operates within an existing organization as well as in the effort to get persons to join in the first place, unless the members are receptive to participation itself as a selective incentive, as proposed earlier in this chapter.

Practical and Strategic Considerations

A few final practical and strategic considerations affect the degree to which clients actively participate in lawsuits, judging from the transit access cases. Sometimes a decision must be made too quickly to permit consultation. This may result in an absence of client voice in major decisions. For instance, the lawyers in the East Bay state case decided on the spur of the moment in the courtroom to combine the hearings for preliminary and permanent injunctive relief rather than go to trial. The Marin County initiating plaintiff also mentioned occasions when there was no time to consult with the other plaintiffs, so that he and the lawyer made the decisions.

A second obvious factor is the time and money costs of participating. Especially in the Transbus case, which included plaintiffs from several cities, representatives from all the groups could not always afford the trips to Philadelphia and later Washington for planning meetings. This was also a problem in the East Bay case, where one of the group plaintiffs was a statewide organization. Time demands were particularly severe on those individuals who were the sole actively involved client, as in the D.C. and Marin County cases. The D.C. client suggested that his crusade had become quite unpopular with his family because it took up so much time.

Finally, clients may participate more if they perceive that it influences decision makers favorably. This consideration is most important when the formal litigation is combined with extra-judicial strategies. There is no indication that clients believed that *judges* noticed their degree of participation (as they did seem to believe the judges noticed their numbers), but the Transbus clients in particular felt that an appearance of participation was important in other contexts. As one Transbus client reported:

> The [American Public Transit Association] group and General Motors have at times tried to combat our efforts by portraying them to Congress and to the press as efforts that are headed by some aggressive, take-charge Philadelphia lawyers. And what they're really thinking is the poor disabled people don't really know what's going on.

A similar strategic consideration occurs in the choice of the individuals to be named plaintiffs or to take an active role on any given occasion. The Minnesota plaintiffs mentioned planning which of their members would be the most influential spokespersons at different times. This strategic factor is related to the clients' normative belief that they should take the lead role, imputing this norm to the people they seek to influence.

Conclusion

This lengthy survey of determinants of client participation is merely exploratory at this time. It is apparent that there is considerable overlap among the variables. For instance, corporate clients are organized, have a favorable financial nexus with the lawyers, are generally of high socioeconomic and educational status, and work with lawyers who subscribe to professional norms calling for largely passive behavior from the lawyers.

Distinguishing the independent influence of each variable is unlikely, but perhaps at least the propositions put forth about determinants of client participation can be summarized here as questions for future research. Some will appear commonsensical because of knowledge already acquired about participation in other collective activities. Others should be more provocative.

I. Personal Characteristics

A. Clients with more education will participate more than clients with less education.

B. Clients from higher socioeconomic strata will participate more than clients from lower socioeconomic strata.

C. Clients with generally assertive personalities will participate more than clients with more retiring personalities.

D. Clients will participate more with lawyers with less dominant personalities than they will with lawyers with more dominant personalities.

E. Clients will participate more with lawyers whose demographic characteristics are similar to their own (age, sex, race, etc.) than they will with lawyers whose characteristics are different from theirs.

II. Norms about Participation

A. Professional norms do influence client participation, and norms encouraging participation will tend to increase such participation.

B. Clients who subscribe to norms which expressly encourage independence and self-reliance will participate more than clients who hold no such explicit norms.

1. Norms expressly encouraging autonomy and, indirectly, participation are more characteristic of members of organized groups than of unaffiliated individuals.

2. Some social groups, such as women, racial minorities, and disabled persons, are more likley to hold norms favoring participation than are other social groups that are organized on bases other than stigmatized ascriptive personal characteristics.

3. Persons who hold norms challenging the authority of any professional group will be more active legal clients than persons who hold no such norms.

III. Complexity of the Law

Client participation is related little or not at all to the inherent complexity of the subject matter of the litigation.

IV. The Social Organization of Legal Services

A. Lawyers who practice in organizational settings rather than in solo practice will have their attitudes toward client participation influenced by norms prevailing within the organization. The norms of some organizations will be conducive to client participation, while the norms of others will inhibit it.

B. Client participation will be greater in decentralized litigation than in litigation coordinated through lawyer networks.

C. Clients will participate more if they are paying for the services of the lawyer, either directly or indirectly, than if the services are paid for entirely by a third party.

D. Client participation will be greater when the relationship with the lawyer is one-time or sporadic and narrowly focused than when the relationship is continuous, long-term, and multifaceted, so that both parties begin to take the relationship for granted.

V. Organization among Clients
   Clients who are organized will participate more than unorganized clients.
   A. Collective financial leverage achieved thorugh organization will encourage client participation.
   B. Moral support or consciousness raising achieved through organization will encourage client participation.
   C. Clients with organizational leadership experience will participate more than clients without such experience.
   D. Organized clients will participate more than unorganized clients by sharing the work involved in being active clients.

VI. Other Considerations
   A. Clients will participate more when the costs of participation in time and money are modest than when they are high.
   B. Clients will participate more when they perceive that their involvement will positively influence decision makers than when they perceive it makes no difference.

In this review of possible determinants of client participation, a number of reasons appear to show why the clients in the accessible transit litigation were more active clients than we could have expected on the basis of the literature on social reform litigation, which primarily examines litigation in the antipoverty movement or the civil rights movement. In the first place, although some disabled people are also dependent, inarticulate, and intimidated by legal situations, there are more disabled clients than poor clients who are well-educated, articulate, and assertive. Some disabled persons with low current incomes grew up in middle-class homes with higher expectations of political efficacy. Some may have become disabled only after acquiring the expectations and communication skills of middle-class people.

Secondly, the disability rights movement in all of its facets puts great emphasis on independence, autonomy, and doing-for-oneself. Self-help groups in which members give each other both material and psychological assistance in living independently are an important part of the movement. Militant disabled activists, moreover, have the experience of resisting the dominance of professionals, even if these are typically medical and rehabilitation professionals rather than lawyers. Although there was certainly some emphasis on "community control" and accountability to consumers in the antipoverty movement as well, the normative support for assertive behavior seems less personally focused and generally more diffuse. "Culture of poverty" rhetoric notwithstanding, organizing around low income is less intimately linked to personal identity than organizing around physical disabilities. Similarly, looking largely at public interest rather than identity-based social reform groups made Handler underestimate the power of solidary incentives.

A further difference is that the disability rights groups were already organized when they began their lawsuits. Poverty litigation was more likely to involve class action suits with perhaps some attention to organizing people as a by-product of the litigation. Tension between lawyers and community organizers testifies to the secondary place which most of the antipoverty lawyers gave to organizing.[104] The result of this difference is that the disabled clients were more able to take advantage of the benefits of being organized discussed above.

Some of the lawyers in the transit access cases were in occasional communication with each other, but they had no organizational ties comparable to those of the NAACP lawyers or Legal Services Corporation lawyers. The lawyers, then, had no coordinated strategy they might have been tempted to impose on the clients. Furthermore, their contacts with the clients were limited in most cases to handling the one lawsuit, and they did not get involved in other organizational matters of the groups. Especially those clients who were paying the lawyers could hardly afford to become dependent on them. Finally, some of the transit access lawyers were ideologically committed to client participation, and others took it for granted because of their experience with corporate clients.

Random factors, such as the personalities of individual clients and lawyers, clearly were important in some of these cases, too. Nevertheless, the pattern of some substantial client participation in all five cases suggests that nonrandom factors account for the greater client participation than that which occurred in most antipoverty and NAACP litigation.

Notes

1. David Horton Smith, Richard D. Reddy, and Burt R. Baldwin, eds., *Voluntary Action Research: 1972* (Lexington,Mass.: Lexington Books, 1972), pt. 2; and Lester W. Milbrath and M. L. Goel, *Political Participation: How and Why Do People Get Involved in Politics?*, 2d ed. (Chicago: Rand McNally, 1977).
2. Neil Smelser, *Theory of Collective Behavior* (New York: Free Press, 1963).
3. Eric Hoffer, *The True Believer* (New York: Harper and Row, 1951), and T. W. Adorno et al., *The Authoritarian Personality* (New York: Harper and Row, 1950).
4. Lewis S. Feuer, *The Conflict of Generations* (New York: Basic Books, 1969), and James W. Vander Zanden, *Race Relations in Transition* (New York: Random House, 1965).
5. Gian Sarup, "A Reference Group Theory of Social Movements and Identity," *Social Science* 50 (1975): 225.
6. Truman, *Governmental Process*.
7. Mancur Olson, Jr., *The Logic of Collective Action: Public Goods and the Theory of Groups*, rev. ed. (New York: Schocken Books, 1971).
8. Handler, *Social Movements and the Legal System*, p. 10.

9. Historically, the lawyer's participation is derivative, of course. To the extent that litigation is an abstraction of combat, as Jerome Frank suggests in *Courts on Trial* (Princeton: Princeton University Press, 1949), the participation of the client is prior to the participation of the agent-lawyer. See also Lester J. Mazor, "Power and Responsibility in the Attorney–Client Relation," *Stanford Law Review* 20 (1968): 1120. From a client's perspective, however, in the now-specialized realm of law the participation of a lawyer may be that which defines the activity as legal.

10. Handler, *Social Movements and the Legal System*, p. 25.

11. Brill, "Uses and Abuses of Legal Assistance," and Wexler, "Practicing Law for Poor People."

12. Suzann R. Thomas Buckle and Leonard G. Buckle, *Bargaining for Justice: Case Disposition and Reform in the Criminal Courts* (New York: Praeger, 1977), p. 115; and Abraham S. Blumberg, "The Practice of Law as Confidence Game: Organizational Co-optation of a Profession," *Law and Society Review* 1 (1967): 28–38.

13. John Baldwin and Michael McConville, "Plea Bargaining and Plea Negotiation in England," *Law and Society Review* 13 (1979): 295–96; and William L. F. Felstiner, "Plea Contracts in West Germany," *Law and Society Review* 13 (1979): 321.

14. Jack Katz, "Legality and Equality: Plea Bargaining in the Prosecution of White-Collar and Common Crimes," *Law and Society Review* 13 (1979): 447.

15. Roman Tomasic, *Lawyers and the Community* (Sydney, Australia: The Law Foundation of New South Wales and George Allen & Unwin, 1978), p. 99.

16. Rosenthal, *Lawyer and Client*, p. 184.

17. Sorauf, *Wall of Separation*, p. 155.

18. Ibid., pp. 150 and 154.

19. Raymond Payne, Barbara Pittard Payne, and Richard D. Reddy, "Social Background and Role Determinants of Individual Participation in Organized Voluntary Action," in Smith, Reddy, and Baldwin, *Voluntary Action*, pp. 214–20.

20. Milbrath and Goel, *Political Participation*, pp. 90–106.

21. Rosenthal, *Lawyer and Client*, p. 189.

22. Payne, Payne, and Reddy, "Social Background and Role Determinants," pp. 225–26; Milbrath and Goel, *Political Participation*, pp. 118–19.

23. Sorauf, *Wall of Separation*, p. 146.

24. Rosenthal, *Lawyer and Client*, pp. 183–84.

25. Ibid., p. 184.

26. Milbrath and Goel, *Political Participation*, pp. 114–16.

27. Constantina Safilios-Rothschild, *The Sociology and Social Psychology of Disability and Rehabilitation* (New York: Random House, 1970), p. 124.

28. Rosenthal, *Lawyer and Client*, pp. 200-01.

29. Richard D. Reddy and David Horton Smith, "Personality and Capacity Determinants of Individual Participation in Organized Voluntary Action," in Smith, Reddy, and Baldwin, *Voluntary Action*, pp. 285–86.

30. Ibid., passim.

31. Milbrath and Goel, *Political Participation*, chap. 3.

32. Peirce, "Great Wheelchair Flap."

33. Bowe, *Handicapping America*, p. 41.

34. Robert Kleck, "Emotional Arousal in Interactions with Stigmatized Persons," *Psychological Reports* 19 (1966): 1226, as cited in Safilios-Rothschild, *Social Psychology of Disability*, p. 122. See also Goffman, *Stigma*, pp. 116ff.

35. Safilios-Rothschild, *Social Psychology of Disability*, p. 117.

36. Rosenthal, *Lawyer and Client*, p. 58.

37. Jerome E. Carlin, *Lawyers on Their Own: A Study of Individual Practitioners in Chicago* (New Brunswick, N.J.: Rutgers University Press, 1962), pp. 17–18; and Carlin, *Lawyers' Ethics: A Survey of the New York City Bar* (New York: Russell Sage, 1966), chap. 2.

38. But see Ethical Considerations 7.7 and 7.8, quoted in text on pp. 139–40.

39. Rosenthal, *Lawyer and Client*, p. 57.

40. Ibid., p. 133.

41. In the context of personal legal problems rather than social reform litigation, Joseph Lobenthal, Jr., suggests that clients—especially the most passive ones—see their relations with their lawyer as a partnership, "because they feel most assured that the lawyer understands the nature of their concern." *Power and Put-on: The Law in America* (New York: Outerbridge and Dienstfrey, 1970), p. 62.

42. E.g., Harrop A. Freeman, *Legal Interviewing and Counseling: Cases With Comments* (St. Paul: West Publishing Co., 1964); Percival B. Hamilton, "Counseling in the Legal Profession," *American Bar Association Journal* 58 (1972): 39–42; Donald L. Very, "The Human Element in the Attorney–Client Relationship: The Answer to Malpractice," *Pennsylvania Bar Association Quarterly* 48 (1977): 515–24; Gary S. Goodpaster, "The Human Arts of Lawyering: Interviewing and Counseling," *Journal of Legal Education* 27 (1975): 5–52.

43. E.g., Walter O. Weyrauch, *The Personality of Lawyers: A Comparative Study of Subjective Factors in Law, Based on Interviews with German Lawyers* (New Haven: Yale University Press, 1964); Robert S. Redmount, "Attorney Personalities and Some Psychological Aspects of Legal Consultation," *University of Pennsylvania Law Review* 109 (1961): 972–88.

44. A few articles which do look at the interactional dynamics include Mark K. Schoenfield and Barbara P. Schoenfield, "Interviewing and Counseling Clients in a Legal Setting," *Akron Law Review* 11 (1977): 313–31; John D. Donnell, "The Corporate Counsel and His 'Client': Use of Role Analysis to Illumine Strains in the Lawyer–Client Relationship," *Indiana Law Journal* 45 (1970): 514–49; Andrew Watson, "Lawyers and Professionalism: A Further Psychiatric Perspective on Legal Education," *University of Michigan Journal of Law Reform* 8 (1975): 248–85; Charles D. Kelso and C. Kevin Kelso, "Conflict, Emotion, and Legal Ethics," *Pacific Law Journal* 10 (1978):69–93.

45. *Code of Professional Responsibility*, American Bar Association, 1969, Canon 2 generally. Advertising was entirely banned until 1977, when the U.S. Supreme Court ruled that such a ban violated the First Amendment in *Bates v. State Bar of Arizona*, 433 U.S. 350 (1977).

46. *Code of Professional Responsibility*, Disciplinary Rules 7–101.

47. Ibid., Ethical Considerations 7–7.

48. Ibid., Ethical Considerations 7–8.

49. Richard Wasserstrom, "Lawyers as Professionals: Some Moral Issues," *Human Rights* 5 (1975): 17.

50. Ibid., p. 16.

51. Ibid., p. 23.

52. William H. Simon, "The Ideology of Advocacy: Procedural Justice and Professional Ethics," *Wisconsin Law Review* (1978): 29–144.

53. Jonathan D. Casper, *Lawyers Before the Warren Court: Civil Liberties and Civil Rights, 1957–66* (Urbana, Ill.: University of Illinois Press, 1972), pp. 80–87.

54. Rabin, "Lawyers for Social Change," pp. 233–35; Harrison and Jaffe, "Public Interest Law Firms."

55. 371 U.S. 415 (1963).

56. 436 U.S. 412 (1978).

57. Erwin O. Smigel, *The Wall Street Lawyer: Professional Organization Man?* (Bloomington, Ind.: Indiana University Press, 1969), pp. 242 and 262.

58. The table is adapted from table 2 in Casper, *Lawyers Before the Warren Court*, p. 84.

59. Ann Fagan Ginger, "The Movement and the Lawyer," *Guild Practitioner* 26 (1967): 12, 14, and 17; Cahn and Cahn, "Power to the People," p. 1041.

60. Gilhool, "Uses of Courts," p. 174.

61. Rosenthal, *Lawyer and Client*, p. 15.

62. Alfred H. Katz and Eugene I. Bender, eds., *The Strength In Us: Self-Help Groups in the Modern World* (New York: New Viewpoints, 1976), p. 30.

63. Ibid., p. 31.

64. Michael Barkun, "The Political Functions of Utopian Experiments: Two Ironies in the Formulation of Group Identity," paper presented at the Third Annual Conference on Utopian Studies, University Park, Pa., 1978, p. 9. A more extensive version is now available as Michael Barkun, "Utopian Politics and the Future of Governance," *Alternative Futures: The Journal of Utopian Studies* 4 (1981): 34–49.

65. Ibid.

66. Ibid., p. 10.

67. Goffman, *Stigma*.

68. See also the list of "essential preconditions for insurgent collective identity" in Sara Evans, *Personal Politics: The Roots of Women's Liberation in the Civil Rights Movement and the New Left* (New York: Knopf, 1979), pp. 219–20.

69. Barkun, "Ironies in the Formulation of Group Identity," p. 10.

70. Terry M. Moe, *The Organization of Interests: Incentives and the Internal Dynamics of Political Interest Groups* (Chicago: University of Chicago Press, 1980), p. 119.

71. Katz and Bender, *Strength In Us*, p. 114.

72. Scott, *The Making of Blind Men*.

73. "Alternative Conference Report, White House Conference on Handicapped Individuals," p. 5.

74. Marie R. Haug and Marvin B. Sussman, "Professional Autonomy and the Revolt of the Client," *Social Problems* 17 (1969): 153. See also Harold J. Laski, *The Limitations of the Expert*, Fabian Tract No. 235. (London: The Fabian Society, 1931); and Howard S. Becker, "The Nature of a Profession," in Nelson B. Henry,

ed., *Education for the Professions: The 61st Yearbook of the National Society for the Study of Education*, pt. 2 (Chicago: University of Chicago Press, 1962).

75. The following discussion is based on table 1, pp. 166–68, and table 2, pp. 169–71, in Edward O. Laumann and John P. Heinz, "Specialization and Prestige in the Legal Profession: The Structure of Deference," *American Bar Foundation Research Journal* (1977).

76. The same expert panel also rated the "intellectual challenge" of the different specialties, responding to the following question: "The legal doctrines, cases, statutes, and regulations involved in some types of practice are characteristically more difficult, complex, and intellectually challenging than are those in others. Would you say that the degree of intellectual challenge presented by the *substance* (as opposed to the strategic considerations) of this type work is: very great, higher than average, lower than average, or very little?" (original emphasis).

Despite the apparent similarity between the experts' "intellectual challenge" question and the practitioners' "professional expertise" question, there were significant differences in the two groups' ranking of the specialties. The most striking differences were in antitrust law, which the experts rated high in intellectual challenge while the practitioners rated it low in professional expertise required, and in municipal law, which the experts rated low and the practitioners high.

The inverse relationship with "freedom of action" appears more clearly with the "professional expertise" variable than with the "intellectual challenge" variable, which is why the former is reported in the text. The gap between the two rankings of legal difficulty and complexity would be an interesting subject for further investigation.

77. The rank-order correlation is -.3263, using Kendall's tau (significant at .009), and -.4169, using the Spearman correlation coefficient, r_s (significant at .016).

78. Even by 1960, 82 percent of all male professional, technical, and kindred workers in the United States were salaried. Wilbert E. Moore, *The Professions: Roles and Rules* (New York: Russell Sage, 1970), pp. 187–88.

79. Carlin, *Lawyers' Ethics*, chaps. 6 and 7; Frances Kahn Zemans, "Socialization to Professional Responsibility: The Profession's Perspective," paper presented at the annual meeting of the Law and Society Association, San Francisco, 1979.

80. Zemans, "Socialization to Professional Responsibility," p. 8.

81. Samuel J. Brakel, *Judicare: Public Funds, Private Lawyers, and Poor People* (Chicago: American Bar Foundation, 1974), chap. 7.

82. *Clearinghouse Review* is published by the Legal Services Corporation and is the main channel of communication among legal services lawyers. It contains reports of case developments from offices around the country and other information of interest to poverty lawyers.

83. Judith V. May, *Professionals and Clients: A Constitutional Struggle*, Administrative and Policy Studies Series, no. 03-036 (Beverly Hills: Sage Publications, 1976), p. 13.

84. Casper, *Lawyers before the Warren Court*, pp. 194–96; Borosage et al., "New Public Interest Lawyers," pp. 1124–28.

85. Cahn and Cahn, "Power to the People," p. 1041.

86. Casper, *American Criminal Justice: The Defendant's Perspective* (Englewood Cliffs, N.J.: Prentice-Hall, 1972).

87. Jack Ladinsky, "The Traffic in Legal Services: Lawyer-Seeking Behavior and the Channeling of Clients," *Law and Society Review* 11 (1976): 207–23.

88. Rosenthal, *Lawyer and Client*, p. 129.

89. F. Raymond Marks, "Some Research Perspectives for Looking at Legal Need and Legal Services Delivery Systems: Old Forms or New?" *Law and Society Review* 11 (1976): 201.

90. Rosenthal, *Lawyer and Client*, pp. 98–99.

91. Mazor, "Power and Responsibility," p. 1138.

92. Casper, *Lawyers Before the Warren Court*, p. 85.

93. Galanter, "Why the 'Haves' Come Out Ahead," p. 151.

94. Scheingold, *Politics of Rights*, p. 135; Cahn and Cahn, "Power to the People," pp. 1005 and 1041.

95. Richard O. Lempert, "Mobilizing Private Law: An Introductory Essay," *Law and Society Review* 11 (1976): 176, summing up F. Raymond Marks, Robert Paul Hallauer, and Richard Clifton, *The Shreveport Plan: An Experiment in the Delivery of Legal Services* (Chicago: American Bar Foundation, 1974).

96. Denvir, "Theory of Public Interest Litigation," p. 1144; Borosage et al., "New Public Interest Lawyers," p. 10791; Cahn and Cahn, "Power to the People," p. 1040.

97. Linda Medcalf, *Law and Identity: Lawyers, Native Americans and Legal Practice* (Beverly Hills: Sage Publications, 1978), pp. 68–69 and n. 4, describes how legal services attorneys came to dominate many decisions of the Native Americans they regularly served, but they collaborated in this with a small faction of college-educated Native Americans.

98. Handler, *Social Movements and the Legal System*, pp. 32–33.

99. May, *Professionals and Clients*, pp. 24–31.

100. Galanter, "Why the 'Haves' Come Out Ahead."

101. Maureen Cain, "The General Practice Lawyer and the Client: Towards a Radical Conception," *International Journal of the Sociology of Law* 7 (1979): 343.

102. Ibid., pp. 344 and 346.

103. Jeffrey M. Fitzgerald, "The Contract Buyers League and the Courts: A Case Study of Poverty Litigation," *Law and Society Review* 9 (1975): especially pp. 184–87.

104. Wexler, "Practicing Law for Poor People," and Brill, "Uses and Abuses of Legal Assistance."

Chapter 8

Long-Term Success: Other Considerations

The degree of client participation in litigation-related activities has been emphasized thus far because it appears to be a major contributor to achieving success. Actively involved clients can provide the perseverance and continuity needed to follow an issue to fruition longer than most lawyers could unless they had a continuing source of financial support for that particular issue. Moreover, much of the monitoring work to be done does not require special legal skills anyway. If a *number* of clients are actively involved, they can also pursue a variety of tactics simultaneously, as some of the disabled groups successfully did.

The presence of active clients does not constitute a necessary *and* sufficient condition for successful litigation, however, even for remedy-oriented litigation. Numerous other variables affect ultimate success. Joel Handler has proposed a comprehensive theory of success in social reform litigation that considers long-term field-level implementation as well as court victory.[1] Although, as argued in chapter 2, Handler's theory underestimates the abilities of clients and lawyers to pursue an issue beyond the courtroom phase, he does identify three other variables affecting success: judicial remedy, the bureaucratic contingency, and cost-benefit distribution.

First, the nature of the judicial remedy available influences the likelihood of success. Courts are much more willing to issue simple preventive injunctions than they are regulatory or structural injunctions, which involve the court in lengthy administrative supervision. A problem which can be solved by the imposition of a preventive injunction or an easily monitored remedy, such as money damages, is much more likely to be successfully taken care of than a problem requiring a complex order. This is especially true if the issue has to be referred back to the original agency for further consideration, as is likely when procedural errors or omissions by the agency are found to be the cause of the plaintiff's injury.[2]

The second variable, which Handler finds to be the most important in predicting success, he calls the bureaucratic contingency. The chances of success are much greater if the benefit sought can be provided with a one-time decision made at the top, requiring minimal administrative discretion at the field level and minimal time to implement. Decisions which must be implemented by many scattered decision makers are much more difficult to monitor. Furthermore, problems which are technically complex require a great deal more expertise to monitor, expertise which social reform groups or their lawyers often lack.[3]

Third, the distribution of costs and benefits of the issue in contention influences the likelihood of success. One favorable cost-benefit configuration is concentrated benefits and distributed costs, for then the beneficiaries have an incentive to work to obtain the benefits and the persons who will be paying the costs are likely to be unorganized and unaware of the impending costs. Another favorable situation is where both costs and benefits are distributed. In this case, many pay but many also benefit, so opposition is again unlikely. Concentrated benefits and concentrated costs are an unfavorable configuration, because both sides are likely to be very aware of their respective advantage or disadvantage, leading to prolonged, intense struggle over the issue. The most unfavorable conditions, Handler believes, are concentrated costs and distributed benefits, for then the measure's opponents are often mobilized and its potential beneficiaries are not. This last configuration is characteristic of many public interest issues, such as environmental pollution and industry regulation.[4]

If the clients are able to monitor the outcome of a court decision or a negotiated settlement, as the disabled clients in this study were, then these variables become somewhat less important, but they are not rendered irrelevant. Clients still vary considerably in their abilities to persevere with an issue, and virtually any group of persons can be worn down eventually if the opposition holds out long enough.

This chapter returns to the five transit cases to report their status roughly two years after final court actions. Then Handler's three variables are used as a framework to help sum up the evidence from the transit access cases about factors other than client participation which contribute to successful use of litigation as a political strategy.

The Cases Two Years Later

In remedy-oriented litigation, success may mean either a court order against the defendant or a defendant's decision to negotiate an agreement. Neither outcome, however, is self-executing. Handler is correct in recognizing that an out-of-court victory does not eliminate the implementation or bureaucratic contingency problem.[5] If active client participation does reduce the importance of favorable bureaucratic conditions, then the disabled clients whose initial success was a matter of winning a negotiated settlement must also be able to see that the settlements are heeded. If the biggest problem with interest groups' precedent-oriented constitutional litigation is the danger that the rights won may not convert into changed behavior,[6] that danger is not completely eliminated by a consent agreement.

In fact, some of the accessible transit cases where the plaintiffs got the defendants to agree to give them at least some of what they wanted had compliance problems over the long run. Of the four groups of plaintiffs who won at least partial victories, two groups were well satisfied with developments in the two years following the termination of legal activities and two groups were quite unsatisfied. In the fifth case, in Marin County, where the most plaintiffs could claim as a victory was a verbal promise in open court not to buy any inaccessible buses in the future, that promise had been kept, but the transit authorities had made little progress in actually providing accessible service.

One of the satisfied groups was the Washington, D.C. plaintiffs, who had won the major battle outright when the judge enjoined the subway system from opening without elevators. The consent agreement, which finally ended the suit several years after the injunction, focused on the installation of a second elevator at a station still under construction and the provision of modified gates and fare collection machines to serve disabled patrons better. Although the transit authority fell behind the schedule specified in the settlement for making these improvements, the principal D.C. client, who remained personally involved in supervising the changes as chair of the elderly and handicapped advisory committee, believed that the delays were justifiable and were not an indication of bad faith or foot-dragging.

The other satisfied group was the East Bay plaintiffs, even though they won no significant legal victory. Their state suit, which ended in mootness, did have the effect of stopping Alameda-Contra Costa Transit from buying the additional nonaccessible buses it had intended to buy. The federal suit ended in a consent agreement which even the plaintiffs' lawyer described as committing the transit agency to no more than it was going to do anyway. Nevertheless, the transit agency did carry out its plans so that one of the original plaintiffs could say after two years, "We have one of the best accessibility programs in development in the country."

The transit agency ordered 165 accessible buses to go on the road beginning in midsummer of 1981. Here, too, an advisory committee became a vehicle for regular consumer involvement in decisions, such as the type of lifts to be ordered, which bus routes to make accessible first, and so forth. Committee members worked with transit staff on educational and public relations materials aimed at bus drivers, disabled riders, and the general public. One pleased former plaintiff reported, "Every chance we get, we always praise A-C Transit to the skies."

Emphasizing the good work of the East Bay transit agency was particularly important for the disabled community there because it decided next to challenge the San Francisco transit agency. San Francisco remained a "gaping hole" (in the words of one advocate) while transit was becoming accessible in most other parts of the metropolitan area. Because San Francisco is the hub to which many trips are directed, it was a particularly important target for the disabled activists. A group including some of the plaintiffs and one of the lawyers from the East Bay suits in this study filed a complaint in federal court against the San Francisco agency for failing to comply with federal regulations on accessibility. Again using litigation in combination with press conferences and other forms of political pressure, the plaintiffs were trying to repeat their success with the East Bay transit agency.

The Minnesota plaintiffs, whose strategy was much like the East Bay plaintiffs' and whose short-term success seemed even greater, had a much more difficult struggle in the long term. The out-of-court settlement which the Minnesota plaintiffs signed with their local transit agency called for 50 percent of the disabled community to receive public transit service by whatever means the agency could provide by early 1979, 75 percent to be served by early 1980, and 100 percent by 1981. Those goals were not met. At the beginning of April 1981, the Metropolitan Transit Commission (MTC) claimed to be serving about 57 percent of the disabled community, while a representative of the United Handicapped Federation claimed it was less than 50 percent.[7]

The whole issue became bound up in complex political relations among the MTC, the Metropolitan Council, the Minnesota Department of Transportation, and the state legislature. Service consisted of small buses, vans, and subsidized taxis providing door-to-door service with only five lift-equipped full-size buses, although bids for sixty more large buses were released in late May 1981.

The biggest difference between the situations in California and Minnesota seems to be the attitude and working relationship between disabled advocates and transit officials. The atmosphere in Minnesota was still strongly adversarial. Indeed, the transit commissioner whose name appeared first among the defendants in the suit stated publicly in April 1981 that the transit commission had won the suit and had no legal commitment to serve the disabled community.

The legal ambiguity of the settlement made such a claim possible. On the one hand, the federal district court judge did rule in favor of the defendants, and the plaintiffs failed to appeal because they had signed the out-of-court agreement with the defendants. On the other hand, the federal court of appeals awarded the plaintiffs $13,000 in attorney's fees on the ground that the plaintiffs' actions were a "factor of importance" and a "catalyst which prompted the defendant to take action." The legal status of the resolution passed by the MTC agreeing to provide service by the specified dates was uncertain, and the plaintiffs were debating whether to go back into court to try to have it enforced.

In terms of its direct goals, the initially successful Transbus case was the greatest failure. When Secretary of Transportation Adams mandated the Transbus design for all recipients of federal funds in 1977, mooting the lawsuit, the plaintiffs appeared to have won an unequivocal extra-judicial victory. Adams' mandate was only the beginning of a long-running struggle, however. Transit operators and industry officials first fought to have the mandate reversed by Congress, but the plaintiffs lobbied successfully to save it. When the first cities released bids for buses of the Transbus design, however, no manufacturers responded to the bids. The Department of Transportation then asked the National Research Council to review a technical study it had commissioned to assess the viability of producing a bus according to the Transbus specifications. The technical study and the NRC panel agreed that "The decisions of U.S. bus manufacturers not to bid were reasonable and understandable business judgments," and that "The Transbus mandate should be delayed until DOT has reexamined the options to achieve the Transbus goals."[8] On August 5, 1979, DOT indefinitely delayed the order to build Transbus.[9]

The "Transbus Group," the plaintiff coalition, devolved to its original local and national associations, which were working to obtain compliance with other transit regulations in their various localities or to fight changes in the federal regulations, to be discussed below, which aided the plaintiff groups in bringing accessible transportation to their communities. The idea of a low-floor, wide-door, ramped bus was shelved, but the redesign of more conventional buses to include lifts proceeded.

Conditions for Success

In these five cases, several variables besides client participation appear to contribute to the successful use of litigation as a political strategy. Handler's three variables—judicial remedy, the bureaucratic contingency, and cost-benefit distribution—provide a framework for discussing the findings, but it is necessary to adapt them to the circumstances of the transit cases, emphasizing especially the significance of public support, federal regulations, and absolute costs.

Judicial Remedies

The important questions concerning judicial remedies are (1) whether courts can be persuaded to act against agencies at all, (2) if so, whether they will take substantive rather than merely procedural actions which remand the decision to the original agency, and (3) how detailed a substantive order will be if one can get it. The conditions which are most conducive to getting a substantive judicial ruling are clear support from existing law and blatant resistance to it by the other side.

The 1970 Amendment to the Architectural Barriers Act so clearly applied the law to the D.C. subway system that the judge did not have difficulty rejecting the transit authority's arguments to the contrary. Furthermore, the transit authority had shown little or no interest in accommodating disabled persons in any way. As scholars have noted, "American courts *are* willing to substantially intervene in issues concerning the organization, timing, and magnitude of 'positive' government programs, provided that the statutory language is sufficiently specific and the state's deviation from those standards sufficiently great."[10] Courts are much less willing to act when the defendants demonstrate some efforts to comply with the law even if the efforts are inadequate or when the law is insufficiently specific.[11]

The type of judicial relief is still crucial, however. As with most of the law reform efforts Handler studies, normal judicial remedies are usually inadequate to solve the transportation problems of disabled people. Specifically, a preventive injunction can impair the functioning of existing transit, as it did with the Gallery Place station in Washington, D.C., or would have with the purchase of new inaccessible buses in the Minnesota and East Bay cases, had the plaintiffs prevailed, but it cannot directly provide accessible transportation. In Washington, however, the preventive injunction, which prohibited the Metro system from being opened to the public until elevators had been installed, was sufficient pressure to get transit officials to make it accessible.

The statutory language relied on in the bus lawsuits was much more vague than the Architectural Barriers Act amendment, so the judges were even more reluctant to issue regulatory or structural injunctions requiring affirmative steps to provide transportation. In fact, it was the promulgation of more detailed administrative regulations specifying the transit operators' obligations under the law which helped to persuade the Eighth Circuit Court of Appeals to find in favor of the plaintiffs, and then it was only a procedural ruling. The court of appeals ruled that the statute did create affirmative duties on the part of transit operators and gave the plaintiffs a private cause of action, remanding the case to the lower court for further findings.[12]

No court has been willing to make a substantive ruling requiring one type of service in the controversy between the regular-route and demand-responsive approaches. A constitutional ruling that separate-but-equal bus service is impermissible would settle that question, but such a ruling is highly unlikely in view of the Supreme Court's apparent hesitation to apply strict scrutiny standards of equal protection analysis to persons with disabilities.[13]

In the absence of strong law and of the degree of resistance it takes to get a judge to enforce it, the variable most conducive to the plaintiffs' achieving some success is a willingness on both sides to negotiate. Typically, plaintiffs initially propose a discussion of the issue with the defendants and are turned down or left unsatisfied before they ever go to court, as happened in the transit cases. In some instances, the seriousness established by going to court may then give the plaintiffs sufficient leverage that the defendants agree to talk, but as these cases have shown, the litigation may also have to be accompanied by ongoing pressure in several forums, such as the media and the political arena.

The Bureaucratic Contingency—Two Types of Technical Complexity

A major barrier to success in the transit cases was the technical complexity of the issue, which Handler includes as part of his bureaucratic contingency variable.[14] Handler considers issues to be technically complex if their resolutions require actions which extend over a considerable period of time, making a one-time, at-the-top decision difficult. But the accessible bus problem was technically complex in a different way. During the Seventies, there was debate about whether building a bus that was both accessible to wheelchairs and functional for daily, regular-route service was technically feasible at all.

Evidence that an agency's policy on accessibility is a top-down decision appears in the case studies. Plaintiffs in three of the cases—East Bay, D.C., and Minnesota—indicated that the personality of a particular official within the transit agency was a major stumbling block to achieving an agreement. In the East Bay and D.C. cases, these individuals did leave their positions during the course of negotiations over the transit issue, and agreements were subsequently reached. According to the plaintiffs, the different attitude of the new official was largely responsible.

Once buses are brought, there is little discretion in whether or not they will be used, because transit agencies do not generally have so many buses that they can choose not to use some of them. A city's bus fleet is not usually replaced in one purchase, however, so that disabled activists might need to watch that a city would not resume buying inaccessible buses after it once bought accessible ones; but the number of such occasions to monitor would be few. The advantage of the approach of the Transbus case, of course, was that getting the federal government to agree to provide its eighty percent funding only for accessible buses would virtually ensure that local transit operators would purchase only that kind.

The absence of frequent, discretionary decisions was also an advantage cited by the supporters of accessible regular-route buses over demand-responsive special service. The latter would have an operating budget separate from the major transit budget and could therefore be an easy target for budget cutters during annual appropriations debates.

The technical problem in the nonbureaucratic sense of designing and building a fully accessible bus suitable for use on regular routes has many facets, which go beyond the scope of this study. The greatest debate was over the feasibility of a low-floor, ramped bus in accord with the Transbus specifications. Supporters and opponents both lined up engineers who believed the bus could or could not be built, and the opponents apparently had the last word.

Short of a wholly redesigned bus, the possibility of "retrofitting" existing buses to accept wheelchairs was also debated. The relative desirability of access by ramp or lift was at times a subject of contention. Technical problems were an issue in the D.C. subway case for awhile, too, with a debate over whether vertical or inclined elevators would be preferable. Although some plaintiffs believed that at times technology was a convenient cover for other reasons for resistance, such as a lack of guaranteed profits or sheer fear of integrating people with disabilities, the technical issue was influential in the lawsuits. The unavailability of appropriate technology was noted by the courts in both the Marin County and East Bay (state) cases in denying the plaintiffs' motions for injunctive relief.

Over time, the technology issue proved to be less insurmountable than the transit industry originally argued. Although the wholly redesigned Transbus was stymied, both General Motors and Grumman Flxible Corporation, the two American manufacturers of full-sized buses, were able to develop wheelchair lift options for their standard buses which met most of the expectations of disabled riders. One complaint was that the lifts are at the rear door, but most disabled people seemed ready to accept that as a lot better than nothing. The incentive of the transit regulations to be discussed below created a market for such a lift, and it was purchased in many cities, including Washington, D.C., St. Paul/Minneapolis, and Oakland.

While the narrow but crucial technological question of the feasibility of a functioning accessible bus is well on its way to being solved, there still remain some technical problems, more broadly defined, in achieving accessible bus systems. Particularly in the interim period before all the buses in an area are accessible, there are problems in making a system that is only partially accessible usable by disabled riders, such as making sure that accessible buses on one line coordinate with accessible buses on other lines at transfer points, minimizing the time needed to board disabled passengers, making bus stops free of barriers, and training drivers to operate the new lifts.

These kinds of problems do mean that a lot of discretion remains in the hands of the transit agencies, reducing the favorableness of the bureaucratic contingency factor of success, in Handler's terms, but the problems do not seem crucial. Among the plaintiff groups, those which established good cooperative working relationships with the transit agencies felt these factors to be much less important than the groups did which still had a mainly adversarial relationship with the transit agency.

Cost-Benefit Distribution

The resolution of these remaining problems hinges largely on costs. According to Handler, the most important issue is the relative concentration or distribution of the costs and benefits, with concentrated costs and distributed benefits the most difficult situation to overcome. The accessible transit issue, however, demonstrates that the cost-benefit distribution may be less objective and more subjective than Handler expects and that absolute costs may be just as or more important than the relative distribution.

How one analyzes the transit issue in these terms differs dramatically depending on one's point of view. As the plaintiffs presented the issue, the costs are concentrated on the transit industry, which explains the great resistance of bus manufacturers and transit operators to providing accessible service, and the benefits are distributed. Plaintiffs argued that accessible transit would mean better service for all transit customers and would not benefit only people completely excluded from buses now. On the other hand, as the defendants presented the issue, the costs are distributed (higher taxes for all) and the benefits concentrated on a very few people with disabilities, mostly persons in wheelchairs.

The defendants were right that ultimately the costs are distributed to taxpayers, of course, but this is true of all public programs. One can hardly attribute the defendants' resistance solely to altruism on behalf of the taxpayer. This is especially true for local transit operators because the federal government paid for eighty percent of the cost of buses, so that the tax burden was not even concentrated on local resources. Handler suggests one general explanation for bureaucratic resistance to changes in public programs. Agencies "want to carry out their programs without interference from outsiders. When ordered to do otherwise, an agency will often do the absolute minimum needed to comply with the letter of the order."[15]

The specific problem in the accessible transit issue is that transit operators perceived the requirement to provide transportation for people with mobility handicaps to be a major change in the service expected of them. They perceived it as a social service rather than as part of their usual responsibilities for providing transportation in urban areas. In the words of a top staff member of the American Public Transit Association, the principal industry organization:

> The original language of Section 16 was interpreted by both DOT and HEW to require special efforts to provide elderly and handicapped persons mass transportation service which they could effectively use. This was a new public policy, and it added a new and very different dimension to transit's efforts to widen its attractiveness to the general public! This new dimension is a social service objective which was little understood by transit managers. It necessitated a new process of resource allocation, requiring measurement of "need" for social services—something transit operators were not staffed to do![16]

The disabled consumers were aware of the transit operators' attitude and condemned it. Participants in at least two of the lawsuits complained about the tendency of operators to treat their transportation needs as "social work." According to the staff member of a national disability organization:

> [Transit operators] are the least forward-looking segment of service deliverers in this country, I would say. They lack imagination; they lack any sense of planning for the future; they lack innovation, and they're extremely political. All they really care about are the economics of it, and they aren't really looking to providing quality service to the people they ostensibly serve.

Another source of resistance to accessible transit has been the bus manufacturers. One might assume that bus manufacturers would support mandated changes in bus design or equipment because a change would create a demand for new products from them. Designing a new, more accessible, bus and retooling to manufacture it, however, require considerable investment capital and a long lead time. On the other hand, the federal government had funded research and development of a Transbus prototype in the early Seventies, so the manufacturers were not left to support the technological development entirely alone.

The problem, as the plaintiffs saw it, was that General Motors, the biggest by far of the few manufacturers of full-sized buses in this country, had developed an interim "advanced design" bus, which offered several new features to make it more convenient for passengers with mild physical disabilities but was not a low-floor model easily accessible to persons in wheelchairs. Since GM had had this model available only a short time, it would not have had sufficient sales to recover the development and retooling costs of this model if a Transbus design were required after September 1979, as was announced in Adams' original mandate. For this reason, the disabled groups allege, General Motors led the lobbying in Congress to delay Adams' order. There is little question that the bus manufacturers, like the transit operators, acted as if they were the targets of concentrated costs of a policy decision.

Similarly, the vigorous efforts of the disabled groups were characteristic of the recipients of concentrated benefits, despite their arguments that the benefits would be distributed. While it would be hard to deny that people presently excluded completely from buses would benefit relatively more, the Transbus advocates, in particular, emphasized repeatedly the benefits of a low-floor, wide-door model to many others, such as parents pushing strollers and shoppers burdened with packages.

Another argument of the disabled plaintiffs that the benefits of accessible transportation would be widely distributed was that every person might someday be the victim of a disabling accident or illness. Thus, accessible transportation should be seen as a form of social insurance for everyone, and the costs of accessibility should be viewed per capita for the region's whole population, not just for the present disabled population. Disabled persons occasionally drove this point home by referring only half-facetiously to nondisabled persons as "T.A.B.s," meaning the "temporarily able-bodied."

Public Support

The arguments emphasizing the large number of beneficiaries and potential beneficiaries of accessible transit were intended to increase public support for the issue. In general, the disabled plaintiffs believed that public support was very important for their success. Studies of other social reform efforts confirm that a generally supportive political climate and explicit support from influential allies outside the social movement itself are critical.[17] Especially if one is conducting a multi-strategy campaign rather than relying solely on the courts and is attempting to force a public agency to negotiate, the appearance of public support for one's cause would certainly help. In fact, most of the major accomplishments of the transit suits occurred at a time of growing public awareness of and support for the rights of disabled people in 1977 and 1978. Public support varied considerably over time and from place to place, however.

The most supportive environment, not surprisingly, was in the San Francisco Bay area. Due in part to its mild climate, California has the highest proportion of disabled people in its population of any state, and the Bay Area is notably receptive to political movements of many kinds. One participant in the suits from the Center for Independent Living in Berkeley reported in 1978, "It seems as if we can do no wrong; anything we do, people think it's okay." When CIL members and others blocked the East Bay transit terminal during the Transbus protest, they got arrested for blocking the terminal only at the very end of the day, and then the district attorney dropped the charges. In the words of one participant:

> I think the absolute acid test of the support was the blocking of the buses at the East Bay terminal because that was something that we knew had tremendous potential to alienate passengers. And it did in fact inconvenience, whatever, 40,000 people or something. But for instance, Channel Five did interviews with people. . . who couldn't get home. Maybe three out of five were super sympathetic and one was medium and one was real pissed off. But people were saying things like "Well, of course I'm inconvenienced, but it's an inconvenience for them every day of their lives and I think they should get what they're fighting for." I think that in general the political climate is one of extreme support from the community that came at the time of the 504 sit-in [the take-over of the HEW building in San Francisco in 1977 to protest the failure to sign the regulations for Section 504 of the Rehabilitation Act of 1973]. Support came from organizations as diverse as the American Legion and the Black Panther Party.

Not all of California was as supportive as the East Bay, however. At the time of the above remark, the president of the California Association of the Physically Handicapped, CIL's co-plaintiff in the federal suit, hailed from Southern California. He felt as if his area was less receptive and was already expressing some backlash reaction to accommodations made for disabled people.

Similarly, the plaintiffs in the Marin County suit experienced much less public support than did the East Bay plaintiffs. The Marin plaintiffs never engaged in any activities that tested public support as much as the terminal blocking demonstration did, but they were very disappointed in their inability to generate press attention for their lawsuit or to mobilize public financial or moral support in response to letters they sent out. Their lawyer attributed it to the atmosphere of Marin County:

> Marin County is strange. It's a place where really people have got an awful lot and there's not a whole lot of sympathy or recognition of problems like this in the county. . . . I mean they assume there's not a whole lot of poverty, there's not a whole lot of people who have serious needs and discrimination.

The Minnesota plaintiffs eventually generated considerable public support for their transportation goals. They obtained a large loan from a church group to pursue their lawsuit and endorsements from notable politicians of their drive for adequate legislative funding to implement the agreement they made with the Metropolitan Transit Commission. The puzzle expressed by some of them, however, was why they had had so much trouble with MTC in the first place in light of Minnesota's generally liberal political environment.

I can't understand why the MTC has been so unwilling to really get into it and provide transit, when it is their clear public mandate—legal mandate—to do so. . . . In Minnesota where the environment is liberal and where there's a more of acceptance of, you know, "We really do need to help the minority group," I just don't understand where they are getting the energy to say, "No, we aren't going to do it."

The D.C. suit was the only one which experienced an obvious and dramatic shift in public support during its course. When the judge first issued the declaratory judgment in favor of the plaintiffs in 1973, the *Washington Post* published two editorials which were generally supportive, though calling for "realism" from both sides.[18] The paper also published a column by Senator Charles Percy, totally supporting the right of disabled persons to ride the subway and rejecting the notion of separate-but-equal transportation.[19]

As measured by such editorial opinion, public support turned against the disabled plaintiffs, however, when two years later the judge ordered one station to remain closed because no elevator had been installed while the rest of the system completed at that time opened. When the merchants in the area of the closed station joined with the transit authority to obtain a waiver of the elevator requirement from the General Services Administration, a *Post* editorial supported them.[20] The lawyers in this case and the principal active plaintiff believe that this shift in public opinion influenced the Washington Urban League to withdraw as plaintiffs. With the station functioning, however, the public soon forgot the continuing legal struggle over the interpretation of ready access, which went on for another three years before final settlement, and public opinion played little further role in the events, judging from the lack of press coverage and comment.

The role of public opinion in the national level Transbus suit appeared primarily in the change that occurred when the Democratic Carter administration took over the Department of Transportation from the Republican Ford administration. The Ford administration's decision to shelve the Transbus project, which precipitated the lawsuit, was reopened by the Carter administration. The more liberal public opinion that the Democrats presumably represented may have indirectly led to a new secretary of transportation who was more receptive to the testimony by members of the Transbus coalition at the hearings called to review the project and more responsive to the pressure of the lawsuit.

As national public support for accessible public transportation grew, it eventually manifested itself in the form of federal regulations favorable to the goals of the disabled plaintiffs, no doubt one of the strongest "allies" a group can have. The difficult struggles to obtain such regulations have been recounted earlier, but once passed, the regulations were important influences at two different points in the disability groups' efforts.

The first two bus cases, Marin County and Minnesota, were filed during the long period before any regulations implementing the original 1970 amendments to the Urban Mass Transportation Act had been written. This is one of the reasons why the Marin County case was brought under California state law and the plaintiffs never chose to go into federal court. When these regulations were finally promulgated in 1976, even though they were still quite vague, they led to the pivotal Eighth Circuit court decision for the Minnesota plaintiffs and later provided the leverage for the East Bay plaintiffs to use against the local transit agency in their federal suit. It was the regulations' vagueness, however, that prompted the Transbus plaintiffs to go to court to try to force a more definitive federal policy.

The second major step in federal regulations developed separately from but parallel to these plaintiffs' litigation. The nationwide protests of disabled persons in the spring of 1977 persuaded the Department of Health, Education and Welfare to sign the regulations implementing Section 504 of the Rehabilitation Act of 1973, the so-called Civil Rights Act of the disabled.[21] These HEW regulations then became the guidelines to be followed by all other Federal agencies in writing regulations to implement Section 504 vis-à-vis their respective activities. The Department of Transportation's 504 regulations went into effect on July 2, 1979, shortly after the last of these five lawsuits was settled.[22] Some of the plaintiff groups had participated in the rule-making process.

These regulations provided that new public buses for which bid solicitations were issued after July 2, 1979, must be accessible to all persons, including wheelchair users. Within three years, fixed-route bus systems must achieve "program accessibility," defined as having at least half of the peak-hour bus service accessible with accessible vehicles used before non-accessible vehicles during non-peak hours. There was also a provision for extending the time limit for achieving accessibility to ten years where extraordinary structural changes or vehicle replacement required. Transit agencies were also required to have "adequate citizen participation mechanisms or procedures," which provided means for the clients in several of the groups to maintain some supervision of the activities of the transit operators.[23] These regulations created the market demand for accessible buses, inducing both American manufacturers to produce full-sized buses equipped with lifts.

Since the 504 regulations went into effect shortly after the plaintiffs in the Minnesota and East Bay suits settled their cases, it is admittedly difficult to separate the credit due the regulations and the lawsuits for progress made in the next two years. The regulations were short-lived, however, and the disabled groups were soon thrown back on their own local resources to ensure their gains.

The regulations were especially controversial because they mandated mainline, regular-route accessibility rather than demand-responsive, door-to-door service. A bill giving cities "local option" over how they provide transportation service for disabled riders rather than requiring compliance with the 504 regulations was defeated during 1980, but similar legislation was reintroduced the next year in the new, more conservative Congress.[24] Also, newly-elected Vice President Bush specifically included the 504 transit regulations among the targets of his task force assigned to review costly or unnecessary federal regulations. According to Bush, the regulations "arguably don't serve the handicapped all that well and do raise costs significantly for providing transit services."[25]

Furthermore, the regulations were the target of a lawsuit by the American Public Transit Association and several metropolitan transit operators.[26] Citing *Southeastern Community College v. Davis*,[27] they claimed that the Department of Transportation's 504 regulations exceeded the department's authority and went beyond the intent of Congress. Although the *Davis* case had nothing to do with transportation, it was the U.S. Supreme Court's first full opinion on a claim by a disabled individual under Section 504. The court had ruled that Section 504 did not require the college to take affirmative action to make its nursing program accessible to Ms. Davis, who had a hearing impairment.

The suit failed at the district court level, but the court of appeals of the District of Columbia Circuit overturned the lower court in favor of the transit interests.[28] Shortly thereafter, Drew Lewis, the Reagan administration's transportation secretary, who was sympathetic to the court's ruling, suspended the Section 504 rules and instituted interim rules similar to those in effect between 1976 and 1979.[29] The ramifications of the situation were not immediately apparent, but it clearly was a major blow to the disability rights movement.

Although the court's ruling was officially based on its finding that the department had exceeded its authority, it is tempting to speculate whether growing public concern about the costs of accessibility had some influence. Despite the efforts of the disabled activists to present accessibility as having widely distributed benefits, the considerable public support they had gained seems to have been based more on altruism than on enlightened self-interest. Accessible transit was and is still largely perceived as a distributed cost and a concentrated benefit. In Handler's analysis this should be a configuration advantageous for the disabled persons. The problem, however, is the tremendous absolute costs. During the height of the Transbus battle, manufacturers' estimates of the cost of a low-floor, wide-door, ramped design ranged from $125,000 to $250,000 per bus, compared to a cost of about $90,000 for the leading non-accessible bus.[30] In a highly controversial study issued after the Department of Transportation's regulations for implementing Section 504 came out in May 1979, the Congressional Budget Office estimated the cost of implementing the regulations at seven billion dollars nationwide.[31]

Since the public has been made more aware of the high costs of accessibility by its opponents and since it never really accepted the disabled advocates' arguments about distributed benefits or social insurance, support has declined.[32] Indeed, public support for the aims of the disability rights movement seems inversely related to public awareness of the actual costs of accessibility. Observers of the black civil rights movement have noted a similar pattern. Scheingold comments:

> Many of those who had been attracted to the civil rights movement or neutralized by its uncertain implications joined the opposition as the costs of change manifested themselves in affirmative action hiring, fair housing plans, school busing, civil disorder, and so forth.[33]

The argument that "rights are rights regardless of cost" has not borne up well against figures, such as those from the Congressional Budget Office study to the effect that making the nation's public transit accessible would cost $400,000 for each new rider who would gain access to it.[34]

Conclusion

In sum, successful use of litigation as a political strategy is aided first, of course, by strong law in one's favor and blatant resistance to it. In the absence of that, active clients may be able to bring about negotiations with the defendants, if necessary by the use of pressure in multiple forums. Successful negotiations and compliance with an agreement over the long term will be more likely if the costs are moderate, if the public supports the plaintiffs' goals, if individual personalities do not create unusual difficulties, and if there are not insurmountable technical barriers.

As the Seventies came to an end, the public at large was becoming more and more concerned about the economy generally and convinced of the need for public budget cutting. Disability rights groups faced an uphill struggle not just to expand, but even to preserve the gains they made toward accessible public transportation during the Seventies. It is ironic that the courts, which disabled groups used with considerable success to pressure local transit agencies, were eventually the same institution that stripped them of their most valuable ally to date, the Section 504 transportation regulations. At the start of the Eighties, the groups were left without this source of national support in their efforts to ensure the implementation of the settlements and consent agreements they had negotiated as a result of their lawsuits. The coming years will be a strong test of the hypothesis that active client participation in litigation decision making can encourage client groups to persevere in pursuing their interests.

Notes

1. Handler, *Social Movements and the Legal System.*
2. Ibid., pp. 24–25.
3. Ibid., pp. 19–22. This point is also made by Jeffrey Pressman and Aaron Wildavsky, *Implementation: How Great Expectations in Washington Are Dashed in Oakland; Or, Why It's Amazing that Federal Programs Work at All, This Being a Saga of the Economic Development Administration as Told by Two Sympathetic Observers Who Seek to Build Morals on a Foundation of Ruined Hopes* (Berkeley: University of California Press, 1973).
4. Handler, *Social Movements and the Legal System,* pp. 17–18.
5. Ibid., p. 214.
6. Scheingold, *Politics of Rights,* pt. 1.
7. Doug Killian, "Handicapped, MTC Still at Odds," *Minnesota Daily,* 3 April 1981, p. 9.
8. Commission on Sociotechnical Systems, National Research Council, *NRC Transbus Study* (Washington, D.C.: National Academy of Sciences, 1979), p. 3.
9. Helen Meier, *Accessible Public Transit: A History and Overview of Accessible Transit Provision in the United States* (San Francisco: United Cerebral Palsy Association of San Francisco, 1981), p. 23.
10. Peterson, *Legal Challenges to Bureaucratic Discretion,* p. 44. See also Handler, *Social Movements and the Legal System,* p. 197.
11. Peterson, *Legal Challenges to Bureaucratic Discretion,* p. 22. A recent example of the Supreme Court's unwilingness to enforce vigorously an arguably ambiguous law is *Pennhurst State School and Hospital v. Halderman,* 451 U.S. 1 (1981). In this case the Court ruled that the Developmentally Disabled Assistance and Bill of Rights Act "does no more than express a congressional preference for certain kinds of treatment," at 19, and that "Congress intended to encourage, rather than mandate, the provision of better services to the developmentally disabled," at 20. For a discussion of the ramifications of the *Pennhurst* decision for the disability rights movement, see Judith A. Baer, "The Burger Court and the Rights of the Handicapped," paper presented at the annual meeting of the American Political Science Association, New York, 1981, especially pp. 14–22.
12. *United Handicapped Federation v. Andre,* 558 F. 2d 413 (8th Cir. 1977).
13. The Supreme Court stated in *dicta* in *Frontiero v. Richardson,* 411 U.S. 677, (1973): "And what differentiates sex from such non-suspect statutes as intelligence or physical disability, and aligns it with the recognized suspect criteria, is that the sex characteristic frequently bears no relation to ability to perform or contribute to society" (p. 686). For arguments that disabled persons should be considered a "suspect class," see Burgdorf and Burgdorf, "A History of Unequal Treatment," and Baer, "The Burger Court and the Rights of the Handicapped."
14. Handler, *Social Movements and the Legal System,* p. 19.

15. Ibid., p. 23.

16. Stanley G. Feinsod, "Perspectives on Barrier-Free Transit Policy," speech presented at the Annual Meeting of the American Public Transit Association, Atlanta, Ga., 1977 (mimeograph), pp. 1–2.

17. Craig Jenkins and Charles Perrow, "Insurgency of the Powerless: Farm Worker Movements (1946–72)," *American Sociological Review* 42 (1977): 249–68; Joyce Gelb and Alice Sardell, "Organizing the Poor: A Brief Analysis of the Politics of the Welfare Rights Movement," *Policy Studies Journal* 3 (1975): 346–54.

18. Editorial, "Metro and the Rights of the Handicapped," *Washington Post*, 14 July 1973, p. A18, and 17 August 1973, p. A24.

19. Charles H. Percy, "Serving the Handicapped," *Washington Post*, 17 August 1973, p. A25.

20. Editorial, ". . . And a Station Break," *Washington Post*, 16 December 1976, p. A18. See also, Richard Cohen, "Merchants at 9th and G Stood Up by Subway, *Washington Post*, 6 June, 1976, p. B1.

21. U.S., *Code of Federal Regulations*, vol. 45, secs. 84.1–84.61 (1980).

22. Ibid., vol. 49, secs. 27.1–27.129 (1980).

23. Ibid., sec. 27.101(b).

24. U.S., Congress, House, H.R. 2553, 97th Cong., 1st sess., 1981.

25. Quoted in "Bush: Handicapped Transit Rules are Among 'Most Burdensome' Requirements," *Handicapped Americans Reports*, 26 Feburary 1981, p. 7.

26. *American Public Transit Association v. Lewis* (originally *APTA v. Goldschmidt*), reported in Jack Eisen, "Transit Group Files Suit to Block Rules on Handicapped," *Washington Post*, 30 June 1979, p. A8.

27. 442 U.S. 397 (1979).

28. *APTA v. Lewis*, 655 F. 2d 1272 (D.C. Cir. 1981).

29. "DOT Rules Let Localities Decide on Transit Services for Disabled," *Handicapped Americans Reports*, 30 July 1981, p. 3.

30. Young, "Transbus Compromise," p. 14, and Hackney, "Elderly, Disabled See Transbus as Last Hope," pp. 18 and 19.

31. U.S., Congress, Congressional Budget Office, *Urban Transportation for Handicapped Persons: Alternative Federal Approaches* (1979).

32. See, for example, Timothy B. Clark, "Regulation Gone Amok: How Many Billions for Wheelchair Transit?" *Regulation*, March/April, 1980, pp. 47–52; Norman Macrae, "Wheelchairs Run Amok," *The Economist*, 27 December 1980, p. 23; David L. Andelman, "M.T.A. Rejects Laws That Require Gear to Aid Handicapped," *New York Times*, 20 September 1980, p. 1; David Berreby, "Rights for Handicapped: A Narrowing Legal Path?" *The National Law Journal*, 29 June 1981, p. 7.

33. Scheingold, *Politics of Rights*, p. 146.

34. Congressional Budget Office, *Urban Transportation for Handicapped Persons*. On the other hand, Dennis Cannon and Frances Rainbow, *Full Mobility: Counting the Costs of the Alternatives* (Washington, D.C.: American Coalition of Citizens with Disabilities, 1980), p. xi, argue that the CBO study "grossly underestimated" the cost of specialized service in contrast to mainline service by studying specialized service that was not truly equivalent to regular bus service in terms

of number of trips available and hours of service. They also charge that the report overestimated the cost of fixed-route service by underestimating its potential ridership. A good analysis of the debate over relative costs of paratransit versus fixed-route service appears in Meier, *Accessible Public Transit*.

Chapter 9

Beyond the Disability Rights Movement

The considerations influencing success discussed in chapter 8 are likely to be important for any issue and any advocacy or social reform group. Obviously, however, some factors play a larger role in some movements than others. A case study of one movement, like this book, is limited in the extent it can generalize about the applicability of its findings to other groups and movements, even when variations within the movement are studied, as with the five cases here.

Nevertheless, some attempt to generalize is desirable. This chapter discusses the distinguishing characteristics of the disability rights movement and an important characteristic it shares with other contemporary social movements to see how these affected its ability to adopt the new style of social reform litigation. Then, a more detailed examination of one other movement, the women's movement, reveals that it shares enough characteristics with the disability rights movement to suggest that it could feasibly adopt a decentralized, remedy-oriented, client-centered litigation strategy for at least some issues.

Is the Disability Rights Movement Unique?

Two features immediately appear to differentiate the disability rights movement from other similar movements: costs and inherent public sympathy. The former may indeed be unique, but it should make success more difficult, if anything. The impact of the latter may well be deceptive.

Because of the need for changes in the physical environment, the cost issue looms much larger in the civil rights claims of disabled persons than it does for other groups suffering discrimination. In theory, all that is needed to end most discrimination on the basis of race or sex is simply to cease discriminating (ignoring for the moment claims for compensation for past discrimination and the relatively few situations where duplicate facilities for each sex are required, as in some sports). Ending discrimination against persons with disabilities, on the other hand, often requires physical accommodations which do cost money.

There is little question that disabled activists have faced less *overt* resistance to their claims and certainly less violence directed against them than have blacks in their civil rights movement or anti-Vietnam War demonstrators, for example. Especially early in their organized political movement, disabled demonstrators experienced a kind of immunity which reflected the great ambivalence able-bodied persons have felt toward disabled persons. The account of a participant in one of the country's earliest obstructive demonstrations by disabled people in 1972 makes this point.

> When I was involved in demonstrations in New York and we shut down Times Square and Madison Avenue two days within a four day period at peak rush hour, they did not touch us. I mean they would not, you know. Forty-five minutes we sat on Madison and Second four days before the election outside of Nixon headquarters, and totally paralyzed the city....In any other group the cops would have come in swinging. Didn't touch us. In those demonstrations where nondisabled people were visible, the cops would go after the nondisabled people, so clearly it's a guilt thing. It's this whole thing with "Here, you've got these cripples, who you give your dimes to, and if we do anything to them, the public is going to be against us, because we're hurting them."...You know, you can hit an antiwar person because they're against the country, but I think it's because nondisabled people don't view us as equals, so it's very bizarre.

Since changing people's attitudes away from the idea that people with disabilities are helpless children who need to be taken care of is such an important part of the disability rights movement, another activist could say sincerely: "The fact that we're getting opposition means that we're meeting with some success." The cost issue is certainly bringing out some opposition, and disabled persons see it as crucial in distinguishing their friends from their adversaries. The same activist continued: "Of course, everybody's for a cripple....Everybody wants disabled people to be able to have what they deserve except if it's going to cost money."

The most militant believe that the cost issue is largely a front for a deeper psychological resistance to integration with people with disabilities.

> [Opposition] is really coming to the surface, and I think that's really far out. Because I think it's going to make the movement become a lot stronger once

we can make disabled people see that all of their niceness, and all of their sweetness, and all of the ass-kissing that's gone on has been in vain. And that the legislators and your local churches, your local charities, really don't want us to be integrated. They're afraid. Money is one issue, but I think it gets to the fact that nondisabled people don't want to see us. We're a real threat to them because they could become like us. And I think it's all of those things, separate transportation systems, all of that.

If such attitudes truly underlie the initial sympathy typically shown the disability rights movement, then it is very unlikely that sympathy would be a significant counterweight to the large costs involved in ending discrimination against disabled persons. That the disabled plaintiffs were able to accomplish what they did, considering the added liability of the costs, is particularly striking and bodes well for the adoption of similar strategies by other groups. In other words, if other groups, which are not burdened with the large costs that burden disabled persons in their quest for equality, adopt some of the same strategies, their chances of success should be quite good.

The observations in this book about the feasibility of a decentralized, remedy-oriented, client-centered approach to social reform litigation are not necessarily limited to persons with disabilities or to the disability rights movement. In particular, I hypothesize that the findings are adaptable to other identity-based social movements, such as women, ethnic and racial groups, homosexuals, and perhaps elderly persons.[1] Such social movements are based on a principal facet of a person's identity which individuals find difficult to subordinate to—or are not allowed by others to subordinate to—other aspects of their personality or social role.

These characteristics are not only central to the individuals' identity, but they also tend to be devalued, or in Goffman's term, stigmatized by society as a whole. This generalization is obviously oversimplified, as images of the esteemed elder or the woman on the pedestal illustrate, but these groups live in a society that is in most ways politically and socially dominated by heterosexual white males. Women are perhaps the group most parallel to persons with disabilities because the oppression of both has mainly taken the form of paternalism more than overt opposition. Breaking out of a pattern of paternalism may create a need for autonomy for its own sake, to prove that one is capable of taking care of oneself.

For persons in this situation, the opportunity to participate in a group with both substantive goals and organizational processes oriented to reinforcing the sense of autonomy can be very attractive. Such groups may be able to attract and hold members in support of collective goods better than a group with goals that are not so intimately related to its members' personal identities.[2] In short, the opportunity to participate may be a more effective selective incentive in some groups than others.

This is not the only similarity between the women's movement and the disability rights movement, however. They are also products of the same political era; there are similarities in the structural characteristics of the organized movements; some issues are equally amenable to decentralized resolution, and the participants have certain characteristics in common. The remainder of this chapter will compare these two movements in an effort to generalize the observations about litigation strategy in the transit access cases to another social reform group.

Litigation Strategies of Women's Groups

Accounts of litigation by women's groups focusing on the clients' role are virtually nonexistent, so I do not know if such remedy-oriented, client-centered litigation has occurred in fact. What has been written tends to focus on traditional lawyer-dominated, precedent-oriented litigation. For example, Karen O'Connor's *Women's Organizations' Use of the Courts* describes recent litigation activities only from the perspective of national organizations and the lawyers who largely compose them, but her accounts of past historical periods suggest other possibilities.[3]

O'Connor recognizes the litigation of the National Women's Suffrage Association in the 1870s as publicity-oriented litigation rather than outcome-oriented litigation (O'Connor's equivalent of precedent-oriented litigation). The litigation was accompanied by innumerable speeches delivered and pamphlets distributed. And certainly the indomitable Susan B. Anthony was an extraordinary example of an active client vis-à-vis her lawyer, Henry Selden, although he did undermine part of Anthony's strategy by bailing her out of jail when she preferred to remain for the sake of publicity.[4]

In another vein, the sponsorship by the National Consumers' League of litigation defending protective legislation for women in the first third of the twentieth century revealed a group of women recruiting a lawyer and doing the bulk of the research for lawsuits in pursuit of their policy goals.[5] That the upper-class women who belonged to the NCL were not the personal beneficiaries of the litigation makes them somewhat different from the disabled clients in the transit litigation, however, and more like social reform lawyers. The working-class women who were the beneficiaries of the laws were not parties to the litigation because the suits were challenges to existing laws brought by disgruntled employers against the states.

One rare client-focused account of a recent women's rights lawsuit demonstrates the pattern noted by Sorauf in some church–state litigation of clients' initiating the lawsuit but largely withdrawing after the lawyer becomes involved.[6] A *Ms.* magazine story of a class action employment discrimination suit against Chase Manhattan Bank shows the women actively recruiting supporters, interviewing lawyers, organizing financial support, collecting necessary data, and debating strategy. For the last year or more that the story follows the suit, however, the client role sharply diminishes:

> Since the filing of the federal court papers in January, 1976, the burden of the suit has shifted from the group onto [the lawyer's] shoulders. The group now averages one meeting every two months. Their active planning sessions have gradually evolved into more passive informational meetings to discuss legal developments in the suit, which has now been reduced to its essentials—legal motions, polite professional confabs among the opposing lawyers, and statistical analyses.[7]

A lawsuit itself inevitably involves some waiting for the court to act, of course, and this account is not sufficiently detailed to tell exactly how much the women's involvement continued. It leaves the impression once again, however, of a lawyer coming in and taking over from clients. The women's movement has enough similarities to the disability rights movement, though, that this pattern should not be any more necessary than it was in the transit cases.

The Political Context

In the first place the women's movement is a product of the same post-*Brown* era as the disability rights movement and thus would share the same political environment for social reform litigation. Indeed, both movements demonstrate the emergence of rights consciousness and were influenced by the civil rights, New Left, and antiwar movements.[8] The women's movement, even more than the disability rights movement, developed the institution or technique of consciousness-raising groups to translate personal problems into political problems.

Women litigating for their rights can also take advantage of new statutory and regulatory laws in their favor, though perhaps somewhat less so than disabled people. While women have had to concentrate more on removing overtly discriminatory legislation, such as the preference for male over female administrators of estates struck down in the Supreme Court's first modern women's rights case, *Reed v. Reed*,[9] there has been more affirmative legislation to meet the special needs of disabled people for physical access, such as the Architectural Barriers Act of 1968 and the various transportation laws discussed in chapter 3. Both groups have benefited from civil rights legislation outlawing discrimination in employment, federal programs, and so forth, which are enforced by a variety of administrative agencies and regulations on local, state, and federal levels.

The development of greater access to the courts for groups would apply to all bona fide groups, of course. The women's movement also has some problems of representation similar to those the disability rights movement faces in that women also are a large dispersed group with many crosscutting loyalties. It is not surprising that one sees women trying to appeal to the courts by stacking groups of ideologically diverse participants just as disabled litigants have done.[10]

Characteristics of the Movement

In addition to the women's movement's sharing the same litigational environment, the movement as a whole has some structural characteristics similar to those of the disability rights movement. First, certain political developments helped to galvanize the movements. State Commissions on the Status of Women served as did the President's and governors' Commissions on Employment of the Handicapped to bring together disabled leaders.[11] Similarly, the efforts for passage of the Equal Rights Amendment created a network among women's groups—equivalent to the effect on disability groups of the struggle to get regulations promulgated for Section 504 of the Rehabilitation Act of 1973.

A second similarity, one very important to this study, is that the women's movement also has a participatory ideology, which ought to help women's groups persist despite the centrifugal free rider tendency created by the largely collective goods sought by both movements. Joyce Gelb and Marian Lief Palley note the importance of what they call "in-process" benefits in the women's movement, citing Allen Buchanan: "This notion of 'in-process' benefits helps explain the nature of participation in feminist interest groups. 'The individual will gain certain benefits from the process of participation itself, regardless of the outcome of the process... [and] these in-process benefits will outweigh [the] costs of contribution.' "[12]

Participatory ideology and consciousness-raising groups notwithstanding, the organized feminist movement has a predominance of leadership groups over mass membership groups.[13] This is reminiscent of the emphasis of the American Coalition of Citizens with Disabilities on national issue lobbying more than grassroots development. Both movements have the potential for politicizing a vast network of traditional voluntary groups. This has occurred to some extent, as with the litigation by the San Raphael Indoor Sports Club and the involvement in Equal Rights Amendment lobbying and *amicus curiae* participation in two lawsuits by the National Federation of Business and Professional Women.[14]

The women's movement recognizes that grassroots involvement is important in a variety of tactics, which should encourage it to continue to expand local participation. Feminist leaders acknowledge "the importance of constituency-based groups" and that "the absence of such mass organizations significantly weakens efforts to influence policy at every level of the political process."[15] Specifically, constituency pressure is an important backup to other strategies, such as professional lobbying.[16] Even in Supreme Court-oriented litigation O'Connor notes the importance of local affiliates for litigating groups to notify national leaders of potentially good test cases and keep them abreast of current issues.[17] Gelb and Palley recognize a role for grassroots members that is remarkably like that played by the disabled client groups. "It is undeniable that as laws and their regulations reach the stage of implementation in issue areas such as education, grassroots efforts provide the information on compliance or noncompliance as well as the general feedback necessary to determine to what extent the laws are effective."[18]

Another similarity between the women's movement and the disability rights movement is that their goals are largely assimilationist or, in the words of Gelb and Palley, "gaining equal rights within existing society rather than creating a new society based on new values."[19] As a result some legislation favorable to women or disabled people seemed so logical or appropriate that it passed initially without pressure from the organized beneficiaries or much public notice. Opposition arose only later. This pattern occurred with the statutes calling for public transportation accessible to handicapped and elderly people and also with Title IX of the Education Amendments of 1972, which outlawed sex discrimination in education. In both instances the big battle has come in fending off opposition to the existing legislation and getting regulations passed that would "put teeth" into the laws.[20]

As the groups have faced opposition, both have had internal conflicts about appropriate strategy. The debate within the disabled movement during the congressional examination of the Transbus mandate about the relative desirability of obstructive protests or supportive demonstrations is mirrored in the debate among pro-choice advocates on the abortion issue about whether to adopt the more emotional appeals used by their opponents (e.g., pictures of women dead from self-induced abortions to counter pictures of aborted fetuses) or to continue with more moderate, traditional political techniques.[21]

There are similarities between the two movements as well in the characteristics that have been conducive to their success. Gelb and Palley note the women's willingness to compromise. They were successful when they "showed themselves ready to accept less than total victory."[22] This is very reminiscent of the successes attained by the disabled plaintiffs in the East Bay, Minnesota, and D.C. cases. Choosing a narrow issue that did not divide potential supporters was important in women's success on the equal credit and pregnancy disability issues.[23] Similarly, the issue of public transit was one on which both disabled persons themselves and parent or professional groups, such as National Easter Seal Society and United Cerebral Palsy Associations, could unite.

Despite these similarities between the women's and disability rights movements, there are also a couple of differences between them which might incline them to adopt dissimilar strategies. Both differences are rooted in the larger number of women than disabled persons.[24] In the first place, women may have less need for a litigation strategy at all because their numbers give them more strength at the polls and in the legislature. Indeed, Gelb and Palley note that feminist interests are better established in Congress and the bureaucracy than in the courts.[25]

Also because of their numbers, women have been able to use a divide-and-specialize strategy among different women's groups. Gelb and Palley consider the efficiency and expertise obtained from issue specialization to be an important factor in their success.[26] Not only the smaller numbers of disabled people, but also their need to minimize divisions along disability lines—the most likely way to divide the issues given historical patterns—makes this approach more difficult. The disability rights movement would have to find ways of specializing among issues that would not destroy the emphasis on cross-disability cooperation that is crucial for their numerical strength.

This problem suggests that it is not only the characteristics of the organized movement that affect the strategies chosen. The specific policy issues pursued also affect the choice. Even if a group decides to use the courts as its principal focus, some issues may be amenable to the style of litigation of the accessible transit cases and others more appropriate for traditional, precedent-oriented social reform litigation. An attempt to generalize about the characteristics of issues that make them amenable to decentralized, remedy-oriented litigation will suggest certain women's issues that might be thus suited.

Characteristics of the Issues

In the first place, remedy-oriented litigation works best with issues that can be negotiated, because it often ends in some degree of compromise. Previous chapters have argued that having a defendant yield without a court order to do so is as good as or better than winning in court. It is possible, of course, that the defendant might do so unilaterally, as the secretary of transportation did when he issued the Transbus mandate, but it is more likely that the resolution will require some willingness to compromise on both sides, as the other transit cases show. In contrast, an adjudicated decision is noted for its zero-sum quality.[27]

Material goods are likely to be more negotiable than symbolic goods. Symbolic goods are principles or values to which one has a strong emotional attachment, while material goods are tangible objects or services which one wants or needs. As Stuart Scheingold has noted: "By and large the emotional issues tend to be the most inelastic, since they are the most difficult to compromise. Whatever can be translated into dollars and cents can be subdivided and bargained."[28]

Any social reform issue is bound to have both symbolic and material implications, but some issues are more heavily one or the other. Racial segregation and church–state separation, early subjects of social reform litigation, are highly symbolic issues and were very appropriately directed toward a constitutional interpretation by the United States Supreme Court. By comparison, public transportation for people with disabilities is a very tangible issue and more suitable for remedy-oriented litigation. It does have its symbolic aspects, of course, precisely at the point of its greatest similarity to the issue of racial segregation—i.e., the debate over whether specialized, demand-responsive service is unacceptable separate-but-equal treatment.

Emphasis on either symbolic or tangible aspects will influence the choice of litigation strategy. The Transbus plaintiffs, with their focus on a newly designed bus for regular-route service, were the most ideologically committed against separate-but-equal, and they were occasionally critical of other groups of plaintiffs who were less insistent about the type of service provided. The Minnesota plaintiffs, in contrast, felt they had gotten the best of their opponents by suddenly shifting their strategy from insisting on regular-route accessibility to accepting the demand-responsive service the transit agency had argued was preferable. This made it possible to negotiate an agreement which provided for incremental increases in the number of people and the geographical areas served.

A number of the issues that the women's movement has pursued are very tangible, such as equal credit, pregnancy benefits, and equivalent athletic facilities and budgets. Notably, these three were initially obtained through legislative action, another strategy oriented toward negotiation and compromise. Other issues are much more heavily symbolic: preeminently, the Equal Rights Amendment. The struggle to amend the Constitution to outlaw sex discrimination has been necessary, in part, because the women's movement has been unable to persuade the Supreme Court through a precedent-oriented litigation campaign to extend to women the same degree of protection it has given racial minorities under the Equal Protection Clause.[29] If constitutional litigation is better suited for symbolic issues than remedy-oriented litigation, then constitutional amendments are even more the province of symbolic issues than constitutional litigation.

The greater divisibility of a material issue also makes it amenable to localized litigation instead of centrally coordinated litigation.[30] Constitutional litigation must ultimately aim to reach the United States Supreme Court and, at least in the hands of the NAACP, has involved careful coordination of suits in different areas. Remedy-oriented litigation, on the other hand, can often be conducted independently and locally.

When a particular public policy issue can be handled somewhat differently in different locales, without violating fundamental symbolic norms, it is amenable to decentralized litigation. Pregnancy disability benefits and athletic programs for women under Title IX do not inherently seem to require identical resolutions nationwide any more than modes of accessible public transit do. Market considerations in building accessible buses or underwriting disability insurance may require some uniformity, as the Transbus plaintiffs saw, but in these issues there is room for some local variation.

This suggests the last factor which makes use of remedy-oriented litigation more feasible. Once a principle has been established, its implementation may be more locally varied, especially if the subject matter is divisible and tangible. The transit access cases were much more rights-enforcing lawsuits than rights-establishing suits. The laws which established the right, at least in principle, of disabled people to accessible public transportation preceded the litigation.

Once again, Title IX would seem to be a women's issue with characteristics that would make it amenable to the basic approach used in the transit access cases. The legislation was passed without much organized support or opposition, conflicts arising first in the process of enforcing it. This permits supporters of the law to use rights-enforcing rhetoric and strategies which present claims as efforts to obtain only that which has already been granted as legitimate.

In fact, this strategy was used in regard to Title IX. The only recognition of use of litigation for leverage in the sense of using courts to get some (usually bureaucratic) defendant to do its job that appears in Gelb and Palley's study is a suit brought against the Department of Health, Education, and Welfare to get it to issue guidelines implementing Title IX. Gelb and Palley's description of this activity sounds exactly like the litigation approach of the disabled plaintiffs: "In addition to setting precedents, litigation is also used as a tool to prod the political process into action regarding enforcement, by establishing seriousness of purpose and credibility."[31]

A final observation about rights-enforcing versus rights-establishing litigation in the women's movement concerns the likely impact of the Equal Rights Amendment, had it survived the ratification process. The establishment once and for all of this fundamental principle nationwide would have facilitated the use of decentralized, remedy-oriented litigation in issues appropriate for differential localized treatment. As it is, women's efforts must continue to go heavily into rights-establishing litigation.

In sum, decentralized, remedy-oriented litigation is compatible with issues which are more material than symbolic and are divisible, localized and grounded in established law. No issue is likely to have all these characteristics unequivocally, however, and there are few local issues that cannot be aided by pressure from a central source, as the federal regulations helped in the transit issue.

Indicators of Client Participation

The last comparison to be made between the women's and the disability rights movements is in the likelihood of active client participation if a litigation strategy is chosen. The hypotheses in chapter 7 identifying conditions of client participation include a number which predict that women clients in remedy-oriented litigation might be expected to be quite active.

In the first place, even more than in the disability rights movement, there are many women involved who have high educational levels and socioeconomic status. In addition, Gelb and Palley characterize feminist activists on the national level as "predominantly attorneys."[32] The large number of women attorneys suggests a high "compatibility factor," the hypothesis that clients participate more when they share common characteristics with their lawyer. On the other hand, if most of the attorneys are women, this might (rightly or wrongly) diminish their sense of the importance of the client perspective and reinforce the belief that they know what is best for their clients.

Any such tendency in this direction might be tempered by the general participatory ideology of the women's movement. The norms of the women's and disability rights movements are very similar in their emphasis on resistance to paternalism, personal responsibility, independence, and assertiveness. For some women this has included a challenge to male gynecologists through the "women's health" movement that is parallel to disabled activists' challenge to doctors and rehabilitation professionals. To the extent that women clients and lawyers, either personally or as expressed formally by feminist law firms, share these values, they should contribute to client participation.

Furthermore, many grassroots women's organizations exist which give their members the kind of moral support, leadership experience, and opportunity to share work that we have found to be conducive to client participation. If long-standing moderate women's groups become politicized and undertake litigation, the number of potential clients with these supports for participation would be huge.

Just as the clients have great potential organizational support, the lawyers are not organized, at least not monolithically organized. Although a couple of the national feminist litigating groups are attempting to emulate the NAACP in developing a group of cooperating attorneys around the country, there is certainly no one group that has the central influence and control possessed by the NAACP in its heyday. The distribution of foundation funding, the presence of several strong personalities, and issue specialization among groups has kept any one group from dominating.[33] As a result, the hypothesis that strong ties among lawyers incline them to do more planning in consultation with each other rather than with their clients suggests another reason for potentially high client participation among women.

Finally, the prediction that clients will participate more if they perceive that such participation is valued by the decision makers they are trying to influence would also apply to women. Feminist leaders perceive that the "image of broad-based support" is important to their success.[34] Since women clients in a remedy-oriented, multi-strategy litigation effort might have the same perception, they would likely make the same assumption that the disabled clients did, that is, that judges, too, react positively to demonstrations of widespread support.

Conclusion

For these reasons, then, if decentralized groups of women do choose to undertake litigation as a strategy to achieve their goals, the chances are good of their becoming active clients and being able to pursue the style of litigation discovered among the disabled litigants. And as this book has argued, being an active client includes following up the outcome of the lawsuit; and it can lead to other political involvement.

Participation in the decisions involved in a lawsuit may be the missing link in the visions expressed by some poverty lawyers of litigation raising consciousness and creating a feeling of competence and efficacy in clients. If participation occurred at this level, then perhaps litigation would not create dependence on lawyers nor be incompatible with organizing, as some critics of litigation as a political strategy believe it to be.[35] In apolitical contexts, greater client participation might reduce complaints about lawyers and, according to Rosenthal, even improve tangible results for clients.

Treating client participation in litigation like any other form of participation in interest group activities, however, risks losing sight of the role of lawyers in litigation and their relation to clients. The beneficial effects on clients do not address the possible effects on lawyers of a changed lawyer–client relationship. To the extent that the emphasis on professional control in what Rosenthal calls the traditional model of lawyer–client relations cloaks a psychological need to dominate in persons who become lawyers, as some have argued, one can expect lawyers to oppose client participation at every turn.[36] Rosenthal argues, in contrast, that being relieved of impossible ideals of professional omniscience and the burden of full responsibility for solving people's problems can actually increase a lawyer's satisfaction.[37] At the least, lawyers presumably are as interested in successful outcomes as clients, so lawyer satisfaction may increase if client participation does promote successful lawsuits.

The study of client participation is important for lawyers and potential litigants, of course, but it also contributes to an understanding of the use of litigation as a political strategy in our democratic system. If litigation is a form of political participation at all, it typically has been in the tradition of representative democracy. Increased client participation would make it more a form of direct democracy rather than social engineering by experts.

Notes

1. The reservation about including the elderly is simply uncertainty on my part whether elderly persons tend to find themselves defined in terms of old age as much as the other groups are defined according to their categories.
2. Barkun, "Utopian Politics," pp. 44–47.
3. Karen O'Connor, *Women's Organizations' Use of the Courts* (Lexington, Mass.: Lexington Books, 1980).
4. Ibid., p. 41.
5. Ibid., chap. 4.
6. Sorauf, *Wall of Separation*, pp. 150 and 154.
7. Jacqueline A. Thompson, "Step-By-Step Through a Class-Action Suit," *Ms.*, February 1978, p. 84.
8. Evans, *Personal Politics*.
9. 404 U.S. 71 (1971).
10. O'Connor, *Women's Organizations' Use of the Courts*, pp. 101 and 122.
11. Joyce Gelb and Marian Lief Palley, *Women and Public Policies* (Princeton: Princeton University Press, 1982), p. 19.
12. Ibid., pp. 17–18, citing Allen Buchanan, "Revolutionary Motivation and Rationality, *Philosophy and Public Affairs* 9 (1979): 68.
13. Gelb and Palley, *Women and Public Policies*, p. 4.
14. Ibid., p. 20; and O'Connor, *Women's Organizations' Use of the Courts*, p. 101.
15. Gelb and Palley, *Women and Public Policies*, p. 50.
16. Ibid., p. 172.
17. O'Connor, *Women's Organizations' Use of the Courts*, p. 26.
18. Gelb and Palley, *Women and Public Policies*, p. 51.
19. Ibid., p. 38.
20. Ibid., pp. 95–97.
21. Ibid., pp. 150–51.

22. Ibid., p. 173.
23. Ibid., p. 170.
24. Although the number of mobilized members of a population is probably a more significant figure than the total number of the population, since no data is available about the relative proportion of mobilization within the two groups, one must look at the whole group as potentially mobilizable for this purpose.
25. Gelb and Palley, *Women and Public Policies*, p. 5.
26. Ibid., p. 172.
27. J. Woodford Howard, Jr., "Adjudication Considered as a Process of Conflict Resolution: A Variation on Separation of Powers," *Journal of Public Law* 18 (1969): 348–49; William P. McLauchlan, *American Legal Processes* (New York: John Wiley & Sons, 1977), pp. 16–18; Horowitz, *Courts and Social Policy*, pp. 34–35.
28. Scheingold, *Politics of Rights*, p. 129.
29. The closest that gender ever came to being recognized as a "suspect classification," and thus having laws using such classifications receive strict scrutiny from the Supreme Court, was in a plurality opinion joined by four justices in *Frontiero v. Richardson*, 411 U.S. 677 (1973). Since that case the Court has backed further away from scrutinizing gender classifications as strictly as racial classifications and has created a standard for reviewing the former. They must bear a "substantial relation to an important governmental objective." Disability as a classification has typically received even less scrutiny by the Court. See *Frontiero*, at 686.
30. An exception to this generalization would be a material issue with considerable physical externalities that could not be geographically contained, such as air or water pollution. Such issues, while material, may also require centrally coordinated attack.
31. Gelb and Palley, *Women and Public Policies*, p. 54.
32. Ibid., p. 40.
33. Ibid., p. 32.
34. Ibid., p. 170.
35. Wexler, "Practicing Law for Poor People"; Brill, "Uses and Abuses of Legal Assistance."
36. Freeman, *Legal Interviewing and Counseling*, p. 236; Weyrauch, *The Personality of Lawyers*.
37. Rosenthal, *Lawyer and Client*, p. 170.

APPENDIX A

Initial Questionnaire

This questionnaire was used early in the research process to help select the cases to receive detailed study. It was sent to all groups that could be identified as having participated as named plaintiffs in lawsuits seeking accessible public transportation by the summer of 1978. Ten questionnaires were sent and six were returned. I was eventually able to contact all but one of the groups. In most instances, only one questionnaire per lawsuit was sent because the presence of multiple organizational plaintiffs was not evident from the case names.

APPENDIX A

INITIAL QUESTIONNAIRE

1. Briefly state the purpose of your organization.

2. What is the approximate size of your membership? ____________

3. What proportion of the membership actively attends functions? _____

4. Is membership in your organization open to any interested person, or are there some criteria for membership? Please specify.

5. Briefly describe the structure of your organization (e.g., paid staff, officers, board of directors, subdivisions, etc.).

6. How is the organization and especially the litigation funded? If possible, rank order sources in order of importance. If funding source is different for litigation than other activities, please note this.

   Membership dues _____ Government funding ____

   Fees for services _____ Foundation grants ____

   Donations _____ Other (specify) _______________

7. What types of activities, in addition to litigating, does your organization pursue? If possible, rank order most important activities to least important.

   Direct provision of services (specify) ________________________

   Contacting public officials to support interests of handicapped persons by:

   Occasional letters ____ Personal phone calls or visits ____

   Letter writing campaigns ____ Other (specify) ___________

   Informing the public of the interests of handicapped people through use of:

   Brochures ____ Public meetings ____

Schools _____ | Newspapers/magazines _____ | TV/radio _____

Sending speakers to other groups _____ | Street leafleting _____ | Other (specify) _______________

Marching or picketing _____ Sit-in type demonstrations _____

Providing social and/or educational activities for handicapped people _____

Other (specify) ________________________________

8. When was your organization founded? ________________

9. Is your organization an affiliate of a national organization _____, an independent local group _____, or other (specify) ____________?

10. Is this the first time your organization has brought a lawsuit?

_____yes _____no

If no, how many other suits have you brought? __________

If yes, have you been involved in litigation in any other capacity than being a named plaintiff, such as support for individual litigants? Explain briefly.

11. Is your organization the only named plaintiff to this suit?

_____yes _____no

If not, please name and identify your co-plaintiff(s).

12. Please list all the named defendants to your suit and identify them if they are individuals, as opposed to agencies or organizations.

13. Briefly describe what the suit is about. What relief are you specifically asking for (e.g., money damages, injunction against purchase of new buses, establishment of new services of some kind, other)?

14. What is the source of your legal counsel?

Legal aid or legal services ____

American Civil Liberties Union ____

A member of your organization ____

Retained privately for this case ____

Public interest law firm ____

Retained by organization on an ongoing basis ____

Other (specify) ________________________________

15. Are any of your lawyers handicapped themselves? ____yes ____no

16. Please state the name and address of your lawyer(s).

17. When was the lawsuit first filed? ____________________

18. How and when was the decision to litigate made? Were other strategies for achieving your goals tried first? If so, what strategies?

19. Is this litigation still in progress ____, or terminated ____? If still in progress, what is the present status of the case?

If terminated, what was the outcome?

Decision for the plaintiff ____

Decision for the defendant ____

Consent agreement ____

Other (specify) ________________________________

20. Briefly describe what you feel the effect of the litigation has been on the long-range activities of your organizational goals? Does this differ from its short-range effects? Have you noticed any effects on the organization itself?

Name of person completing questionnaire ______________________

Your role with the organization ______________________

For further information, whom should I contact?

Name ______________________

Address ______________________

APPENDIX B

Summary of Facts About Six Transit Access Cases

APPENDIX B

SUMMARY OF FACTS ABOUT SIX TRANSIT ACCESS CASES

Name of Case and Citation or Number	Bohlke v. Golden Gate Bridge, Highway and Transportation District ("the Marin County case") No. 73362	Washington Urban League v. Washington Metropolitan Area Transit Authority (later Paralyzed Veterans of America v. WMATA) ("the D.C. case") Civil Action No. 776-72	United Handicapped Federation v. Andre ("the Minnesota case") 409 F.Supp 1297 (1976) and 558 F.2d 413 (8th Cir. 1977)
Location	Marin County, California	Washington D.C.	Minneapolis/St. Paul, Minnesota
Federal or State Court of Filing	California Superior Court	U.S. District Court, District of Columbia	U.S. District Court, Minnesota
Counsel	Sterling L. Ross, Jr., solo practitioner	James A. Dobkin and David Towey, Arnold & Porter Institute for Public Interest Representation	William M. Mahlum, solo practitioner
Number of Plaintiffs	1 organization/4 individuals	3 organizations/1 individual	2 organizations/6 individuals
Defendants	Golden Gate Bridge...District and president; Marin County Transit District and chairman of board	Washington Metropolitan Area Transit Authority; Downtown Progress (added 1976); General Services Administration (added 1977)	Officials of Metropolitan Transit Commission; Administrator of the Urban Mass Transportation Administration; Secretary of the U.S. Department of Transportation; AM General Corporation
Principal Causes of Action	Calif. Gov't Code 4500 Calif. Civil Code 54.1	P.L. 91-205, 42 U.S.C. 4151	49 U.S.C. 1602(a)(1) and 1612(a); 29 U.S.C. 794
Date Filed	November 18, 1974	April 19, 1972	December 8, 1975
Date of Final Court Action on Merits	August 16, 1978	October 12, 1978	May 3, 1978

		("the East Bay case")	
Name of Case and Citation or Number	Disabled in Action of Pennsylvania v. Coleman ("the Transbus case") No. 76-1913	Center for Independent Living v. Alameda-Contra Costa Transit District No. 496609-8	Zukas v. Alameda-Contra Costa Transit District No. C 780
Location	Philadelphia, Pennsylvania	Alameda and Contra Costa Counties, California (Oakland, Berkeley, etc.)	
Federal or State Court of Filing	U.S. District Court, Eastern District of Pennsylvania	California Superior Court, Alameda County	U.S. District Court, Northern District of California
Counsel	James J. Raggio, et al., Public Interest Law Center of Philadelphia	Katherine Bartlett and Evelyn Frank, Legal Aid Society of Alameda County	
Number of Plaintiffs	12 organizations/7 individuals	3 organizations/4 individuals	3 organizations/5 individuals
Defendants	Secretary of U.S. Department of Transportation; Administrator of the Urban Mass Transportation Administration; Administrator of the Federal Highway Administration	Alameda-Contra Costa Transit and officials	Alameda-Contra Costa Transit and officials; Metropolitan Transportation Commission and officials; Secretary of U.S. Department of Transportation; Administrator, UMTA; Administrator, FHA
Principal Causes of Action	49 U.S.C. 1602(a)(1) and 1612(a); 23 U.S.C. 142 nt.; 29 U.S.C. 794; P.L. 93-391, 9315; U.S. Constitution, 5th and 14th Amendments	Calif. Civil Code 54.1 Calif. Gov't Code 4500 Calif. Constitution: Art. I, Sec. 1 & 7; Art. IV, Sec. 16	49 U.S.C. 1601, et seq.; 29 U.S.C. 794; 23 U.S.C. 142, as amended (88 Stats., 2283); U.S. Constitution, 5th and 14th Amendments; 42 U.S.C. 1983
Date Filed	June 17, 1976	June 21, 1977	April 13, 1978
Date of Final Court Action on Merits	March 17, 1978	December 27, 1978	June 1979

Bibliography

Books

Adorno, T. W.; Frenkel-Brunswik, E.; Levinson, D. J.; and Sanford, R. N. *The Authoritarian Personality*. New York: Harper & Row, 1950.

Alinsky, Saul. *Reveille for Radicals*. New York: Vintage, 1969.

Becker, Theodore, and Feeley, Malcolm M., eds. *The Impact of Supreme Court Decisions*, 2d ed. New York: Oxford University Press, 1973.

Benjamin, Roger, and Choong Nam Kim. *American Indians and the Criminal Justice System in Minnesota*. Minneapolis: Center for Urban and Regional Affairs, 1979.

Berger, Raoul. *Government By Judiciary: The Transformation of the Fourteenth Amendment*. Cambridge: Harvard University Press, 1977.

Berry, Jeffrey M. *Lobbying for the People: The Political Behavior of Public Interest Groups*. Princeton: Princeton University Press, 1977.

Bickel, Alexander. *The Least Dangerous Branch*. Indianapolis: The Bobbs-Merrill Co., Inc., 1962.

———. *The Supreme Court and the Idea of Progress*. New York: Harper & Row, 1970.

Black, Charles L., Jr. *The People and the Court: Judicial Review in a Democracy*. New York: The Macmillan Co., 1960.

Bowe, Frank G. *Handicapping America: Barriers to Disabled People*. New York: Harper & Row, 1978.

Bowe, Frank G.; Jacobi, Jan E.; and Wiseman, Laurence D. *Coalition Building: A Report on a Feasibility Study to Develop a National Model for Cross-Disability Communication and Cooperation*. Washington, D.C.: American Coalition of Citizens with Disabilities, 1978.

Brakel, Samuel J. *Judicare: Public Funds, Private Lawyers, and Poor People*. Chicago: American Bar Foundation, 1974.

Buckle, Suzann R. Thomas, and Buckle, Leonard G. *Bargaining for Justice: Case Disposition and Reform in the Criminal Courts*. New York: Praeger, 1977.

Cannon, Dennis, and Rainbow, Frances. *Full Mobility: Counting the Costs of the Alternatives*. Washington, D.C.: American Coalition of Citizens with Disabilities, 1980.

Carlin, Jerome E. *Lawyers' Ethics: A Survey of the New York City Bar*. New York: Russell Sage, 1966.

———. *Lawyers on Their Own: A Study of Individual Practitioners in Chicago*. New Brunswick, N.J.: Rutgers University Press, 1962.

Casper, Jonathan D. *American Criminal Justice: The Defendant's Perspective*. Englewood Cliffs, N.J.: Prentice-Hall, 1972.

———. *Lawyers Before the Warren Court: Civil Liberties and Civil Rights, 1957–66*. Urbana, Ill.: University of Illinois Press, 1972.

Commission on Sociotechnical Systems, National Research Council. *NRC Transbus Study*. Washington, D.C.: National Academy of Sciences, 1979.

Dean, Howard E. *Judicial Review and Democracy*. New York: Random House, 1966.

Dworkin, Ronald. *Taking Rights Seriously*. Cambridge: Harvard University Press, 1977.

Edelman, Murray. *Politics as Symbolic Action: Mass Arousal and Quiescence*. New York: Academic Press, 1971.

Evans, Sara. *Personal Politics: The Roots of Women's Liberation in the Civil Rights Movement and the New Left*. New York: Knopf, 1979.

Feuer, Lewis S. *The Conflict of Generations*. New York: Basic Books, 1969.

Frank, Jerome. *Courts on Trial*. Princeton: Princeton University Press, 1949.

Freeman, Harrop A. *Legal Interviewing and Counseling: Cases with Comments*. St. Paul: West Publishing Co., 1964.

Gamson, William A. *The Strategy of Social Protest*. Homewood, Ill.: Dorsey Press, 1975.

Gelb, Joyce, and Palley, Marian Lief. *Women and Public Policies*. Princeton: Princeton University Press, 1982.

Goffman, Erving. *Stigma: Notes on the Management of Spoiled Identity*. Englewood Cliffs, N.J.: Prentice-Hall, 1963.

Gusfield, Joseph R. *Symbolic Crusade: Status Politics and the American Temperance Movement*. Urbana, Ill.: University of Illinois Press, 1963.

Hall, Donald R. *Cooperative Lobbying—The Power of Pressure*. Tucson: University of Arizona Press, 1969.

Handler, Joel F. *Social Movements and the Legal System: A Theory of Law Reform and Social Change*. New York: Academic Press, 1978.

Handler, Joel F.; Hollingsworth, Ellen Jane; and Erlanger, Howard S. *Lawyers and the Pursuit of Legal Rights*. New York: Academic Press, 1978.

Held, Virginia. *The Public Interest and Individual Interests*. New York: Basic Books, 1970.

Hobbes, Thomas. *Leviathan*. Edited by Michael Oakeshott. New York: Collier Books, 1962.

Hoffer, Eric. *The True Believer*. New York: Harper & Row, 1951.

Horowitz, Donald L. *The Courts and Social Policy*. Washington, D.C.: The Brookings Institution, 1977.

Hyneman, Charles. *The Supreme Court on Trial.* New York: Atherton Press, 1963.

Jacob, Herbert. *Justice in America: Courts, Lawyers, and the Judicial Process,* 2d ed. Boston: Little, Brown and Co., 1972.

Katz, Alfred H. *Parents of the Handicapped: Self-Organized Parents' and Relatives' Groups for Treatment of Ill and Handicapped Children.* Springfield, Ill.: Charles C. Thomas, 1961.

Katz, Alfred H., and Bender, Eugene I., eds. *The Strength In Us: Self-Help Groups in the Modern World.* New York: New Viewpoints, 1976.

Kluger, Richard. *Simple Justice: The History of Brown v. Board of Education and Black America's Struggle for Equality.* New York: Vintage Books, 1977.

Krislov, Samuel. *The Supreme Court in the Political Process.* New York: MacMillan, 1965.

Laski, Harold J. *The Limitations of the Expert.* Fabian Tract No. 235. London: The Fabian Society, 1931.

Lobenthal, Joseph, Jr. *Power and Put-on: The Law in America.* New York: Outerbridge and Dienstfrey, 1970.

Lowi, Theodore J. *The End of Liberalism: The Second Republic of the United States,* 2d ed. New York: Norton, 1979.

Lusky, Louis. *By What Right? A Commentary on the Supreme Court's Power to Revise the Constitution.* Charlottesville, Va.: The Michie Co., 1975.

McDaniel, James W. *Physical Disability and Human Behavior.* New York: Pergamon, 1969.

McLauchlan, William P. *American Legal Processes.* New York: John Wiley & Sons, 1977.

Marks, F. Raymond. *The Lawyer, the Public, and Professional Responsibility.* Chicago: American Bar Foundation, 1972.

Marks, F. Raymond; Hallauer, Robert Paul; and Clifton, Richard. *The Shreveport Plan: An Experiment in the Delivery of Legal Services.* Chicago: American Bar Foundation, 1974.

May, Judith V. *Professionals and Clients: A Constitutional Struggle.* Administrative and Policy Studies Series, no. 03-036. Beverly Hills: Sage Publications, 1976.

Mayhew, Leon H. *Law and Equal Opportunity: A Study of the Massachusetts Commission Against Discrimination.* Cambridge: Harvard University Press, 1968.

Medcalf, Linda. *Law and Identity: Lawyers, Native Americans and Legal Practice.* Beverly Hills: Sage Publications, 1978.

Meier, Helen. *Accessible Public Transit: A History and Overview of Accessible Transit Provision in the United States.* San Francisco: United Cerebral Palsy Association of San Francisco, 1981.

Milbrath, Lester W., and Goel, M. L. *Political Participation: How and Why Do People Get Involved in Politics?* 2d ed. Chicago: Rand McNally, 1977.

Moe, Terry M. *The Organization of Interests: Incentives and the Internal Dynamics of Political Interest Groups.* Chicago: University of Chicago Press, 1980.

Moore, Wilbert E. *The Professions: Roles and Rules.* New York: Russell Sage, 1970.

Obermann, C. Esco. *A History of Vocational Rehabilitation in America.* Minneapolis: T. S. Denison & Co., 1965.

O'Connor, Karen. *Women's Organizations' Use of the Courts.* Lexington, Mass.: Lexington Books, 1980.

Olson, Mancur, Jr. *The Logic of Collective Action: Public Goods and the Theory of Groups*. rev. ed. New York: Schocken Books, 1971.

Peltason, Jack W. *Federal Courts in the Political Process*. Garden City, N.Y.: Doubleday & Co., 1955.

Pressman, Jeffrey, and Wildavsky, Aaron. *Implementation: How Great Expectations in Washington Are Dashed in Oakland: Or, Why It's Amazing that Federal Programs Work at All, This Being a Saga of the Economic Development Administration as Told by Two Sympathetic Observers Who Seek to Build Morals on a Foundation of Ruined Hopes*. Berkeley: University of California Press, 1973.

Raggio, James J.; Lipman, B. G.; Gilhool, T. K.; and Wolf, E. D. *The Disabled and the Elderly: Equal Access to Public Transportation*. Washington, D.C.: The President's Committee on Employment of the Handicapped, 1975.

Report of the National Advisory Commission on Civil Disorders. By Otto Kerner, Chairman. New York: Bantam, 1968.

Rosenthal, Douglas E. *Lawyer and Client: Who's in Charge?* New Brunswick, N.J.: Transaction Books, 1977.

Safilios-Rothschild, Constantina. *The Sociology and Social Psychology of Disability and Rehabilitation*. New York: Random House, 1970.

Scheingold, Stuart A. *The Politics of Rights: Lawyers, Public Policy, and Political Change*. New Haven: Yale University Press, 1974.

Schubert, Glendon. *The Public Interest*. Glencoe, Ill.: The Free Press, 1960.

Scott, Robert A. *The Making of Blind Men: A Study of Adult Socialization*. New York: Russell Sage, 1969.

Shaposka, Bert. *The N.A.D. Story—A History of Enlightened Self-Interest*. Silver Spring, Md.: National Association of the Deaf, 1964.

Shklar, Judith N. *Legalism: An Essay on Law, Morals, and Politics*. Cambridge: Harvard University Press, 1964.

Smelser, Neil. *Theory of Collective Behavior*. New York: Free Press, 1963.

Smigel, Erwin O. *The Wall Street Lawyer: Professional Organization Man?* Bloomington, Ind.: Indiana University Press, 1969.

Smith, David Horton; Reddy, Richard D.; and Baldwin, Burt R., eds. *Voluntary Action Research: 1972*. Lexington, Mass.: Lexington Books, 1972.

Sorauf, Frank J. *The Wall of Separation: The Constitutional Politics of Church and State*. Princeton: Princeton University Press, 1976.

Tomasic, Roman. *Lawyers and the Community*. Sydney, Australia: The Law Foundation of New South Wales and George Allen & Unwin, 1978.

Truman, David B. *The Governmental Process: Political Interests and Public Opinion*, 2d ed. New York: Knopf, 1971.

Vander Zanden, James W. *Race Relations in Transition*. New York: Random House, 1965.

Varela, Rita A. *Self-Help Groups in Rehabilitation*. Washington, D.C.: American Coalition of Citizens with Disabilities, 1979.

Vose, Clement E. *Caucasians Only: The Supreme Court, the NAACP, and the Restrictive Covenant Cases*. Berkeley: University of California Press, 1959.

———. *Constitutional Change: Amendment Politics and Supreme Court Litigation Since 1900*. Lexington, Mass.: Lexington Books, 1972.

Wasby, Stephen. *The Impact of the United States Supreme Court: Some Perspectives*. Homewood, Ill.: Dorsey Press, 1970.

Wechsler, Herbert. *Principles, Politics and Fundamental Law.* Cambridge: Harvard University Press, 1961.

Weyrauch, Walter O. *The Personality of Lawyers: A Comparative Study of Subjective Factors in Law, Based on Interviews with German Lawyers.* New Haven: Yale University Press, 1964.

Wolfensberger, Wolf. *A Balanced Multi-Component Advocacy/Protection Schema.* Law and Mental Retardation: A Monograph Series. Toronto: Canadian Association for the Mentally Retarded, 1977.

Articles

Achtenberg, Jack. "Law and the Physically Disabled: An Update with Constitutional Implications." *Southwestern University Law Review* 8 (1976): 847–87.

Ashbrook, John M. "Are Judges Abusing Our Rights?" *Reader's Digest,* August 1981, pp. 77–80.

Auerbach, Jerold S. "A Plague of Lawyers." *Harper's,* October 1976, pp. 37–44.

Baer, Judith A. "The Burger Court and the Rights of the Handicapped." Paper presented at the annual meeting of the American Political Science Association, New York, 1981.

Baldwin, John, and McConville, Michael. "Plea Bargaining and Plea Negotiations in England." *Law and Society Review* 13 (1979): 287–307.

Barkun, Michael. "The Political Functions of Utopian Experiments: Two Ironies in the Formulation of Group Identity." Paper presented at the Third Annual Conference on Utopian Studies, University Park, Pa., 1978.

———. "Utopian Politics and the Future of Governance." *Alternative Futures: The Journal of Utopian Studies* 4 (1981): 34–49.

Barkun, Michael, and Levine, James. "Protest in Suburbia: Case Study of a Direct-Action Movement." *Syracuse Law Review* 20 (1968): 21–44.

Becker, Howard D. "The Nature of a Profession." In *Education for the Professions: The 61st Yearbook of the National Society for the Study of Education,* pt. 2, pp. 17–46. Edited by Nelson B. Henry. Chicago: University of Chicago Press, 1962.

Bell, Daniel. "The Revolution of Rising Entitlements." *Fortune,* April 1975, p. 98+.

Bell, Derrick A., Jr. "Serving Two Masters: Integration Ideals and Client Interests in School Desegregation Litigation." *Yale Law Journal* 85 (1976): 470–516.

Birkby, Robert H., and Murphy, Walter F. "Interest Group Conflict in the Judicial Arena: The First Amendment and Group Access to the Court." *Texas Law Review* 42 (1964): 1018–48.

Blumberg, Abraham. "The Practice of Law as Confidence Game: Organizational Co-optation of a Profession." *Law and Society Review* 1 (1967): 15–39.

Borosage, Robert; Brown, B.; Friedman, P.; Gewitz, P.; Jeffress, W., Jr.; and Kelly, W., Jr. "The New Public Interest Lawyers." *Yale Law Journal* 79 (1970): 1069–1152.

Brill, Harry. "The Uses and Abuses of Legal Assistance." *The Public Interest* 31 (1973): 38–55.

Buckley, William F. "Curb the Courts?" *National Review*, May 26, 1972, pp. 606–07.

Burgdorf, Marcia Pearce, and Burgdorf, Robert, Jr. "A History of Unequal Treatment: The Qualifications of Handicapped Persons as a 'Suspect Class' under the Equal Protection Clause." *Santa Clara Lawyer* 15 (1975): 855–910.

Cadden, Vivian. "The Case Against Divorce Lawyers." *McCall's*, November 1976, p. 169+.

Cahn, Edgar S., and Cahn, Jean Camper. "Power to the People or the Profession?—The Public Interest in Public Interest Law." *Yale Law Journal* 79 (1970): 1005–48.

Cain, Maureen. "The General Practice Lawyer and the Client: Towards a Radical Conception." *International Journal of the Sociology of Law* 7 (1979): 331–54.

Cappelletti, Mauro. "Vindicating the Public Interest Through the Courts: A Comparativist's Contribution." *Buffalo Law Review* 25 (1976): 643–90.

Clark, Timothy B. "Regulation Gone Amok: How Many Billions for Wheelchair Transit?" *Regulation*, March/April 1980, pp. 47–52.

Cochran, Clarke E. "Political Science and the 'Public Interest.' " *Journal of Politics* 36 (1974): 327–55.

Daly, Margaret. "What Are Your Rights with a Lawyer?" *Better Homes and Gardens*, November 1975, p. 40+.

Denvir, John. "Towards a Political Theory of Public Interest Litigation." *North Carolina Law Review* 54 (1976):1133–60.

di Suvero, Henry. "The Movement and the Legal System." In *Radical Lawyers: Their Role in the Movement and in the Courts*, pp. 51–69. Edited by Jonathan Black. New York: Avon Books, 1971.

Donnell, John D. "The Corporate Counsel and His 'Client': Use of Role Analysis to Illumine Strains in the Lawyer–Client Relationship." *Indiana Law Journal* 45 (1970): 514–49.

Felstiner, William L. F. "Plea Contracts in West Germany." *Law and Society Review* 13 (1979): 309–25.

Fitzgerald, Jeffrey M. "The Contract Buyers League and the Courts: A Case Study of Poverty Litigation." *Law and Society Review* 9 (1975): 165–95.

Footlick, Jerrold K. "Too Much Law?" *Newsweek*, January 10, 1977, pp. 42–47.

———. "We've Got Too Much Law!" *Reader's Digest*, May 1977, pp. 96–100.

Galanter, Marc. "Why the 'Haves' Come Out Ahead: Speculations on the Limits of Legal Change." *Law and Society Review* 9 (1974): 95–160.

Gelb, Joyce and Sardell, Alice. "Organizing the Poor: A Brief Analysis of the Politics of the Welfare Rights Movement." *Policy Studies Journal* 3 (1975): 346–54.

Gest, Ted. "Why Lawyers Are in the Doghouse." *U.S. News and World Report*, May 11, 1981, pp. 38–41.

Gilhool, Thomas K. "The Uses of Courts and of Lawyers." In *Changing Patterns in Residential Services for the Mentally Retarded*, pp. 155–83. Edited by R. Kugel and A. Shearer. Washington, D.C.: President's Committee on Mental Retardation, 1976.

Ginger, Ann Fagan. "The Movement and the Lawyer." *Guild Practitioner* 26 (1967): 12–17.

Goodpaster, Gary S. "The Human Arts of Lawyering: Interviewing and Counseling." *Journal of Legal Education* 27 (1975): 5–52.

Gronemeier, Dale. "From Net to Sword: Organizational Representatives Litigating Their Members' Claims." *University of Illinois Law Forum* (1974): 663–74.

Hackney, David C. "Elderly, Disabled See Transbus as Last Hope." *Mass Transit*, January/February 1979, pp. 16–19 +.

Hakman, Nathan. "Lobbying the Supreme Court—An Appraisal of 'Political Science Folklore.' " *Fordham Law Review* 35 (1966): 15–50.

Halpern, Charles R., and Cunningham, John M. "Reflections on the New Public Interest Law: Theory and Practice at the Center for Law and Social Policy." *Georgetown Law Journal* 59 (1971): 1095–1126.

Halpern, Stephen C. "Assessing the Litigative Role of ACLU Chapters." In *Civil Liberties: Policy and Policy-Making*, pp. 159–68. Edited by Stephen Wasby. Lexington, Mass.: Lexington Books, 1976.

Hamilton, Percival B. "Counseling in the Legal Profession." *American Bar Association Journal* 58 (1972): 39–42.

Handel, Richard C. "The Role of the Advocate in Securing the Handicapped Child's Right to an Effective Minimal Education." *Ohio State Law Journal* 36 (1975): 349–75.

Harrison, Gordon, and Jaffe, Sanford M. "Public Interest Law Firms: New Voices for New Constituencies." *American Bar Association Journal* 58 (1972): 459–67.

Haug, Marie R., and Sussman, Marvin B. "Professional Autonomy and the Revolt of the Client." *Social Problems* 17 (1969): 153–61.

Heddinger, Richard W. "The Twelve Year Battle for a Barrier Free Metro." *American Rehabilitation*, May/June 1976, pp. 7–10.

Horn, Jack. "Attitudes: Reactions to the Handicapped—Sweaty Palms and Saccharine Words." *Psychology Today*, November 1975, pp. 122+.

Howard, J. Woodford, Jr. "Adjudication Considered as a Process of Conflict Resolution: A Variation on Separation of Powers." *Journal of Public Law* 18 (1969): 339–70.

Hunt, F. "Lawyers' War Against Democracy," *Commentary*, October 1979, pp. 45–51.

Jenkins, Craig and Perrow, Charles. "Insurgency of the Powerless: Farm Worker Movements (1946–72)." *American Sociological Review* 42 (1977): 249–68.

Katz, Jack. "Legality and Equality: Plea Bargaining in the Prosecution of White-Collar and Common Crimes." *Law and Society Review* 13 (1979): 431–59.

Kelso, Charles D., and Kelso, C. Kevin. "Conflict, Emotion, and Legal Ethics." *Pacific Law Journal* 10 (1978): 69–93.

Kleck, Robert. "Emotional Arousal in Interactions with Stigmatized Persons." *Psychological Reports* 19 (1966).

Kort, Fred. "Content Analysis of Judicial Opinions and Rules of Law." In *Judicial Decision-Making*, pp. 133–97. Edited by Glendon Schubert. New York: Free Press, 1963.

Kriegel, Leonard. "Uncle Tom and Tiny Tim: Some Reflections on the Cripple as Negro." *The American Scholar* 38 (1969): 412–30.

Krislov, Samuel. "The Amicus Curiae Brief: From Friendship to Advocacy." *Yale Law Journal* 72 (1963): 694–721.

———. "The OEO Lawyers Fail to Constitutionalize a Right to Welfare: A Study in the Uses and Limits of the Judicial Process." *Minnesota Law Review* 58 (1973): 211–45.

Ladinsky, Jack. "The Traffic in Legal Services: Lawyer-Seeking Behavior and the Channeling of Clients." *Law and Society Review* 11 (1976): 207–23.

Laumann, Edward O., and Heinz, John P. "Specialization and Prestige in the Legal Profession: The Structure of Deference." *American Bar Foundation Research Journal* (1977): 155–216.

"Lawyers Giving Public a Raw Deal?" *U.S. News and World Report*, December 1, 1980, pp. 45–46.

Lempert, Richard O. "Mobilizing Private Law: An Introductory Essay." *Law and Society Review* 11 (1976): 173–89.

Macrae, Norman. "Wheelchairs Run Amok," *The Economist*, December 27, 1980, pp. 22–25.

Marks, F. Raymond. "Some Research Perspectives for Looking at Legal Need and Legal Services Delivery Systems: Old Forms or New?" *Law and Society Review* 11 (1976): 191–205.

Matthews, Arthur R., Jr., and Weiss, Jonathan A. "What Can Be Done: A Neighborhood Lawyer's Credo." In *Bureaucracy and the Public: A Reader in Official–Client Relations*, pp. 438–49. Edited by Elihu Katz and Brenda Danet. New York: Basic Books, 1973.

Mazor, Lester J. "Power and Responsibility in the Attorney–Client Relation." *Stanford Law Review* 20 (1968): 1120–39.

Mitnick, Barry M. "A Typology of Conceptions of the Public Interest." *Administration and Society* 8 (1976): 5–28.

Nagel, Stuart S. "Using Simple Calculations to Predict Judicial Decision." *American Behavioral Scientist* 4 (1960): 24–28.

Neier, Aryeh. "Protest Movements among the Disenfranchised." *Civil Liberties Review* 1 (1973): 49–74.

"New Rehabilitation/Developmental Disabilities Act Amendments Become Law." *Amicus* 3 (November/December 1978): 8–16.

O'Connor, Karen. "Litigation as a Form of Political Activity: How Women's Groups Have Used the Courts." Paper presented at the annual meeting of the American Political Science Association, Washington, D.C., 1978.

Orren, Karen. "Standing to Sue: Interest Group Conflict in the Federal Courts." *American Political Science Review* 70 (1976): 723–41.

Payne, Raymond; Payne, Barbara Pittard; and Reddy, Richard D. "Social Background and Role Determinants of Individual Participation in Organized Voluntary Action." In *Voluntary Action Research: 1972*, pp. 207–50. Edited by David Horton Smith, Richard D. Reddy, and Burt R. Baldwin. Lexington, Mass.: Lexington Books, 1972.

Peterson, Eric. "Legal Challenges to Bureaucratic Discretion: The Influence of Lawsuits on the Implementation of EPSDT." Working Paper No. 27, Health Policy Project Series, Department of Epidemiology and Public Health, Yale University, 1975.

Rabin, Robert L. "Lawyers for Social Change: Perspectives on Public Interest Law." *Stanford Law Review* 28 (1976): 207–61.

Rains; Kitsuse; Duster; and Freidson. "The Labeling Approach to Issues in Deviance." In *Issues in the Classification of Children* 1 (1975): 88. Edited by N. Hobbs.

Reddy, Richard D., and Smith, David Horton. "Personality and Capacity Determinants of Individual Participation in Organized Voluntary Action." In *Voluntary Action Research: 1972*, pp. 277–98. Edited by David Horton Smith, Richard D. Reddy, and Burt R. Baldwin. Lexington, Mass.: Lexington Books, 1972.

Redmount, Robert S. "Attorney Personalities and Some Psychological Aspects of Legal Consultation." *University of Pennsylvania Law Review* 109 (1961): 972–88.

Salzberg, C. "Should You Trust Your Lawyer?" *Working Woman*, September 1980, pp. 30–31.

Samerotte, George C., and Harris, Mary B. "Some Factors Influencing Helping: The Effects of a Handicap, Responsibility, and Requesting Help." *The Journal of Social Psychology* 98 (1976): 39–45.

Sarup, Gian. "A Reference Group Theory of Social Movements and Identity." *Social Science* 50 (1975): 219–26.

Schoenfield, Mark K., and Schoenfield, Barbara P. "Interviewing and Counseling Clients in a Legal Setting." *Akron Law Review* 11 (1977): 313–331.

Selznick, Philip. "Social Advocacy in the Legal Profession in the United States." *Juridical Review* (1974): 113–26.

Settle, Russell F. and Weisbrod, Burton A. "Financing Public Interest Law: An Evaluation of Alternative Financing Arrangements." In *Public Interest Law: An Economic and Institutional Analysis*, pp. 532–49. Edited by Burton A. Weisbrod, Joel F. Handler, and Neil K. Komesar. Los Angeles: University of California Press, 1978.

Simon, William H. "The Ideology of Advocacy: Procedural Justice and Professional Ethics." *Wisconsin Law Review* (1978): 29–144.

Sorauf, Frank. "The Public Interest Reconsidered." *Journal of Politics* 19 (1957): 616–39.

Thompson, Jacqueline A. "Step-By-Step Through a Class-Action Suit." *Ms.*, February 1978, pp. 81–84.

"Those #*%&!!! Lawyers." *Time*, April 10, 1978, pp. 56–59+.

Varela, Rita A. "Power to the Disabled." *Social Policy* 4 (March/April 1974): 46–48.

Very, Donald L. "The Human Element in the Attorney–Client Relationship: The Answer to Malpractice." *Pennsylvania Bar Association Quarterly* 48 (1977): 515–24.

Vose, Clement E. "Litigation as a Form of Pressure Group Activity." *Annals of the American Academy of Political and Social Science* 319 (September 1958): 20–31.

Wasserstrom, Richard. "Lawyers as Professionals: Some Moral Issues." *Human Rights* 5 (1975): 1–24.

Watson, Andrew. "Lawyers and Professionalism: A Further Psychiatric Perspective on Legal Education." *University of Michigan Journal of Law Reform* 8 (1975): 248–85.

Wechsler, Herbert. "Toward Neutral Principles of Constitutional Law." In Wechsler, *Principles, Politics, and Fundamental Law*, pp. 3–48. Cambridge: Harvard University Press, 1961.

Weintraub, Frederick J., and Abeson, Alan R. "Appropriate Education for All Handicapped Children: A Growing Issue." *Syracuse Law Review* 23 (1972): 1037–58.

Wexler, Stephen. "Practicing Law for Poor People," *Yale Law Journal* 79 (1970): 1049–67.

Williams, Michael. "This Issue." *The Independent*, Summer 1977, p. 6.

Young, David. "The Transbus Compromise." *Mass Transit*, January/February 1979, pp. 12–15.

Zemans, Frances Kahn. "Socialization to Professional Responsibility: The Profession's Perspective." Paper presented at the annual meeting of the Law and Society Association, San Francisco, 1979.

Newspapers

Andelman, David L. "M.T.A. Rejects Laws That Require Gear to Aid Handicapped." *New York Times*, 20 September 1980, p. 1.

Anderson, Jack. "A Formidable Alliance of the Elderly and Disabled." *Washington Post*, 1 April 1979, p. B7.

Berreby, David. "Rights for Handicapped: A Narrowing Legal Path?" *The National Law Journal*, 29 June 1981, p. 7.

Bowe, Frank. "Civil Rights for the Disabled." *Washington Post*, 9 January 1979, p. A19.

Cohen, Richard. "Merchants at 9th and G Stood Up by Subway." *Washington Post*, 6 June 1976, pp. B1 and B9.

Editorial. ". . . And a Station Break." *Washington Post*, 16 December 1976, p. A18.

Editorial. "Metro and the Rights of the Handicapped." *Washington Post*, 14 July 1973, p. A18, and 17 August 1973, p. A24.

Eisen, Jack. "Transit Group Files Suit to Block Rules on Handicapped." *Washington Post*, 30 June 1979, p. A8.

Feaver, Douglas B. "Metro Bows to Demands of Handicapped." *Washington Post*, 13 October 1978, p. C5.

Killian, Doug. "Handicapped, MTC Still at Odds." *Minnesota Daily*, 3 April 1981, p. 9.

MacPherson, Myra. "Back: The Vietnam Veterans, Forcing Their Way Into America's Attention." *Washington Post*, 31 May 1979, p. D3.

Peirce, Neal R. "The Great Wheelchair Flap." *Washington Post*, 28 December 1978, p. A23.

Percy, Charles H. "Serving the Handicapped." *Washington Post*, 17 August 1973, p. A25.

Ridder, Walter T. "Minority Tyrannies." *New York Times*, 29 July 1976, p. 31.

Shaffer, Ron. "Church of Scientology Attacks Investigators and Critics." *Washington Post*, 16 August 1978, p. A4.

Wascoe, Dan, Jr., "Lawyers Don't Get Fees from MTC Suit." *Minneapolis Tribune*, 12 June 1979, p. 1B.

Government Reports, Documents, and Laws

Abt Associates, Inc., *Travel Barriers–Transportation Needs of the Handicapped*. Prepared for U.S. Department of Transportation, Office of Economics and Systems Analysis. Cambridge, Mass., 1969.

Chicago, Ill. Mun. Code 36–34 (1966) (repealed 1974).

United States Code

U.S. Architectural and Transportation Barriers Compliance Board. *Report on Transportation Needs of Handicapped Individuals* (1975).

U.S. Architectural and Transportation Barriers Compliance Board. *Report to the President and to the Congress of the United States* (1975).

U.S. *Code of Federal Regulations.*

U.S. Congress. Congressional Budget Office. *Urban Transportation for Handicapped Persons: Alternative Federal Approaches* (1979).

U.S. Congress. House. *The Effectiveness of the Architectural Barriers Act of 1968. Hearings before the Subcommittee on Investigations and Review of the House Committee on Public Works and Transportation.* 94th Cong., 1st sess., 1975.

U.S. Congress. Senate. *Hearings before a Subcommittee of the Committee on Labor and Public Health on S.1066, S.2273, and S.3465.* 81st Cong., 2d sess., 1950.

———. *Hearings before the Subcommittee on the Handicapped of the Senate Committee on Labor and Public Welfare on H.R. 8395.* 92d Cong., 2d sess., 1972.

U.S. *Congressional Record.*

U.S. *Federal Register.*

U.S. General Accounting Office. *Further Action Needed to Make All Public Buildings Accessible to the Physically Handicapped* (1975).

———. *Mass Transit for Elderly and Handicapped Persons: Urban Mass Transportation Administration's Actions* (1977).

U.S. National Commission on Architectural Barriers. *Design for All Americans* (1968).

U.S. President. Proclamation 4001. *Weekly Compilation of Presidential Documents.* 8 September 1970.

U.S. President. *Public Papers of the Presidents of the United States.* Washington, D.C.: Office of the *Federal Register*, National Archives and Records Service, 1953– . Richard Nixon, 1972, "Memorandum of Disapproval of Nine Bills." 27 October 1972.

Cases

Abilities Unlimited, Inc. v. Villegas, Civil No. 75-0001 (D. Hawaii 1975).

American Public Transit Association v. Lewis, 655 F.2d 1272 (D.C. Cir. 1981).

Atlantis Community, Inc. v. Adams, 453 F. Supp. 825 (D. Col. 1977).

Bagstad v. Orange Co. Transit District, No. 79-3426 (9th Cir. 1980).

Baker v. Bell, 630 F.2d 1046 (5th Cir. 1980).

Bartels v. Biernat, 427 F. Supp. 226 (E.D. Wisc. 1977).

Bates v. State Bar of Arizona, 433 U.S. 350 (1977).
Bohlke v. Golden Gate Bridge, Highway and Transportation District, No. 73362 (Marin Co., Calif. Super. Ct., 1974).
Brown v. Board of Education, 347 U.S. 483 (1954).
Brown v. Board of Education II, 349 U.S. 294 (1955).
Center for Independent Living v. Alameda-Contra Costa Transit District, No. 496609-8 (Alameda Co., Calif. Super. Ct., 1977).
Cherry v. Mathews, No. 76-0255 (D. D.C. 1976).
Craig v. Harney, 331 U.S. 367 (1946).
Disabled in Action of Baltimore v. Hughes, Civil No. 74-1069-HM (D. Md. 1974).
Disabled in Action of Pennsylvania v. Coleman, No. 76-1913 (E.D. Pa. 1976).
Douglas v. California, 372 U.S. 535 (1963).
Eisen v. Carlisle & Jacquelin, 417 U.S. 156 (1974).
Friedman v. County of Cuyahoga, No. 895961 (Cuyahoga, Ohio 1972).
Frontiero v. Richardson, 411 U.S. 677 (1973).
Griffin v. Illinois, 351 U.S. 12 (1956).
Hambrick and Ritter v. California Business and Transportation Agency, No. 180434 (San Bernardino Co., Calif. Super. Ct., 1977).
Health Research Group and Public Citizen, Inc. v. Kennedy, 82 F.R.D. 21 (1979).
Hunt v. Washington Apple Advertising Commission, 432 U.S. 333 (1977).
Leary v. Crapsey, 566 F.2d 863 (2d Cir. 1977).
Levy v. Louisiana, 391 U.S. 68 (1968).
Lloyd v. Regional Transportation Authority, 548 F.2d 1277 (7th Cir. 1977).
Michigan Paralyzed Veterans of America v. Coleman, 451 F.Supp. 7 (S.D. Mich. 1977).
Mobility Impaired Grappling Hurdles Together v. Briscoe, Civil No. A 75 CA 31 (W.D. Tex. 1975).
National Association for the Advancement of Colored People v. Alabama, 357 U.S. 449 (1958).
N.A.A.C.P. v. Button, 371 U.S. 415 (1963).
National Automatic Laundry and Cleaning Council v. Shultz, 443 F.2d 689 (D.C. Cir. 1971).
National Motor Freight Traffic Association, Inc. v. U.S., 372 U.S. 246 (1963).
Paralyzed Veterans of America v. Washington Metropolitan Area Transit Authority, Civil Action 776-72 (D. D.C. 1972).
Pennhurst State School and Hospital v. Halderman, 451 U.S. 1 (1981).
Pennsylvania Association for Retarded Children v. Commonwealth of Pennsylvania, 334 F.Supp. 1257 (E.D. Pa. 1971).
Reed v. Reed, 404 U.S. 71 (1971).
Rodriquez v. Adams, Civil No. 76-281 (W.D. Tex. 1976).
Shapiro v. Thompson, 394 U.S. 618 (1969).
Sierra Club v. Morton, 405 U.S. 727 (1972).
Simon v. Eastern Kentucky Welfare Rights Organization, 426 U.S. 26 (1976).
Snowden v. Birmingham-Jefferson County Transit Authority, 551 F.2d 862 (5th Cir. 1977), affirming 407 F.Supp. 394 (N.D. Ala. 1975).
Southeastern Community College v. Davis, 442 U.S. 397 (1979).
Trageser v. Libbie Rehabilitation Center, 590 F.2d 87 (4th Cir. 1977), cert. denied 442 U.S. 947 (1979).

United Handicapped Federation v. Andre, 558 F.2d 413 (8th Cir. 1977), remanding 409 F.Supp. 1297 (D. Minn. 1976).
U.H.F. v. Andre, 622 F.2d 342 (8th Cir. 1980) (attorney's fees).
United States v. Students Challenging Regulatory Agency Procedures, 412 U.S. 669 (1973).
Vanko v. Finley, 440 F.Supp. 656 (N.D. Ohio 1977).
Warth v. Seldin, 422 U.S. 490 (1975).
Young v. Adams, No. 77-6056 (2d Cir. 1977).
Zahn v. International Paper Co., 414 U.S. 291 (1973).
Zukas v. Alameda-Contra Costa Transit District, No. C78-0824CBR (N.D. Calif. 1978).

Miscellaneous Printed Sources

"Alternative Conference Report." White House Conference on Handicapped Individuals, May 23–27, 1977 (mimeograph).
Code of Professional Responsibility. American Bar Association, 1969.
Encyclopedia of Associations, 11th ed., s.v. "National Congress of Organizations of the Physically Handicapped" and "National Paraplegia Foundation."
Feinsod, Stanley G. "Perspectives on Barrier-Free Transit Policy." Speech presented at the annual meeting of the American Public Transit Association, Atlanta, Ga., 1977 (mimeograph).
Handicapped Americans Reports. Washington, D.C.: Capitol Publications, Inc., 26 February 1981; 30 July 1981.
Indoor Sports Club. Untitled pamphlet, 1974.
National Association of the Physically Handicapped. Untitled pamphlet, n.d.
Paralyzed Veterans of America. *1978 Annual Report*. Washington, D.C.: Paralyzed Veterans of America, 1978.
Raggio, James J., letter to Hull, Kent. March 23, 1978.
United Cerebral Palsy Associations, Inc. *1976 Annual Report*. New York: United Cerebral Palsy Associations, Inc., 1976.
Zukas, Hale. "C.I.L. History." Berkeley, n.d. (mimeograph).

Interviews

People are identified by their position (if known) which is most relevant to the subject of the interview. In some cases they had moved to other jobs when interviewed or have moved since the interview.

Bartlett, Katharine. Attorney, Alameda County Legal Aid Society. Oakland, California, 15 December 1978 (with Evelyn Frank); telephone, 25 June 1979.
Bennett, Irene. State treasurer, California Association of the Physically Handicapped. Concord, California, 12 December 1978.
Benson, Audrey. President, 1974–76, United Handicapped Federation. St. Paul, Minnesota, 23 October 1978; telephone, 23 May 1979.
Bohlke, Russell. Former president, San Raphael Indoor Sports Club. Palo Alto,

California, 11 December 1978; San Francisco, California, 10 May 1979; telephone, 10 May 1981.

Bowe, Frank. Director, American Coalition of Citizens with Disabilities. Washington, D.C., 11 July 1979.

Browne, Jan. Vice president, California Association of the Physically Handicapped. Telephone, 14 December 1978.

Cannon, Dennis. President, California Association of the Physically Handicapped. Telephone, 19 December 1978.

Cone, Kitty. Staff member, Center for Independent Living. Berkeley, California, 12 December 1978; telephone, 11 July 1979, 19 May 1981.

Conklin, Robert. Member, Washington, D.C., chapter of the National Association of the Physically Handicapped. Washington, D.C., 10 January 1979; telephone, 25 July 1979.

Deitz, David. Director, Legal Department, United Cerebral Palsy Associations, Inc. Telephone, 16 January 1979, 9 March 1979.

Dobkin, James. Attorney, Arnold & Porter. Washington, D.C., 13 November 1978 (with David Towey); telephone, 23 February 1979, 29 August 1979.

Dudley, B. Richmond. Assistant advocacy director, Paralyzed Veterans of America. Washington, D.C., 28 December 1978 (with John Lancaster).

Dybwad, Gunnar. Professor, Brandeis University and former executive director, National Association for Retarded Citizens. Telephone, 31 January 1979.

Dystel, John. Director of advocacy, American Coalition of Citizens with Disabilities. Washington, D.C., 11 July 1979; telephone, 29 August 1979.

Frank, Evelyn. Attorney, Alameda County Legal Aid Society. Oakland, California, 15 December 1978 (with Katharine Bartlett); Oakland, 10 May 1979; telephone, 9 March 1979.

Goldman, Charles. General counsel, Architectural and Transportation Barriers Compliance Board. Washington, D.C., 9 January 1979.

Heddinger, Richard. Board of Directors, National Capitol Area Chapter, National Paraplegia Foundation. Washington, D.C., 22 June 1978; telephone, 10 March 1979, 19 May 1981.

Heumann, Judy. Deputy director, Center for Independent Living. Telephone, 2 January 1979.

Hull, Kent. Director of legal services, National Center for Law and the Handicapped. Telephone, 13 July 1979.

Johnson, Alice. Member, California Association of the Physically Handicapped. Telephone, 13 December 1978.

Junilla, Tom. Staff organizer, United Handicapped Federation. St. Paul, Minnesota, 22 May 1978, 7 June 1979; telephone, 25 May 1979, 30 July 1980, 12 May 1981.

Kaplan, Debby. Director, Disability Rights Center. Washington, D.C., 5 January 1979.

Kardenes, Rick. Staff member, National Center for Handicapped Transportation. St. Paul, Minnesota, 23 May 1978.

Kramer, Victor. Former director, Institute for Public Interest Representation, Washington, D.C., 31 October 1978.

Lancaster, John. Advocacy director, Paralyzed Veterans of America. Washington, D.C., 12 October 1978, 28 December 1978 (with B. Richmond Dudley); telephone, 22 August 1980.

Lankasky, Kathleen. Program services coordinator, United Cerebral Palsy of Alameda County. Telephone, 15 December 1978.

Lowder, Fran. President, National Congress of Organizations of the Physically Handicapped. Telephone, 29 January 1979.

Mahlum, William. Attorney. St. Paul, Minnesota, 23 October 1978, 3 June 1979; telephone, 9 March 1979.

Mistler, Sharon. Former president, National Capitol Area Chapter, National Paraplegia Foundation. Washington, D.C., 30 October 1978.

Morse, Darlene. Vice president for transportation, United Handicapped Federation. Minneapolis, Minnesota, 8 June 1979.

Myerson, Irving. Area vice president, Indoor Sports Club. San Francisco, California, 13 December 1978.

Neuman, Jay. President, Disabled in Action of Pennsylvania. Philadelphia, Pennsylvania, 24 January 1979; telephone, 11 March 1979.

Raggio, James. Attorney, Public Interest Law Center of Philadelphia. Philadelphia, Pennsylvania, 24 January 1979.

Robrahn, Reese. Former director of research and governmental affairs, American Council of the Blind. Washington, D.C., 15 January 1979.

Robson, Kathy. President, 1978–79, United Handicapped Federation. Telephone, 24 May 1978.

Rosenberg, Norman. Attorney, Mental Health Law Project. Washington, D.C., 17 October 1978.

Ross, Sterling L., Jr. Attorney. San Francisco, California, 14 December 1978; telephone, 9 March 1979.

Rostron, Scott. President, 1976–78, United Handicapped Federation. St. Paul, Minnesota, 8 June 1979.

Shapiro, Sieglinde. Former president, Disabled in Action of Pennsylvania. Philadelphia, Pennsylvania, 25 January 1979; telephone, 26 July 1979, 14 May 1981.

Shilton, David. Attorney, Urban Mass Transportation Administration. Telephone, 24 July 1979.

Shnaider, Renah. President, East Bay Chapter, California Association of the Physically Handicapped. Telephone, 14 December 1978, 11 March 1979.

Shulman, Eric. Legislative assistant, National Council of Senior Citizens. Washington, D.C., 23 January 1979.

Steinfeld, Edward. Professor, Syracuse University School of Architecture, and director of project to update ANSI accessibility standards. Syracuse, New York, 23 November 1977.

Towey, David. Attorney, Arnold & Porter. Washington, D.C., 13 November 1978 (with James Dobkin).

Van Wagner, Richard. Former vice president, United Handicapped Federation. St. Paul, Minnesota, 8 June 1979.

Varela, Rita. Special projects manager, American Coalition of Citizens with Disabilities. Washington, D.C., 15 January 1979.

Wolfensberger, Wolf. Professor, Syracuse University. Syracuse, New York, 18 January 1979.

Wrbanich, Stephen. Executive director, Twin Cities Chapter, National Paraplegia Foundation. Minneapolis, Minnesota, 23 October 1978; telephone, 9 March 1979.

Zames, Frieda. Former president, Disabled in Action of New York. Telephone, 31 January 1979.

Zukas, Hale. Staff member, Center for Independent Living. Berkeley, California, 10 May 1979.

The following were very brief conversations, by telephone unless otherwise noted, which do not constitute full interviews.

Howard, Angela. Staff member, National Caucus on the Black Aged. Late January 1979.

Jacobs, John. Executive director, Washington Urban League. January 1979.

Rosenberg, Larry. Staff member, Alameda-Contra Costa Transit District. 9 May 1979.

Stone, George. Member, D.C. Chapter, National Association of the Physically Handicapped, at a meeting of the same. 10 January 1979.

Tucker, Sterling. Former executive director, Washington Urban League. 30 January 1979.

Wicks, Jack. Aide to Senator Alan Cranston. 13 July 1979.

Index

About the Author

SUSAN M. OLSON is Assistant Professor of Political Science at the University of Minnesota. Her writings have appeard in *Judicature* and *Governing Through Courts*.

www.ingramcontent.com/pod-product-compliance
Ingram Content Group UK Ltd.
Pitfield, Milton Keynes, MK11 3LW, UK
UKHW041639031026
15587UKWH00001B/375

9 780313 241055